THE
LAST HUMAN
CANNONBALL

THE
LAST HUMAN
CANNONBALL

AND OTHER SMALL JOURNEYS
IN SEARCH OF GREAT MEN

Byron Rogers

First published in Great Britain
2004 by Aurum Press Ltd
25 Bedford Avenue, London WC1B 3AT

These pieces appeared in earlier form in the *Daily* and *Sunday Telegraph*, *Guardian*,
Sunday Times, *Sunday Express*, *Evening Standard* and *Saga* magazines.

A catalogue record for this book is available from the British Library.

ISBN 1 84513 041 3

1 3 5 7 9 8 6 4 2
2004 2006 2008 2007 2005

Designed in Linotype Pilgrim by Geoff Green

Printed in Britain by MPG Books Ltd, Bodmin

To Jim Hill

'Consider famous men, Dai bach, consider famous men.'
Idris Davies

CONTENTS

FOREWORD

~~

Long ago, when I was a boy, there was a serial called *The Face in the Rock* on BBC Wales's Children's Hour. This, I found out much later, was a dramatisation of the American novelist Nathaniel Hawthorne's short story 'The Great Stone Face', and it fascinates me now as much as it did then, for the story has the power of myth.

Above a valley, time and the winds have carved a face in the rock, inspiring the tradition that one day he will come, the man whose face it is, and when he does this will be the great man of his time. A small boy, growing up in the valley, believes in this so completely that he makes it his life's work to meet them in turn: the general, the preacher (it was BBC Wales after all), the writer, the politician. Only none of these is the face. It is only in the man's old age, as he is dying, that his grandson sees that the face on the pillow is the face in the rock, his quest having been so ennobling that in the process he himself has become the great man. I never did like the ending: it was the idea of the quest I loved, and the weighing in the balance of fame. It set the pattern of my life.

The Last Human Cannonball

For say it were possible for there to be a job that allowed a man to meet his heroes: not just those of his middle age, but those of his childhood whom he wished he could have met, who wrote the comics, and in one case a collector who still had *all* the comics (so, forty years on, all interrupted, or lost, serials could be resumed). And from these to go on to meet his legendary contemporaries, the pop idol, the film star, the great beauty – and not only the famous, but also the truly astonishing folk heroes who loom up in one- or two-paragraph news stories, like the OAP who on a SAGA holiday, and with nothing better to do, swam the piranha-infested Amazon.

And say that job allowed him to realise his fantasies, to walk through the mud of Agincourt with the weapons provided (which would make him the first man since the Middle Ages able to put a long-bow on expenses), peer into the locked cabinets of the British Museum (one the bequest of a mayor of Bedford who, having got it into his head that all religions started with phallic worship, bought every sculpted erection of the Old World and left his collection to the Museum, which immediately turned the key on the lot), and to attend one of Miss Cynthia Payne's remarkable orgies (where only red, not pink, tinned salmon was provided). And to walk the most familiar streets of all, those of a Western film town in Spain, as well as the most unfamiliar, those of Tombstone, the real Western town, where nothing was where it should have been. Then, beyond these, where all roads of fantasy and hero-worship lead, Hollywood.

In the pages which follow you will visit such places and meet such people, for in my lifetime it was still, just, possible to get a job that allowed me to do so. They start with the most mysterious report ever issued, that on Average Man, weighed, measured, his chemistry and specific gravity established, and quietly issued to higher civil servants in the case of nuclear attack. Here is poor 'bare, forkèd man' in all his constituents. They end with the last human cannonball in European circuses, booted up the arse every night and sent hurtling helplessly towards an uncertain landing, which, more than the sparrow fluttering through the hall, seems to me the perfect metaphor for the human condition.

In between you will meet the quick and the very quick, some in the past, like the greatest shit who ever lived, Colonel Charteris, who on his death-bed offered £20,000 to anyone who could disprove the existence of Hell, adding he was indifferent to that of Heaven; also the merry little judge who at the last witchcraft trial observed 'There be no law against flying', and with that one remark laughed the Middle Ages out of England.

You will have transsexuality explained by Burt Lancaster. You will be there when it is revealed to two OAPs that their mother, cranky old mum whom they thought had never been out of the town, had been Ethel le Neave, and Dr Crippen's mistress. You will meet a photographer who took a stand on pubic hair like other men took a stand on the Rhine (a line the solicitous *Sunday Telegraph* took out of the piece on first publication), and who was in and out of court because of his un-airbrushed prints until he sold his Soho Square studio at the height of a property boom, and retired to a mansion the size of Longleat. You will hear a man say, 'I think that was the day I got crucified ... first', the most wonderful quote I have ever recorded.

In its ramshackle way, this has been my quest for the Face in the Rock.

Byron Rogers
Carmarthen 2004

S EE HOW THE NAILS GROW

~

I t is possibly the strangest book ever written. Not The Egyptian Book of the Dead, nor any of those helpful Latin treatises which horror story writers allege are kept locked in the British Museum to prevent the conjuring up of horned demons in the middle of the Reading Room, even come close.

The book was lent to me by a senior civil servant. He is retiring now and after a working life spent consulting it he has thankfully put it away, just as a used car dealer would his much-thumbed *Glass's Guide*.

It is on sale to the public, though you will probably never see it in any book shop. Published by the Pergamon Press at £45, it will never be a best seller or a paperback. A large blue volume entitled *Report of the Task Group on Reference Man*, it comes without illustrations or even a dust-jacket.

It begins with man's average height, his surface area, his weight. His surface area, for example, is broken down into head and neck (nine per cent), outstretched palm and fingers (one per cent) and so on.

The Last Human Cannonball

It goes on to determine the specific gravity of man, his total body water, the volume of his blood. The tone is that of a map-making team.

But what follows is a voyage underground, just as in that science fiction film in which Raquel Welch and some others were miniaturised and sent on a voyage through the blood system.

You begin sinking through the skin, the body fat and the meat. Weight of body fat, male 29.76 lbs. Much of this data was based on the bodies of 17 men who met deaths from violence, and you cannot get out of your mind the picture of a vast cauldron with someone boiling them down.

Weight of total fat, female 35.27 lbs. And this is just the beginning.

Weight of the skin of a new-born infant 7.2 oz. Weight of the skin of an adult man 5.8 lbs. Nothing is too much trouble to calibrate.

The total weight of fingernails and toenails for the adult male come to 0.075 of an ounce.

There is even a set of figures based on the growth of the third fingernail. EVERY 24 HOURS: until the age of three, 0.00276 of an inch; between 20 and 30, 0.00492 of an inch; in the eighties, 0.00332 of an inch.

Nails grow faster in summer. Toenails grow faster than fingernails. The fastest growth rate in fingernails is the third, followed by the second, fourth, first and fifth.

The weight of hair on an adult male is 0.7 of an ounce. (No allowance, says the *Report* primly, being made for sideburns or a beard). The weight of female hair is 7.5 oz. And so on.

We are sinking now, past the heart ('a hollow muscular organ shaped like a blunt cone'). No, we have taken another turn.

We are weighing tongues: 2.450 oz in an adult male, 2.10 oz in an adult female.

We are in the digestive system now ('In the mouth food is prepared for digestion, but the time of residence is relatively short').

An idea of the worldwide nature of the research all this is based on is given in one short sentence: the dimensions of the tongue are based on 'data for a Japanese population'.

There is no difference in capacity between the male and female bladders whatever the evidence gleaned in every saloon bar in the world. Frequency of urination, states the *Report*, is based only on habit.

The male ejaculation is measured, and its range.

The width of the adult vagina is measured, the wall thickness, its length. Breasts are weighed and their chemical composition noted. Testicles are weighed.

Did I say everything has been measured? No, not quite. The one statistic not given is the one Dr Kinsey also never gave. The insides and outsides of women are ransacked but no measurement is given for the penis.

And why was this astonishing project, assembled by a task force over thirty years, undertaken? Was it a vote of confidence in man? No.

It was carried out by Committee Two of the International Commission on Radiological Protection. And it was used during his working life by the civil servant as a work of reference to see how much radiation the poor old human creature, weighed, measured, mined, could take, and still stagger on into an uncertain future.

There is no need to conjure up horned demons.

1984

PART ONE
BEGINNINGS

Where eagles dared

~

I t existed for only twenty years, and for half that time was past its best. But the man who finally killed it is still, seven years later, defensive about his action, for a sense of outrage persists in men in their middle thirties: it was simply that in their childhood in the 1950s there was the finest comic ever produced, and there passed away a small glory from the earth.

It is just before nine o'clock in the morning on Friday, 14 April 1950. In Lammas Street, Carmarthen, two boys are waiting for a newsagent to open. Each has a small card in his hand and has been waiting half an hour. In that time they have punched each other, tried not to walk on the cracks of pavements and been twice to the municipal lavatories. But mostly they have read their cards.

They have had them a week now, taking them to school, hiding them under their pillows, reading them over and over with a mixture of incredulity and joy. For this is 1950, and in 1950 nobody gives anything away. But there it is, a crumpled print: on production of this card the bearer will be given the first copy of a new comic. There occurred in Carmarthen on April 14 1950, the longest half hour in the history of the world.

It is difficult to explain to anyone older or younger the effect *Eagle* had that first Friday. There were comics enough – the D. C. Thomson circus was in full cry, all slapstick and jokes about food. There were even the last of the old American horror comics, which a solicitous Government was to twitch away from our rocksteady hands. Things crept out of sewers; Desperate Dan ate his cow-pie; the Germans were endlessly defeated. It was a predictable little world.

Then came *Eagle*.

It was the quality of it which was so staggering. Of something like sixteen pages half were in full colour. Even the paper was better, and bigger. But the drawings were like nothing we had ever seen. When the great Frank Hampson, creator of Dan Dare, drew the Venusian city of Mekonta across the entire front page, the image of it was so vivid that seeing it again after twenty-seven years you can immediately pick out familiar features.

When Hampson again, on the back page this time, drew the light streaming out of the night on Saul making his way to Damascus, you realised that the morning texts that had been mumbled at you were astonishing reading.

But at no time did you feel you were being got at, as you did with Arthur Mee's *Children's Newspaper*, where they were always slipping in facts about frog-spawn and volcanoes and seeds in blotting paper. You were taught useful things, like how to bowl googlies. You even had an *Eagle* Special Investigator who did practical everyday things, like crossing deserts or being a knife-thrower's target.

But mainly *Eagle* was Dan Dare; and with Hampson Dan Dare was pointed at infinite space, and you with him. You braved the terrible silicon swamps and flame belts, saw the skies darken with space fleets, and looked on the evil green brain who went about on a kind of flying commode because his body had withered. You were told of Atlantis, and dark moons, and a sort of Welwyn Garden City which floated in the balmy southern airs of a Venus peopled by golden-haired men.

After Korky the Cat and Biffo and Lord Snooty, it was as though the horizons had rolled back. But today Korky and Biffo and Snooty are still in the *Dandy* and *Beano*, and *Eagle* is to be found only in the British Library and collectors' shops – at £1 a copy. A new generation has arisen that knows not Dan Dare or Digby or Harris Tweed or the Mekon, or the astonishingly detailed drawings of nuclear subs and jets that once brought the Ministry of Defence scurrying to the *Eagle* offices. The late L. Ashwell Woods had done a drawing of a new military aircraft so detailed that the men at the Ministry thought it violated D Notices. The drawing sprang from Woods's own imagination.

Whither is fled the visionary gleam?

In an office in a skyscraper in London, Marcus Morris, managing director of the National Magazine Company, stubbed out a cigarette and lit another. The room was full of leather chairs and antique furniture: from here Morris directs the fortunes of *Cosmopolitan* and *She*, magazines in which women exhort other women towards orgasm with the energy of cattle drovers. But in 1950, aged thirty-five, his only experience of journalism was his own parish magazine.

A clergyman in a smart Stockport parish who wanted to edit a national magazine, he had, without financial backing of any kind, found Frank Hampson in the local art school and was paying him a regular salary out of his own stipend of £10 a week. They had produced a dummy of *Eagle* which Morris hawked around Fleet Street for over a year before Hulton Press bought it. His debts were Dickensian.

So the comic began not in a boardroom or as the result of elaborate readership surveys, but because of one man completely outside the world of publishing. 'I suppose it does sound a bit astonishing now,' Morris said quietly. He talks so softly the syllables disappear into the leather desk. Imagine a highly-strung racing greyhound with a penchant for pinstripes and chain smoking, and you have an idea of his build. He looks mild, shy, worried. But the appearance is deceptive. Morris, said one of his colleagues, is the only man he has ever met who can shout without raising his voice.

It you talk to people who worked on *Eagle* the conversations always come back to Morris. *Eagle* was Morris. Clifford Makins succeeded him as editor in 1960. 'He was always a bit of an enigma. We'd have conferences and Marcus would say "Hmmm", then "Hmmm", and then again "Hmmm", and you'd come out not knowing what he thought. But he always knew exactly what he wanted, and you didn't argue.'

'I'd always been interested in the strip-cartoon technique, especially in the way it could be used to put over the Christian faith.' The Revd Marcus Morris smiles. 'In the beginning even Dan Dare was envisaged as a flying padre, but that faded out. I just wanted to create a good comic. To preach to children would be fatal.

'We wanted to put across certain values and standards. Some of the stories were rough and tough, but children like that. What we wanted to avoid most of all was the Superman-type story – that there could be some magic way of coping with life. There was a need for something of good quality. Children's comics were such poor things that there was a gap in the market.'

It was then that the fun started. The hard-eyed men at Hulton Press recognised that such a gap existed. John Pearce was then general manager. He grinned wickedly. 'It would be wrong to say that we didn't capitalise on the fact that Marcus was a clergyman. In our promotion in the national press aimed at parents we called it "A Children's Magazine edited by the Reverend Marcus Morris".'

He took another sip of gin. 'But in those days do-goody children's papers were bad sellers. To the trade we called it "*Eagle*, Hulton's great *comic*".'

That was just the beginning. At the same time the *Daily Express* was planning to bring out a children's magazine of its own, and the race was on. Then Hulton announced to the trade that, because of production difficulties, the launch of *Eagle* had to be put back two weeks. The *Express* relaxed. But secretly Hulton had brought their launch date forward by two weeks. 'We broke them,' said John Pearce slowly.

Ironically it was the beginning of Hulton's difficulties. They had been thinking in terms of 250,000 copies an issue. But from the provinces came demands for more and more. The first copy of *Eagle* sold a million, and Hulton were in trouble.

'If a magazine runs away with itself like this you run it at a loss,' said John Pearce. 'You can't put your advertising rates up fast enough.

'So I went away for a few days and thought about it. When I came back I took the decision to put the price up to fourpence. Now you must remember that in 1950 it was virtually unthinkable to put your prices up. It's a daily thing now. Then everyone was very worried. But do you know, we didn't lose a single copy ... and we got a million more pennies a week.' Even after thirty years Pearce recalled the marvel of it.

Morris was installed as editor. Hulton paid off his debts and he began an astonishing regimen of editing all week then catching the Friday night train back to his parish. On Sunday he boarded the night train back to London. A few months later he resigned his parish and moved south, where he became something of a nine-day wonder in Fleet Street. Newspaper profiles were written about this strange clergyman who looked like an actor, wore camel-hair coats and, as a student, had given exhibitions of ballroom dancing at the Randolph in Oxford.

Hulton had a winner (Morris, in his relief and naivety, having neglected to negotiate a royalty). *Eagle* was the first comic to have advertisements (something like two and a half pages out of the sixteen). It was also the first comic to have its own reporter.

MacDonald Hastings, an experienced Fleet Street writer who had shared in the general amusement about Morris's appointment, became *Eagle* Special Investigator. 'I think they wanted someone to emulate Dan Dare. In his heart of hearts I think Marcus Morris was always sorry that I didn't kill myself.'

In the next ten years his tall, owlish figure (as boys we could never quite accept the spectacles) went to the Yukon, to the bottom of the sea, crossed the Kalahari, and became (in an asbestos suit) a living firework. He drove a dog-team (and omitted to tell his young readers that the dogs farted all the time), charmed snakes in India, mined for gold, and became a lumberjack.

'No, nobody I knew thought it was odd working for a comic. You forget that there was a great respect for *Eagle*. Nothing had come anywhere near it. It was on a completely new level. They got the top people to work for them, and paid them the top.'

Among artists were Hampson, the late Frank Bellamy, Thelwell and David Langdon. Even the sixteen-year-old Gerald Scarfe had a cartoon printed in the paper.

Clifford Makins, who was Morris's deputy, remembers the feeling of superiority they had over all rivals. 'I think we ignored them. I can't recall even reading any of them. They were lurching along somewhere in the background, but there was nothing we could have learned from them.'

A whole *Eagle* world grew up. There was an Eagle Club ('with 60,000 applications to join after the first two issues'). Morris added a sort of bar to the badge, which people obtained through some deed of social usefulness. In Christian paradox such graduates were to be known as Mugs. I remember not being able to follow his reasoning there, and did not qualify. There were crowded *Eagle* carol services in St Paul's Cathedral (where most of his editorial staff saw Morris for the first time in a clerical collar).

There was also a Boys and Girls Exhibition at Olympia, at which they encountered their hero MacDonald Hastings bemusedly signing autographs, his words ringing in their ears: 'Without wasting any precious time I asked the knife-thrower if he ever missed. The man replied that no man was infallible.'

Oh, there was no messing about on *Eagle*: I remember those words now.

But children grow up. At fifteen you were too old for *Eagle*. Yet, however much it might dwindle into a background, it was unthinkable that at some future date it should not be there.

In 1960 Morris was offered a job by the National Magazine Company and left. Hulton had already been taken over by Odhams. Morris was succeeded by Clifford Makins, who left a year later when Odhams in its turn was taken over by the Daily Mirror group. In 1970 IPC merged *Eagle* with one of its own comics, *Lion*.

'*Eagle* was a freak, an individual thing, and I think Marcus really did have inspiration. When he went, the thing faded with him.' Makins started to laugh: 'I should know because I succeeded him.'

Why did *Eagle* fail? The people associated with it say it was because IPC kept introducing economies.

John Sanders, editorial director of the IPC Juvenile Group, was the man who killed *Eagle*. 'We've come in for an awful lot of stick from *Eagle* buffs. Most of it is absolute twaddle. We close magazines when they don't make money. When it started there were possibly fifteen other weeklies. When it closed there were fifty. I think it ran out of steam.'

It is significant that whereas most copies of *Eagle* now fetch £1 apiece, those from 1965 on cost only 25p.

But could it be launched again? John Pearce thinks it could, with the right kind of editorship ('Marcus, you must remember, was a kind of mad genius in his way'). John Sanders is adamant that it could not.

'I don't think it would sell 10,000 copies. People who venerate old copies should remember that today's comics are for today's children. It would be like reprinting a 1947 *Daily Telegraph*.'

Two years ago Marcus Morris contacted Makins with the idea of launching a second *Eagle*. 'I think we even got to the stage of a rough dummy. But I found myself thinking in the old ways.' Makins stopped for a moment. 'And I remember saying to Marcus, "We're too old."'

So the war stories lurch on, and the sport serials, and the boys with magic powers: the comics of 1977 are little different from the comics of 1950. But I no longer see small boys waiting for newsagents to open in Carmarthen. *The Best of Eagle* speaks, to quote Wordsworth, of something that is gone.

1977

A LIFETIME WITH AUNTIE

⤳

The greatest writer in the history of the earth can be found most days on the top floor of the BBC offices in the Aeolian Hall, Bond Street. Here, far above the grand entrance hall and where the corridors are low and turn abruptly as in a warren, one suddenly comes upon a door leading into a dusty little office. On the door is a printed card giving his name, rank and regiment: Charles Chilton, Producer, Light Entertainment, Radio.

It is strange they should describe him so. For five golden years, between 1953 and 1958, there were no doubts whatsoever but that Mr Chilton was the greatest writer there had ever been. Stop any man in the street aged between twenty-five and thirty-five, who had a radio in his childhood, and is neither an idiot nor a graduate in English from the University of Cambridge, and he, too, will take issue with the nameless heralds of the BBC. For as a child he would have hurried home from play to listen to *Journey Into Space*, which Mr Chilton wrote and produced in those years. It was broadcast at 7.30, always, in retrospect, on summer evenings:

to get a child home then would normally require some kind of military curfew. But Chilton did it. 'He who pleases the children,' wrote Boswell in a rare moment of perception, 'will be remembered with pleasure by the men.'

And not only the children listened. *Journey Into Space*, in the last of its third series, was heard each week by between 5,000,000 and 6,000,000, the last time that more people listened to radio than to television. Chilton's copious mail included things like an anguished little letter from a monastery asking was it possible to change the time of transmission as it interfered with evensong. Seventeen years later, he still receives at least one letter a week on the subject of *Journey Into Space*. 'If I meet people now, and they realise who I am, I'm absolutely bombarded with questions,' he says, with some bewilderment. It has its responsibilities, being the greatest writer in the history of the earth, but retired.

Only he isn't retired at all. At fifty-eight, he is the BBC's most distinguished radio producer. It is fascinating to speculate just how many millions there must be who know him only as the co-author of *Oh, What a Lovely War*, and the writer-producer of ballad-documentaries. Generations have arisen which knew not Joseph.

Sadly, Mr Chilton himself doesn't seem to have liked being Joseph much. '*Journey Into Space* really drove me up the wall. It was dreadful thinking up something new every week, getting them out of the last impossible situation. I'd only begun it because the BBC wanted to do a science fiction series, and I was slightly interested in astronomy, and had a telescope and so ... I had a go at it. For five years. I was very glad when it finished. I went over to producing *Take It From Here*, with Jimmy Edwards.' Oh my Five – Four – Three – Two – One – WHHOOOOOOSHES, long ago.

The BBC sold it to fifty-eight countries. Yet in its archives the Corporation today has only one record of one complete episode from the first series. Five years of radio have gone as though they had never been: the BBC excuses itself on the grounds of cost and, ironically, space. Yet it perturbs Mr Chilton not at all.

'I don't think it was a bad show. It was good radio. But I'm glad people can't listen to it now.' Mr Chilton smiles suddenly, the sort of baffled smile one turns on someone else's troublesome child.

All that is now left of *Journey Into Space* is a line of bound scripts in Chilton's office, grey with dust. His secretary flicks a duster at each one, and surreptitiously proceeds to dust the lampshade. Borrowing the scripts is an awesome responsibility. What would the other brooders on the land, or rather worlds, of lost content do if these got lost?

The scripts, of course, are very good. The last series of *Journey Into Space* is still, with Kubrick and Clarke's *2001*, the best piece of science fiction drama ever produced. When one considers that each series required something like nine hours of scripts, and that Chilton recorded on a Sunday, having written that week's episode during a sleepless Friday night (the rest of the week he was a BBC producer engaged on other programmes), his achievement is little short of incredible. It is even more incredible when you realise that it was BBC policy in those days not to pay its producers for any scripts they wrote: for those five years Chilton got nothing. 'Mozart died a pauper,' he says blandly.

The three series concern themselves with the adventures of four astronauts, all drawn from the Commonwealth (oh those happy, new Elizabethan days when we'd conquered Everest and the world knew where Woomera was). But when one has said that then it is the sum total of absurdity in the series.

For Chilton didn't put a foot wrong, scientifically. His dialogue was later, rather eerily, echoed by the American astronauts (as when his Jet Morgan says: 'Well, it's not made of green cheese.'). He had roped in a friend engaged in rocket research at Farnborough as consultant. 'If I got into trouble I'd ring him up and say, "They're going round the moon at 2,000 feet. I want to get them down to 1,000 feet. What do I do?" He'd say, "You've got to get them to go faster." And I'd say, "Thanks."'

His scripts also encountered the difficulty on which the American space programme threatens to founder, the boredom of space. 'You've no idea how hard it is to plot something when you've got the whole of the universe. On earth you can have an earthquake, or have people meet people. Up there nothing happens.' Chilton gestured vaguely at the ceiling.

So you make it happen. Electronic music, chilling voices. Chilton uses the shock of having his astronauts, in the flush of achievement, suddenly stumble upon the artefacts of another, superior civilisation (as Clarke was later to do in *2001*). But even that only took the story up to Episode Nine, and there were nine of the first series to be written.

He didn't miss a trick. At the end of Episode Sixteen, in a splutter of horror and awe, they have their first sight of an extra-terrestrial being, a towering armadillo shape glimpsed briefly in shadow. 'I really don't know why I made him look like that,' said Chilton airily. 'Must have been to the Zoo or something.'

But the last series was pure fantasy. Chilton, whom one should really not ask about these things, says unexpectedly, 'You must understand I'd run out of knowledge by then. I had to fall back on ideas.' The series involved a Martian plan to invade Earth, using mass hypnosis through television. Chilton, the old radio hand, denies stoutly that there were any sour grapes in this turn of the plot.

It is almost always disappointing to meet one's idols. But to meet one who regards his highest achievement as a mere comma in a career awash with punctuation is something of a catastrophe. Time's winged chariots hurry into earshot. Yet, within two years of retirement, Chilton's working life is as full as ever, with plans for programmes about musical social history, Christmas in the Trenches, the Boston Tea Party, the Salvation Army.

Deep down in a studio in Broadcasting House he was recording *The Boston Tea Party*, gently lecturing his actors on history. 'Now, you're Tom Paine. He was a Norfolk man.' The actor looks up from his script: 'I can't do a Norfolk accent.' Mr Chilton rattles on breezily, 'Well, not to worry. He lived in Kent for years. His house at Sandwich is still there. Do a Sandwich accent.' The actor looks relieved. 'I've learnt more history in eight years with Charles than I ever did at school,' says the man at the sound control.

The Boston Tea Party is typical Chilton documentary: narrative is broken up by contemporary ballads, and by the speeches and writings of the men who made the events. History bowls past at a cracking rate, the great figures of the past flickering and falling. This is the technique that Chilton has made his own, and which is now widely copied in radio and television.

A short, friendly, voluble man, he scampers through the script assigning part to his actors, dropping little footnotes of history ('He attacked a fort in the Ohio Valley, now known as Pittsburgh by the way'). His forty-two years with the BBC have not erased his Cockney vowels. It is ironic how no one likes his idol to be either friendly, or voluble (as Harold Nicolson noted, this is what put a lot of people's backs up with Lord Byron: the romantic hero made jokes). Chilton, typically, shows no signs of the fact he has spent all Friday night writing this script, and Saturday having it typed and duplicated.

He says roundly, 'If I'm to be remembered as anything I'd like it to be as the originator of this music-and-facts form, which really does fulfil the BBC charter, "to inform, educate and entertain".' Perhaps it is just that Chilton doesn't like pilgrims.

Certainly he has no doubts himself as to what was the high point in his career. Was it … ? 'Oh, no, no, no, it was when I was first appointed a radio producer. I've never ever wanted to be anything else in the BBC. I hope to retire as a producer.' Charles Chilton has now been a radio producer for thirty-six years.

The Last Human Cannonball

That he ever became one is something of a little miracle. He was born into a section of the working class so far down the social spectrum that one needs to go back to something like the horrors of Doré's engravings of the London poor to picture it. In the slums around King's Cross, orphaned in early childhood, he remembers a Christmas Day when there was no food at all in the house. 'My brother wrote "Turkey", and "Potato" and "Pear" on bits of paper and went round the table putting them on plates.'

It was the old working-class London, sunk in its own unchanging misery, far below the rumblings of any effective state education. Until he joined the BBC Chilton had not met a university graduate.

His relationship with the BBC has been a strange and probably unique one: to the slum child it became in turn finishing school, university and career. Even now he cannot get the wonder out of his voice when talking about the Corporation: 'I was so delighted at working there that it seemed always to have been a source of delight just being there at all. If I tried to join it now I wouldn't have a hope in hell. I had no qualifications at all.'

He joined at fifteen as a messenger boy, having been turned down for a job as a milkman. He had written to the BBC largely because he had been impressed by their great new Broadcasting House, 'like a great battleship ... in Portland Place'.

The place seems to have been crammed with mentors. Producers wrote out reading lists for the young Chilton: others invited him to the lunchtime lectures which they themselves gave. The messenger boy became assistant librarian in the record department, began to write short linking scripts for record programmes, became, in an apocalyptic burst of glory, a radio producer. He was nineteen, and things would never be the same again.

He is not bitter about his childhood. 'I don't think I ever realised I wasn't getting enough to eat.' Today he lives with his wife in a rather grand Edwardian villa, built by a Sackville-West who had a weakness for indulging his mistress but this time, thankfully, not his reading public. It stands in its own grounds, back from Bromley Common. The Chiltons met at the BBC, where Mrs Chilton was a secretary. They have three children, one of whom is an actress, another, a son, at London University, and a third, another son, who works for the English Tourist Board.

His family, at least, remember *Journey Into Space*. His wife remembers the hectic weekends. 'He used to smoke all the time. I used to say, "Why can't you get a week ahead?", but he never could. And then when one of the series came to an end he used to feel so lost.' His daughter, Mary, remembers the creepy electronic music. 'It used to terrify me. I was only four, I think.'

Chilton himself still mutters defiantly, 'I've never thought of myself as a dramatist. I only wrote *Oh, What a Lovely War* under protest. When I retire I may write drama, but it would have to be musical drama.'

He survives, a relic of an age when radio was an honourable calling. All day and all night now the inanities of pop music and phone-ins and chat-shows gulp out along the metres: the old master of radio is still there in an age which has debased radio, and language, and music, even its public. Chilton says glumly, 'It's a bad time as I can't stand Radio One. I hope it improves. But the mass audience likes gibberish, and I can't see how they can improve.'

Yet he denies that his budgets have been reduced (he had £180 a week to spend on *Journey Into Space*; today he can get £500 for some programmes). 'I have always liked working for radio. I grew up in it. You became part of it. It is the thing I was born to do. If I'd been in the USA I might have ended up in films. And the BBC, you know, has retained radio as an art form.'

And yet ... for every person who listens to the radio eight watch television. The radio criticism in Sunday reviews seems to occupy less and less space each week. Chilton, who once had full-page articles written about him in the days of *Journey Into Space*, is now restricted to the occasional paragraph. He says, a little sadly, 'I'm still widely known among the people who have stayed with radio. I think the generation who liked me when they were young still listen to me.'

He loves radio for the way it can stimulate people's imaginations, and for the way a producer can really dominate his programme. 'You can't be your own master on television. Someone has to design the sets and do the photography.' Fondly he remembers his own rushed schedules and the howlers during transmission. 'I did a Western series in which someone had to say: "Billy the Kid's been seen in Corydon." That's a Border town. He got everything mixed up and said, "Billy the Kid's been seen in Croydon."'

But talk to him about *Journey Into Space* and he is more amused than anything. He makes jokes about your interest to his wife. Together they try and remember the names of the characters, which you yourself could have supplied with ease, but didn't, out of curiosity. He makes it seem as though it were all so long ago. Perhaps it was, when everyone was younger, but when he was the greatest writer in the history of the earth, and didn't know it. It has been sad, writing this.

1975

DESPERATE DEN

~~

There was a wild list to his curtains. The end of a rail had come away from the wall, but of course had not fallen. Nothing can fall in that room now, at least not to the ground. There is too much in the way.

'Your curtains need fixing,' I said chattily.

He looked at them the way a farmer in the Great Plains might look at what remains of his house after a tornado has passed. Emotion is wasted on natural disaster. 'Yes,' said Dennis Gifford, 'that happened about three years ago.'

He knew it had to be 1984 because before that time he was still able to get to his curtains.

When I was a boy in Carmarthen I had a friend called Tony Meredith. He lived with his grandparents, and he was allowed to keep every comic he bought. I remember the first time I went to his house: I must have stood there blinking like Caernarvon and Carter as the lamps lit up Tutankhamun's tomb. Every issue I had missed, or lost, or had taken from me was there. They were in heaps on the floor, on chairs, on the settee. I was never to forget that room in St David's Street, for I had not known such a house, or such riches existed. Then eight years ago I made an even greater discovery.

There were no guards as there would have been around W. R. Hearst's San Simeon; nor was it under the mud as at Sutton Hoo. It was a modern semi-detached, a lot of right angles and glass, in a street in Sydenham, south-east London, and a summer's evening when I first met Dennis Gifford.

We have been in touch a few times since then, but we did not meet again until this year. Perhaps we could meet in London, said Dennis. It seemed such a long way to come.

'No bother, Dennis. I'll come down, and we'll have a cup of tea.'

There was a long pause. 'It would be a bit difficult for me to make you a cup of tea.'

'Fair enough, I'm not that keen on tea. We'll just sit down and have a chat.'

'You don't understand. There is nowhere for you to sit down now.'

Meredith was a schoolboy. The full resources of two pensions might have been at his disposal, but he only had a front room. Dennis Gifford is fifty-nine and a successful deviser of television programmes such as *Looks Familiar*. He also has a whole house. I think it was Tolstoy who had an image of unbounded possibility when he foresaw Genghis Khan with a telephone; the result is quite similar.

The architects had built a fitted wardrobe in the hall: that is full of American comics, with the exception of the horror ones which are in the kitchen. There are comics on the stove, on the fridge, on the floor. Dennis Gifford can still use his grill, but roasts are a memory for he can no longer open his oven.

The fridge filled up years ago, for Dennis is fascinated by the free gifts which come with some comics and made a bad mistake once when he stored a comic with free chewing gum in it and that melted. There are lollipops in the fridge now, and Desperate Dan nougat.

There is central heating but he cannot remember when it was last on, for no heat can get through the mounds of comics and magazines. A hot air machine clatters away somewhere. A television set is also still visible because Dennis likes to watch old films in the afternoon; you peer gratefully at that as you would at a last sight of land, since it is the last link with a conventional house. A burglar would probably take one look and then walk quietly away, for none of the indices of his trade make any sense here.

The living room is lined with bookshelves, comic annuals, books on film and radio and old entertainers, but they filled up long ago and he has had to build bookshelves at right angles to them, like a breakwater. Where these end, the mounds begin.

'I have outgrown this place,' said Dennis Gifford thoughtfully.

Dickens would have loved such a house, for it is that of a boy who has run away from home, and whom no grown-up will ever pester again. Dennis, who is divorced, lives alone, and there are few visitors: they would create too much tension. For if you come here there is always a third person in the room, the child you were, his outline at once ghostly and precise; your host knows this and watches you warily as a child would watch anyone entering his den.

If a phone rings he says, 'Could you try not to move?', because should you pick up a comic and replace it on another pile, that could mean its disappearance for years. The trouble is that you are dying to move for there is always something, a *Knockout Annual* they sold out of in Carmarthen in 1950, or something you once had, so strange and so familiar you cannot help touching.

His anxiety is prompted as much by scholarship as by avarice, for this is also his work-room. Here, starting at 7.30 every day, inching his way down the stairs from the bathroom, the one space free of heaped paper (steam can damage), Dennis Gifford writes his books. *Victorian Comics. The International Book of Comics. One Hundred Years of Comics.* Most are reference books because he knows his subject so well he no longer wishes to impose his comments. The first *British Comic Catalogue*, in which he identified 1700 titles between 1874 and 1974, and encountered no problems in finding illustrations to reproduce. They were all in his collection.

The Golden Age of Radio, the first guide to the programmes, the people, the catch-phrases. And this year, at £45 a copy, there appeared simultaneously in Britain and America what he regards as his life's work: the updated version of his *British Film Catalogue* which took him twenty years to compile, and which lists every film made in Britain for public entertainment. Films neither he nor anyone else will ever see, films destroyed, films forgotten, they are all here with their stars, directors, even plots ('Disowned girl reunited with father after running him over'; 'Girl takes sister's place when she deserts blinded scientist'; 'Escaped lunatic thinks tin can is bomb').

For the purpose of this catalogue he read the adverts in every issue in every trade paper. He traced men who had retired in 1914 and were still alive, such as the old director Lewin Fitzhamon, then well into his nineties and living in a flat in the Charing Cross Road.

'Everyone had forgotten about him, but he made more than 600 films between 1904 and 1912. He loved children and animals, and usually had dogs or ponies rescuing babies from gypsies. He didn't like gypsies.

'He was the first man to have a convincing narrative, with beginnings and ends, and he was also the first director to go on location. He went to Bognor for a week, and took a pony with him. He had it swim out to rescue a girl from a rock.'

Dennis met old stars from a time when a studio was a rented

house and filming took place in suburban gardens on sunny after-noons. Alma Taylor. Hay Plumb ('Oh, the names they had'), a comedian, the first man to direct a five-reel film of *Hamlet*. Chrissie White.

'She was the first actress to give the industry a romantic inter-est. She married her co-star, the great Henry Edwards. Ever hear of him? No? Dear, oh dear. People seem to be getting younger and younger every day.

'But that shows the necessity for doing all this. We tend to forget. I think that's at the back of my personal crusade.' Dennis has forgotten nothing.

The comics came first. His parents were against them and only allowed him two a week, so at the age of six he went under-ground. Sent to his grandmother's he would walk half the way and pocket the bus-fare.

Occasionally the grown-ups pounced, seeing the outline of a smuggled comic under his sweater, and once the Luftwaffe and his mother conspired to rid him of his greatest treasure, the first issue of the *Dandy* which had a free tin whistle in it.

'When I was evacuated in the first year of the war my mother emptied my comic cupboard. I came back after a year and it was quite empty. She always denied it and I grew old and forgave her as best I could.

'But I can still see that cupboard now. We stored coal in anoth-er part of it, and I remember the black smudges on some of the comics. I have been looking for that copy of the *Dandy* ever since.'

Evacuation to Tonbridge brought a new love – films, which his mother had also disapproved of, and at which his earlier reactions had alarmed other members of his family ('Aunt Florrie stopped taking me after I became very frightened and hid under the seat and made a terrible commotion'). But at Tonbridge there was Harold Lloyd, and an entranced Dennis walked out of the cinema and straight into a lamppost, breaking his glasses.

The Last Human Cannonball

At the age of fourteen, still in school, he began drawing for the *Dandy*, after sending a comic strip to D. C. Thomson of Dundee. He was commissioned to draw Pansy Potter the Strong Man's Daughter and did so after homework, but his pride was dampened when he discovered another boy in the same school drawing for comics. His name was Bob Monkhouse.

Then there was the RAF. Dennis remembers the RAF with much love: it meant he could go to the pictures every night of the week and watch double features. This was the first of the lost worlds in his life, the tiny cinemas (one in Wiltshire was above a butcher's shop), the curtains which their proprietors loved and used to drench with green and pink light so that he could not read the credits, and the medicated peppermints which was all that they were allowed to sell in the Age of Austerity.

For a few years after the RAF he shared a studio with Monkhouse, both of them drawing for comics, and then Monkhouse took off into show business, and he continued with Stoneage Kit, the Ancient Brit, in *Knockout*. He was a freelance artist until the 1960s when he began devising panel games for radio, his greatest success coming with *Sounds Familiar*, in which panellists had to guess the origins of songs and soundtracks.

'It was a way of hearing things I'd missed.' The obsession of his life and the means of financing it had come together. It took him two years to convince the BBC that nostalgia was a valid emotion (the 1960s, he observed dryly, was a bit of a brave new world), but his career as the keeper of the nation's entire stock was under way. *Sounds Familiar* became *Looks Familiar* on television in 1972 and is still running. Last year it was on Channel 4 until that channel decided there was one minority group, the middle-aged, which it did not want to indulge; *Looks Familiar* will return to ITV.

As he became more successful so his comic collection grew and began to include other men's childhoods. The very old comics with characters like catsmeat men; the 1920s comics with Daniel

Dole and Oscar Outofwork; up-market comics set in nurseries where to see your parents was a great treat. In 1976 he organised the first British Comics Convention. Of the 250 people who came, 150 drew professionally for comics. In his lifetime the dealers have emerged, charging anything over £5 for a first issue, though he has still not found the one great gap in his collection, the first *Dandy*, complete with free tin whistle.

And somewhere out there are the comics which the store Lilley & Skinner gave away free when you bought a pair of shoes. There were twelve issues and he has none of them. He used to look at them through the window of the store in Rye Lane, Peckham, and he can still remember his bewilderment when he took his mother there only to have it pointed out to him that to buy a pair of shoes for a free comic did not make sense. Considerations like that no longer apply.

He is a legend now, and his collection an archive. Film-makers borrow his old comics, though the Two Ronnies sat on the ones they borrowed and had to pay an indemnity fee. He lectures in America and, last November, at the Belfast Arts Festival, where his appearance coincided with the furore over the Anglo-Irish Treaty ('I didn't think I was going to get back to my comics').

Somehow he has faced up to the fact that he will never achieve whole sets, just as there are films he will never see. He is even reconciled to the fact that he will never read his collection as it stands now, though every time he goes to London he returns with more annuals.

When it comes to new comics he has now steeled himself to buying only Christmas issues and those which come with free gifts, but it will be still touch and go as to whether he runs out of time or space first. Sometimes he dreams of a British Comics Institute on the lines of the British Film Institute, with himself as curator.

Meanwhile among the yellowing paper the phones ring as old

entertainers vie for his attention. This year he is doing a radio series with Harold Berens ('You don't know Harold Berens? Wot a geezer? You don't remember "Ignorance is Bliss"? Why must I meet youngsters?').

'By trade I am a Resurrectionist,' said Dennis Gifford.

But I had found his Buck Ryan viewer, a small black thing with a spool which turned so you could watch on film, frame by frame, the adventures of the great detective. I last saw that in 1951.

Dennis was in a state of some unease, hovering two feet away. 'You won't break it?' He only has two of them.

1987

PART TWO
THE WORLD

THE LEGENDARY LOST FAIR

∽

I f you want to know what it looks like, think of the Sargasso
Sea in a horror comic, the tattered rigging of wrecks rearing
out of the green slime at sunset. Except that this is a sea of
elder and brambles, right bang in the middle of Leighton Buzzard,
and what has almost disappeared into it is a century of heavy
traction.

This is a story of buried treasure. The cast includes Albert, an
almost spherical gentleman, and Tom, a watchful man in a
leather coat. Together they are the Smith Brothers, who two
decades ago inherited this seven-and-three-quarter-acre yard from
their father, along with his funfair. Then there is Gerry, a man in
a hurry with a black moustache, a mobile phone, and a Mercedes
with the number-plate GC1. Gerry is Gerry Cottle, the circus-
owner, and something that has eluded him for years is finally
within his grasp; Gerry is here to buy a funfair.

Only there is a problem. Soon after they inherited the fair,
Albert and Tom fell out, so solicitors came leaping through the
brambles. The result is that the two brothers, who live next door

to each other in this their winter quarters, have not spoken to each other for nearly twenty years. 'It's like negotiating with the Bosnians and the Croatians,' puffs Gerry, who has spent the morning running backwards and forwards across the yard.

A series of injunctions having kept the fair off the roads ever since the original row, this is the first time that anyone outside the family has seen the dodgems and the Swirl. 'I am a happy man,' whispers Gerry Cottle.

You would not credit the desolation. Bindweed creeps up the cabs of huge Scammell trucks, there are abandoned tyres and batteries, old hot-dog stands, wrecked dodgems and the trucks getting older and older the further into the desolation you go. But at the edge are the rides of the lost fair, which are still in working order.

What makes the whole thing so bizarre is the value of the stuff. An operational set of dodgems can set you back anything from £250,000 to £400,000. The value of the yard, which is just two minutes' walk from the high street, is anyone's guess. It is believed that at the height of the property boom, sums of £1 million an acre were mentioned, though finding that would have been child's play compared to negotiating with the Smiths.

Even people who know them well are baffled by the origins of the row. Yes, money was involved, volunteers Albert, now sixty-two, the only brother who will talk about it. Also the fact that on the rides 'T. Smith & Sons' was overnight mysteriously changed to 'T. Smith & Son'. 'I could tell you more,' says Albert, who doesn't. All that is known is that their father, T. Smith, was a patriarch who took all the decisions and handled all the money. And then T. Smith died.

Talking to the brothers is like talking to men out of the Middle Ages. Tom admits he never went to school; Albert's wife claims her husband did, 'only he never learned nothing'. The result is that neither man can read or write. You are not aware of this until you ask one of them to remember a date or spell a name, when the conversation is abruptly changed.

'It don't bother me,' says Tom, grinning. 'I know right from wrong. I'm a good mechanic. What more is there?'

When Gerry Cottle started negotiating with showmen he found he was in a completely oral culture, a feature of which was the speed at which rumours spread. 'You bargain with one of them in Land's End, and by night they all know about it in John o' Groat's,' said Malcolm Cannon, his right-hand man. 'It's like a bush telegraph, only they've got cellular phones so it's quicker.'

It was also an enclosed little world. 'Outsiders do marry in, but they find it difficult,' said Albert's wife. Many families are dynasties who staked the right to a location in the old street fairs; such rights, on the rare occasion when they change hands, fetch upwards of £40,000. So not only do you meet men seemingly out of the Middle Ages, they probably are.

'My dad did it, and 'is dad before 'im,' says Albert. 'Also my mother's dad, T. Pettigrove, 'e 'ad really big stuff, 'e did. 'Is Golden Carousel is still on the roads, must be well over 100 years old. Used to be steam, that.'

What is up for sale are the big rides the brothers own jointly. They always had rides. They were never in the sideshow business; no bearded ladies wintered here, or snakes. 'One of them snake shows is still touring,' says Albert. 'The old woman got to pay her girls £150 a week to get in amongst 'em now.'

The brothers toured every year from March to November, and what Albert calls 'this lovely old yard' was their winter quarters. They still tour, but separately now, with the new rides they were obliged to buy after the Dispute (the brothers talk of it like the Fall). Albert in particular has been forced out to more and more remote sites. 'Like Sarum,' he broods, and it is some time before I realise he is talking about Salisbury.

The disputed rides, by now a legend among fair people, would probably have stayed where they were in the lovely old yard, had two things not happened. The first was that the brothers acquired a financial adviser, a young man with a BMW. The second was the ambition of Gerry Cottle.

For two years Cottle had been trying to get showmen to tour with his circus. With two circuses on the road for forty weeks a year, and with traditional town grounds closed to him, because of the attitude of councils to performing animals, he had negotiated a whole series of new sites on the outskirts. These were sites so large not even a circus would fill them. So Cottle dreamed of a mixture of circus and fair, 'a travelling theme park'.

The only thing was that the showmen, having always used sites their fathers used, were wary. So this year, in exasperation, he decided to go it alone, to have his own funfair, not with imported modern rides, but with those he remembered from when he was a boy.

But where was he to get stuff that old? He heard there was some in Glasgow, and flew up in February, only to find the rides had been sold an hour before. He heard there were some in Swindon, and was actually in negotiation with the family when they decided to sell to a museum, fearing the reaction of other showmen.

Then, on the grapevine, he heard about the Legend of the Lost Fair. He also heard other things, that despite the dispute the brothers had kept the dodgems and the rides in working order.

And so it proved. A lorry untaxed for over ten years roars into life when Gerry Cottle, burbling excited nothings into his mobile phone, finally comes to Leighton Buzzard. Within an hour he has the lorry taxed in Luton.

'None of this should have happened,' says Albert Smith. Both Smiths are walking very slowly up and down, fifty yards apart.

1992

Back we went to Agincourt

⌒

The mighty McEwen made the bow. He made it of red yew in the old way until it stood taller than a man, a curving beautiful thing. Originally it had been his, with a draw-weight of 120 pounds. McEwen is possibly the only man in England capable of using such a bow. In the Middle Ages he would have been a holy terror; today McEwen of Wanstead is a printer on the *Daily Express*. To accommodate mortal men he had shave the bow down to fifty pounds.

'But how d'you reckon you'll get it through French Customs?' he asked.

'I shall say it's a fishing rod.'

He looked at me sadly. 'Oh no, they'll remember. You watch. They'll remember.'

It is a Thursday morning, 20 June 1415. In the Great Hall of the King's castle at Carmarthen a priest is writing names on a parchment as they are called out. The hall is filled with men: as the names are called each acknowledges his presence. It has been going on like this since dawn, and one man moves impatiently in his seat. It is nearing 10 a.m. and that is dinner time.

This man is the King's Chamberlain, Thomas Merbury, who has been entrusted with the recruitment of archers for the coming French war. Five thousand archers will fight at Agincourt, of whom 240 will be from the county of Carmarthenshire. Merbury knows these men: twelve years earlier some of them, in Owen Glyndwr's uprising, would have tried to kill him. Nothing sharpens an appreciation of skill so much.

They had taken this very castle in 1403 and, again, with French help, in 1405. The uprising petered out, though it devastated Wales. That is one of the reasons why so many men wait patiently in the hall, that and the fact that Henry V is paying foot archers four pence a day for the campaign. Think of that: the Statute of Labourers in 1351 fixed ploughmen's wages at *seven shillings a year*.

The men in the hall are being contracted, with that legalistic obsession of the Middle Ages, to go 'God willing, with our most excellent lord the King in his journey into France' for a period of forty-five and a half days. Sixteen days after the agreement they are all to go on the royal expense account. One has a sudden vision of happy knots of men singing 'Charge it up, charge it up,' as they walk to Portsmouth. In the hall that day, men's imaginations must have raced.

Consider them for a moment. In the history of archery there can never have been men so highly trained. Archery was the sporting obsession of the day, and these were its finest exponents. In 1346 their fathers had brought down the chivalry of France at Crécy (1200 men had gone from the county, one of the heartlands of the bow), and again in 1356 at Poitiers. They can shoot bows with draw-weights of between 80 and 120 pounds (the modern composite bow is between 30 and 40), and release 15 aimed arrows a minute so that the sky turns black. They can wound at 150 yards, their long bodkin spikes brushing mail aside as though it were paper. At fifty, they can send their great clothyard shafts up to the feathers in a charging horse.

As they stand in the hall they look ready for anything. Some lean on their bows as they wait. One or two are in mail, many in brigandines, quilted jackets with iron plates sewn into them. They wear stockings of wool and long hooded cloaks. Their belts bulge with daggers and swords.

Since Crécy these men have walked through Europe, awestruck by its cities and great cathedrals, sleeping as rough as tramps, boozing, living off nuts and berries; and the heavy armoured cavalry that has dominated European history for a thousand years, since the Goths rode down the Roman legions at Adrianople in 378, has melted before them.

Consider these men: *they might have toppled not only dynasties but the entire society of their time.* In other societies where the bow ruled, its greatest exponents were kings and nobles. It is no accident that the record for flight shooting is still held by a Turkish sultan. But in Europe no knight in the early fifteenth century goes to war as an archer. *It has never happened before in the technology of war that its most devastating weaponry is in the hands of the most deprived elements of its population.* A moment like this will never come again. But it passes.

The strange thing is that the names of the men in the hall stand out from the anonymous poverty of the Middle Ages. In the Public Records office in Chancery Lane there is a document heavy with seals and covered with the spiky brown hand of medieval bureaucracy which lists them. You look on something that the man wrote down one July morning in Carmarthen five and a half centuries before. The parchment has arrived.

Most names are patronyms (surnames were not common in Wales until the middle of the sixteenth century): Richard ap Gruffydd of Caeo; Little Evan of Iscennen; Jenkyn ap Henry and David Thomas of Llanstephan; Philip Bennett of St Clears;

The Last Human Cannonball

Thomas Cooke and Philip ap Adda of Laugharne. The surnames are those of English colonials in the boroughs.

None of the heralds, those sports writers of the Middle Ages, will record these names. They are outside the rules of chivalry. No one would have bothered to take these prisoner, for such men have no money for ransoms. They would have been ridden down like chickens by proud French lords like the Dukes of Alençon and Bar and Brabant.

But Little Evan took his bow with him to France, and the dukes of Brabant and Alençon and Bar did not ride home from Agincourt.

'You stand sideways on to the target,' said McEwen. 'Like this, feet apart. Lay the arrow across your hand and bring it to the string. Now draw as though you were opening a chest expander.'

In his great hands the bow opened like a fan. Edward McEwen, forty-three, six feet two, sixteen and a half stone, has been making longbows since as a boy he quietly subtracted branches from yew trees in the local park. He makes them now to test the claims of history: historians, he maintains, have little hope of understanding medieval wars unless they have shot with a bow.

In the moat of the Tower of London, for a film, he used replicas of those arrow-heads which have survived. The Tower provided a medieval coat of mail and an Elizabethan breastplate much thicker than any worn at Agincourt. The Ministry of Defence provided a figure made of compressed polystyrene, the closest approximation of a human body. A butcher provided a mutton carcass.

McEwen put the bodkin head, a six-inch steel spike, through mail as though that had not been there. A direct hit on the Elizabethan plate resulted in an inch of penetration. Another arrow, deflected by the angle of the plate, took off the figure's head. Shot at the carcass the bodkin went straight through to bury itself in the ground. Another head, the terrible forker, a crescent head two inches across which rotated in flight, cut at an angle through four ribs of the carcass. When they show this film in the Tower a quiet falls on the watching schoolboys.

'We all lose arrows,' said McEwen. In a wood in north London we were having a crash course for Agincourt. We prodded the leaves: at the end of an hour I had lost three. 'It happens to the best,' said McEwen.

Later at home I put a phone directory against a sofa and let fly at point-blank range. I missed the directory. Little Evan probably never saw an arrow in a chesterfield.

They sailed from Portsmouth on 11 August 1415, 8000 archers and 2000 men-at-arms in 1500 small ships. Some of the great lords had cauldrons in their baggage: had they died their bodies would have been boiled down and their skeletons returned to England.

The King, Henry V, had a piece of the True Cross in his. He was twenty-seven, an athlete and a religious bigot, and he needed this war. France was a vast adventure playground for the English barons; it prevented their minds turning to civil insurrection at home. The kings who made peace fell: Edward II and Richard II, two of the few attractive figures of the Middle Ages, had been torn down. And so the men of Carmarthen, for the House of Lancaster and four pence a day, went to France.

Five centuries later they did remember the bow in Calais. A clerk in the car-hire office clutched his chest, shouted, *'Un arc,'* and fell on the insurance forms.

The army disembarked at Harfleur on 14 August. For a month they laid siege to it. By the time it fell on 22 September, a third of them were either dead or out of action, chiefly through dysentery. So some piece of public relations was necessary. Abandoning his plan of marching on Paris, the King led his army in an attempt to reach Calais, then an English port, before the French could cut them off.

They marched fast. By 20 October they had covered 200 miles in 12 days. They had been days of rain and river-crossings. There had been little food. On Monday, 21 October, there occurs one of the rare moments of real drama in a medieval chronicle. At Peronne, 'after we had passed the town about a mile we found the roads strangely trodden by the French army, as it had gone before us in many thousands'. You can feel the shock: the French, in vast numbers, were between them and the sea.

Three days later they were just two days' march from Calais. But late in the day scouts came in with news that the French, outnumbering them five to one, were across their line of march. Glumly the little army settled down for the night at the small village of Maisoncelles. It was raining. Through the darkness they could hear the sounds from the French camp a mile away: that night a great party was being held at the castle of Tramecourt.

In the plains of northern France little has changed. There are no hedges, no meadows, no hills. There is just the heavy, ploughed earth that laps the roads, the few villages, the trees. Apart from the metalled roads the landscape is much as it was in 1415.

Maisoncelles, Agincourt and Tramecourt form a small triangle in the back roads south of St Omer. The villages have a dispirited look, a straggle of small houses at a crossroads, a church, a small café. There is no litter for nobody stops. It is very quiet.

It is hard to remind yourself that this is the abattoir of Europe. Crécy is 18 miles to the south-west, the Somme 40 miles to the south-east, and Waterloo 100 miles to the north-east. For millions of men their last memory was of these flat acres.

The family who own the battlefield owned it in 1415. They lost three brothers at Agincourt; on the roadside before the long drive to their château is a memorial to Viscount Chabot de Tramecourt, and his two sons. Three more died in the last war, in German captivity. The family has been here since the eleventh century, and from here they went on the Third Crusade.

Tourists came, 'English tourists', said the Viscountess. Sometimes they were a nuisance. 'It was a defeat for us,' she said gently.

Back We Went to Agincourt

In the last century one of the family had erected a memorial over the French grave pits: he had done it to discourage archaeologists.

In a clump of trees a rusting metal Christ droops from his Cross. The inscription records merely that it was here 'that our valorous warriors fell'. A few biblical quotations follow. There is nothing else, no description of the battle nor the numbers of the slain. It is as though this was a disaster so complete as to admit of nothing but generalities.

At a crossroads a quarter of a mile away a rough standing stone has been erected. '*Agincourt, symbole de courage ...*' More generalities. The de Tramecourt family were annoyed by this. It was put up by a priest who was not of the neighbourhood. And he had not, said the Viscountess, even asked permission.

Tramecourt is wooded, as it was in 1415. The Agincourt woods have been cut back, but you can still, from the odd clump of trees, see where they were. At the narrowest point there was just 1000 yards between the woods. It was here that the battle was fought. A French army, some 30,000 strong, was committed to advancing into a funnel.

McEwen came over on the third day with the sort of outfit a medieval archer would have worn, a suit of mail, a brigandine, woollen hose. He changed on the battlefield, and it was a metamorphosis. His shoulders spread before our eyes, his step lightened. And he began to swagger, he really did. A bully-boy of the Middle Ages was walking the plains of northern France again.

McEwen stretched himself. 'I feel a real berk walking around Wanstead like this. It's very odd but I feel quite at home here.' A heavy-lidded French lorry-driver passed. Twenty yards further on, in a classic double-take, the brake-lights came on and you could see a hand fumbling with the driving mirror.

In the café at the crossroads a fat man with a beer looked out of the door. He was 150 yards away. 'I could drop him from here,' said McEwen professionally. He was moving on his toes and stretching like a boxer. 'Huh,' he said looking across the ploughed ground. 'The French were really asking for it, coming across ground like this.'

The armies deployed at first light, the English in a horn formation, the tips of which were the archers. In the centre the knights had dismounted. The French were in three great lines, the first two on foot, the last mounted. Princes of the blood had jostled and argued their way into the front row of the first line: 8000 men, each in armour weighing between 60 and 75 pounds, waited. On the wings were more heavy cavalry.

For four hours nothing happened. The two armies stood there in the rain. Then commands were given and the English began to advance. The earth had been ploughed and movement was difficult. At about 200 yards from the French lines they halted and the archers began to hammer the stakes they had brought with them against cavalry into the ground. They sharpened the ends. The English front fitted neatly into the 1000 yards between the woods.

Chroniclers do not disagree about the sequence of events which followed. There was an arrow strike, possibly with flight arrows because of the distance, against the French knights on horseback. It was designed to provoke them into attack: at 200 yards such arrows would have had little effect on armour, but the horses would panic. Out of the sky, like dense rain, the arrows were falling.

The French charged. Horses carrying between 250 and 300 pounds of men and armour lumbered through the mud. To a man on foot it would have seemed like the end of the world to see these behemoths against the sky. The archers would have been standing, possibly three deep, each man with a quiver of twenty-four arrows stuck into the ground at his feet. Nobody knows what orders were given, or how they were given. McEwen believes there would have been some concerted plan, with the archers told to hold their arrows until the point of charge about fifty yards away. At that range every arrow would tell.

The horses quickened into a gallop, their riders shouting as the lances came down. Then the word of command, and a hiss as though a great creature had drawn its breath when 5000 heavy war arrows were loosed. The archers were professionals now, drawing, loosing, their fingers as gentle as those of pianists. Horses were screaming and falling. The hiss was uneven now as men shot in their own time. The charge broke and the few men still alive turned their horses.

But they rode into the advancing French first line against whom the archers now turned their bows. They shot at its flanks, so that the mass of men became denser and reminiscent of an advance against machine guns in the Somme, with the men bent forward as though against rain. It must have been like that at Agincourt.

The two lines met and lances scraped against armour. There was a shock as though a rugby scrum, multiplied a thousand times, had clashed. And still the arrows came. Men were falling in the French lines and other men were falling on them. Into the confusion came the French second line and still the front was contracting. Now something very strange happened. Knights fought knights in medieval wars and fought according to honour and custom. A lightly armed archer would have stood little chance in a hand-to-hand encounter with a knight. But the archers dropped their bows and seizing mallets and knives rushed at the French mass.

It was now that the battlefield became a stockyard. The vast scrum collapsed on itself. Chroniclers talk of piles of bodies higher than a man. Some suffocated. Others lay there as the archers inserted their long knives into the visors and cut into their brains. The cries were muffled by the armour. There would have been a great rummaging in these heaps as men looked for the richest armour and ransoms. The third French line did not charge.

The battle was breaking up into scuffles as men chased each other. There was a small French charge led by the Duke of Brabant which broke like rain on glass. Worried by this, and by the large numbers of French prisoners standing about, Henry V ordered them killed. Knights and men-at-arms refused, so he ordered 200 archers in with their knives. But two things about this must be remembered: first, no outrage is reflected in the chronicles of both sides; secondly, over 1000 prisoners reached England, so it could not have been a massacre.

The battle had lasted three hours. Some 10,000 Frenchmen were dead, while the English casualties were probably little more than 100. The battle had begun to assume the proportions of a miracle. That night fires were lit. The English dead were put in a barn and the building set on fire. The bodies of the Duke of York and the Earl of Suffolk were boiled down in the cauldrons. In the morning the archers walked across the field, killing the French wounded.

The Llanstephan men might have recognised one of the dead. Henry Gwyn, lord of Llanstephan, an old Glyndwr man unable to reconcile himself to English victory, had died on the French side. His castle, high above an estuary 400 miles away, was confiscated: more fussy bureaucratic scribblings on parchment. It is an irony that the most important poignant moments were supplied by the civil service. On 29 October the English reached Calais.

Agincourt passed into folklore. Exactly 500 years after it was fought, during one of the darkest periods of the First World War, the writer Arthur Machen wrote a short story, 'The Bowmen of Mons'. In this the British line is about to break, and the grey German hordes are poised to flood through, when there is a cry of 'Harry and St George' and out of the sky the great arrows come. Men actually believed at the time that this had happened.

There was a staff colonel named Shepheard who, travelling behind the lines in fog, suddenly saw 'Hooded, cloaked figures of silent, gazing men, rank beyond rank ... They rose slowly and every man stared fixedly at me. It was a queer wistful sad stare ... their cloaks were grey, almost luminous ... I touched at one and it came off in my fingers like a soft dust.

'Then slowly they sank into the ground, rank after rank of hooded men sinking into the earth, their eyes fixed on me to the last.'

Little Evan would probably have found this the strangest thing of all, romantic folklore and four pence a day. A longbow is such a beautiful thing it is easy to forget its capacity for carnage. I felt a bit uneasy, bringing one back here. But the men in the fields gathering swedes did not look up after the first few glances: Agincourt fades beside the victories of the EEC's agricultural policy.

McEwen had no such scruples. His feet apart, he drew the great bodkin back to his ear and loosed. It rose in an arc then slapped into the ground. It went a little over 150 yards, an indication of its weight, and of his theory that the archery battle was fought at close range. The forker and the barbed arrows followed.

We walked over the mud to where they had sunk deep into the furrows. McEwen picked them up and looked at them. 'The mud of Agincourt,' he said with wonder in his voice. It was a sort of homecoming: he had shot the red bow at Agincourt.

Long after the photographs had been taken of the first war arrows probably to be shot there since the battle, he was in no hurry to change out of his archer's outfit. He sat in the café drinking brandy. A party of French people ostentatiously showed no interest at all. McEwen slowly wiped the mud off his arrows. He seemed very happy.

The landlady sold me a French account of the battle. It was six pages of dull narrative. She brought it from an inner room and it came, like pornography, under plain cover. It cost £1.50. The defeated always make a profit sometime.

1979

WHERE THE BEST WHIPPETS SHOP

⟜

I t takes you aback, the first time: no shop could be that small. The second time, you almost expect to see it gone from the nowhere world of Indian restaurants and army surplus stores behind Euston Station in London, back into the fairy tale out of which it surely strayed.

But when you read the lettering above the tiny window the pavements move a little: 'J. P. WHIPPET SUPPLIES'. No Mayfair gun-makers, no Jermyn Street shirt-makers, have anything on this. Behind Euston is the most exclusive shop in the world.

'Blokes come in looking cross.' John Porter's sturdy red face was expressionless. 'Right, they say, what's it all 'bout then? They think it's a joke. And this Swedish bloke, few months back, wanted to know if he could take a picture for some magazine. Said he'd never seen anything like it in the world.'

It does not surprise him any more. He has grown used to the fact that there is a world in which people hurry past, and another, too small for them to enter, which begins inside his shop: in the land of whippets where falls not hail, nor rain, nor any snow.

Where the Best Whippets Shop

The shop is cluttered. There are tiny leather boots and fur-lined coats and, in an inner room, on which the curtains are drawn, the long melancholy features hang on the walls like the masters of some secret society.

It is impressed on you here that the Creation did not take seven days. On the eighth the Almighty, refreshed after His day off, added a moral guide for mankind. He made the whippet.

'A whippet-owner, I'd trust him with my life,' declared John Porter. 'In my time I've known some rotten people.' He paused. 'And I've known some very nice whippets.'

It is not a pet shop. He does not deal in the dogs, nor does he sell their food. He makes and sells whippet muzzles, whippet blinkers, whippet boots and whippet coats lined in wool. Many of these he designed himself.

There are whippet medicines, whippet figurines in bronze, whippet ties, whippet brushes, whippet etchings and a small library of books and magazines. The monthly *Whippet News* has its own pin-ups: 'Rose loves the walks, hunting, eating and sleeping, and is ready at any hour for any of these.' And what caption-writer can claim as much for any Page Three girl? The magazine also has its Court Page, recording the matings and births, the intricate genealogy and even the occasional sad little obituary.

John Porter, now seventy-four, has no doubts about his role as squire to this aristocratic caste. 'The whippet is a thing of beauty,' he said in his matter-of-fact way. 'He has good ears, good eyes and these long, classical legs. Not like some poor bull terrier.

'And he's so affectionate. You can pull a whippet's earhole, he won't bite yer. He never goes mad or barks, or goes potty. You could leave a whippet alone with a baby and he'd be all right.'

He smoothed down one of his coats thoughtfully. 'Baby would be fine, too.'

He has had the shop since the 1930s. He began as a shoemaker. Then, after the war, when a greyhound auction room opened round the corner from him, he began to make leads and muzzles. Whippets had always been miners' dogs, but around the mid-1950s they moved south and began to rise among the social categories. John Porter went into whippet supplies.

But then came a turning point in his life. In 1967, wearying of what he now calls 'the villainies of the track' (in some of which he had happily joined: 'Bloke likes to win sometimes'), he went over exclusively to whippets. Like all converts, he remembers the date.

There are some 40,000 whippets in Britain, and a racing season lasting from April to October on grass circuits all over Britain. No gambling is allowed. There is just love – in many cases a love exceeding that of women.

John Porter scratched his ear. 'A bloke comes in here, I know if it ever came to a toss-up between his whippet and his old woman, she'd be packing her bags.

'But then, his old woman don't race. And she does cost a lot more.'

A whippet costs between £35 and £100. His coat costs £6.50, his boots 75p each, his racing satins £7.50. Porter's own whippet, usually referred to as 'that bloke', gets through half a pound of the best steak-and-kidney a day. His owner supplements this with brown bread croutons.

'I was up north once, at a meeting, when this man comes up with three whippets and his wife. He was wearing a white choker and a cap. The goods, you know. And he bought three whippet coats, three muzzles and three leads. Must have come to over £25.

'His missus was looking at some whippet brooches I stocked then, and she asked how much they were. They were about 50p each. But this bloke, he suddenly grabbed her by the arm, "Come away, you don't want any of those."

'So I leaned over and gave her one with my compliments. I never saw a bloke look such daggers in my life.'

Like all believers he delights in telling of others further down the path of enlightenment than himself.

'Went to see a bloke once. I'd heard he was off work. But when I got there he seemed perfectly all right. He took me upstairs and there was this nose on the pillow.

'It was the whippet was sick. He'd put him into his own bed and was nursing him.' There was a strange noise, as of a drain clearing. John Porter was laughing.

As the dog has risen socially, so the orders have become more exotic. Porter has made whippet coats to match those worn by their owners. He rummaged in a pile and produced a camel-hair coat ordered by some titled lady in Kensington.

Eighty per cent of his business is postal now, and some of it part of an expanding overseas trade. The other week he had sent off coats to Finland. 'Poor little buggers,' muttered John Porter, 'walking around in twenties below.'

The boots, tiny soft-soled things, are for sore feet. They are bought singly, but at least one of his customers buys a complete set of four. Takes her dogs on ice, he said.

We walked among his medicine stocks, tasting. He and his friends use many of the embrocations on themselves. 'Old boy sends me £12 every two months. Says it does him a world of good.'

Business has never been better. At one race meeting last year he took over £800 in one day. From the Continent come grateful letters, one from Sweden with a paw print acknowledging a new coat.

He travels to meetings with his dog. Sixteen thousand miles a year, said John Porter, and that bloke had never been sick. As a puppy he would eat everything in the shop which did not move. 'His father was a champion,' said Porter.

He reckons on another six years in business, and hopes someone else will then take up the ministry.

A recent issue of *Whippet News* had an arts section. There was a poem addressed by an owner to his dog:

We show, course and race, and
are very faithful and true,
We're obedient and a friend,
what else can a dog do?

Outside the shop the lorries rumbled on to Camden Town.

'You'd like to think there'll be whippets in heaven,' said John Porter suddenly. There was a long pause. 'But I suppose that's what you'd call a fallacy.'

In a small shop in London two men brooded on the vagaries of accepted theology.

1991

WHERE ALL LOST YEARS ARE

F or them no revolution is ever over, no war ends, no dynasty ever falls. In London there is a place where there is no time.

The chain mail was real, and so old they had forgotten how they ever came by it. Probably it was part of the left luggage in some medieval pub. It was rarely called for, they said, as knitted cord looked as good, but the odd actor did sometimes insist on it. The old men tell of Sir Herbert Beerbohm-Tree, the great Edwardian, who once appeared on the West End stage in full plate and chain mail. Just the once. It all went well until Sir Herbert had to kneel, and then a polite if puzzled audience saw Macbeth play the full first act on his knees. Sir Herbert had been unable to get up. A great old trouper, but he never afterwards appeared in real armour anywhere.

In the workroom the cutter had just completed something he had worked on for three years: it had become, he said, almost a way of life. On a peg glittered the full dress uniform of a Napoleonic marshal, the gold braid reaching across the blue doeskin.

The Last Human Cannonball

Even the cutter, a man who has wandered the centuries like Dr Who, with scissors and thread, was quite fascinated by it. Four inches of collar, he muttered, highest collar he had ever made. He could not resist putting it on, blinking through his spectacles in the mirror at the man who had once strutted through the drawing rooms of France in this.

In Camden Town is the Great Attic. Enter a large brick warehouse, under the flag of the Queen's Award for Export Achievement, and fantasy closes round you like a fog, 93,000 square feet of fantasy.

You may remember a story like this. The children are staying with their grandmother: the days are wet and they wander disconsolately through the house. Then one day they come on a corridor they have not seen before, a corridor ending in a small blue door. Beyond that, in the dim light, they blink at rack after rack of old clothes, and nothing is ever the same again.

'You see it in people's faces,' said Gerald Moulin, manager of the head office of Bermans and Nathans Ltd in Irving Street in the heart of London's theatreland. 'They come to us expecting to see about three rails of old clothes, and then they see this ... '

Chiffons, velvets, buckskins; a leather cuirass for a centurion to swagger in along the Appian Way; the furs and fustian of the Dark Ages; the velvet of the fifteenth century; the lace of the seventeenth; the brocade of the eighteenth. Rack after rack; floor after floor, empires and religions and revolutions where once Maples stored their furniture.

On six floors they have in Camden Town, at a conservative estimate, one million costumes. After the great Hollywood studios sold off theirs, this place became unique. 'When we advertise we say, "Largest stock in Europe, *probably* in the world,"' said Monty Berman, the managing director. 'You can't be certain.'

When he was a boy there were eighteen costumiers in London, and Bermans was the youngest and shakiest. The company was founded by his father, a Russian émigré, whose portrait hangs in the reception hall. Nathans, with which they amalgamated twelve years ago, was founded in 1790: there are programmes of the charades it costumed at Windsor and letters written to the firm by Charles Dickens.

Bermans boomed when the young Monty Berman introduced a new concept, the package deal. If a producer came to him he would give one quotation for costumes, manufacture and fitting: it was an approach which recommended itself to the money men who were behind producers. It made for neater budgeting. When *My Fair Lady* was produced on the London stage, Bermans was the first company to have done everything except the wigs.

'Our motto was always "Don't say no". If we had quoted £20,000 we'd stay within that, unless the producer wanted to stage the Charge of the Light Brigade.' (It was a small joke, for upstairs are the frogged uniforms: Bermans helped stage *The Charge of the Light Brigade*).

So a monolith came into being. It is an indication of the size of the firm today that it claims to outfit seventy per cent of all German television costume dramas. There is a staff of 200, including 16 tailors and 40 dressmakers.

Here anything is possible. They have enough uniforms in stock to equip an American division from the Second World War, and enough weaponry to prompt a small medieval insurrection.

Jester's cap after jester's cap after jester's cap. The cowls of the Middle Ages. The coifs of the Middle Ages. The soft-soled shoes of the Middle Ages. The furs of the nobility. In heaps. In boxes. In cupboards.

'You don't have to use real fur all the time, you know,' said Monty Berman seriously. 'I mean, there weren't that many sables knocking about the fields of England in the year 800.' He lowered his voice. 'You can usually get away with a dog.'

I had gone to hire a Roundhead trooper's uniform, ostensibly

The Last Human Cannonball

to be photographed for an article on the Civil War. They brought out the high-waisted leather jerkin, the cloak, the woollen pantaloons. They talked about underwear and fastenings: and what was so staggering was that these men seemed to know as much about everyday life in the seventeenth century as any academic historian.

The costumes are leased out ('We don't like selling,' said Monty Berman) – what the firm calls 'made new, to hire'. After a film they come back to Camden Town and can be hired out to members of the public at upwards of £25 a week. They will hire you a replica of the Imperial State Crown at £25, should your fantasies so take you.

They do not encourage browsers who want fancy dress (another branch, in Irving Street, houses the fancy dress collection).

'People come in here asking to be made up like the Devil,' muttered Monty Berman. 'You have to take them on one side and warn them: "How are you going to push a gin and tonic in through that lot?"'

You find racks awaiting collection: Aladdin for a Gravesend panto; exotic Arabian costumes for a production of *Hassan* at Epsom College; dozens of elves' and goblins' outfits for *Santa Claus* being filmed at Pinewood with Dudley Moore.

You make amazing little discoveries. Among the racks, squeezed in among the velvets, is the black jerkin Laurence Olivier wore when he made *Hamlet* thirty years ago. Landfalls like this are everywhere: Olivier's robes as the Mahdi in *Khartoum*; Burt Lancaster's preaching black from *The Devil's Disciple*; Charlton Heston's robes as Richelieu in *The Three Musketeers*. Inside helmets and jackets are famous names and legendary films. It gets to the point where you find yourself trying to catch them out. 'Incas,' echoed Monty Berman equably. 'Yes, we've got Incas somewhere.'

Solar topis and riding breeches come from here. A man flies

through the air: Superman's red knickers and blue tights are theirs. *Mountbatten: The Last Viceroy* is now in production: civilian and military clothes as well as all Lord Mountbatten's costumes are from here. Trevor Nunn is directing a big budget film about the life of Lady Jane Grey: Bermans and Nathans provided hundreds of period costumes. *Hitler and the Generals* is in production and they have come up with the uniforms for an age which smothered itself in uniforms. They have one department devoted entirely to the uniforms of the Third Reich, and to those of its concentration-camp victims.

At any one time, anywhere in the world, actors in twenty films and forty television dramas are dressed in their clothes.

However much you may have heard about this place, your first experience of it is mind-blowing. You enter what seems to be a waxwork museum in the reception area. Models in glass cases wear the costumes of famous productions and swords line the walls. But it is offstage, among the racks, that bewilderment sets in. 'The Stone Age? Oh yes, we can do you the Stone Age. We did the costumes for *One Million Years BC.*'

For the last twenty-eight years Philip Linke has worked here. He is now the firm's chief cutter and is also on the board. It was Mr Linke who made a marshal's uniform in what was an unusual deal, a private order placed by an American banker who bought the uniform outright so that he might play at war games with his friends. Mr Linke would not be drawn on the price, except to say that there was so much gold braid involved that a rise in the cost of bullion had doubled it.

Across the Atlantic the letters came, specifying cut and buttons and cloth, and with the letters came the photographs. The American and his friends were in the practice of trying to outdo each other. Mr Linke smiled. His client had gone for the ultimate. Every single detail on the uniform was an exact replica.

The Last Human Cannonball

'No, it isn't the most elaborate uniform I've ever made. That was for Charlton Heston as General Gordon.' Gordon wore the full dress uniform of a Turkish pasha, so thick with braid it might almost have stopped a bullet. 'And I only had one fitting. When Heston came my hands were shaking like this. I was younger then, much younger.'

Since then he has made every costume from the beginnings of time until now. It has given him a unique insight into the history of male dress.

'Just about up until the time of Beau Brummell it was more like dressmaking, all the lace and silk and that. But then it became tailoring, for you had fitted garments.'

When asked about his favourite costume, he thought for a long while. After all, he has been obliged to learn the lost arts of tailoring to make the hidden pockets in tight Regency trousers. Mr Linke said he thought the most elegant *and* comfortable clothing was something from around 1946 when, as he put it, people started getting smart again. It seemed an odd choice until you realised that Mr Linke was a young man in 1946. In everybody's life there is a time when the going was good.

'I saw Errol Flynn on television as Robin Hood. Quite ruined my weekend, that did,' said Monty Berman. 'There he was with lovely padded shoulders and all those women floating around in chiffon. Ridiculous. When we made *Alfred The Great* the King looked as though he'd been sleeping in his costume. That's how it was.

'All those thirties and forties films are like that. Magnificent costumes, but today there are too many people about who know how men dressed in the past. I shouldn't watch television. At Monday board meetings I'm unbearable. I've had a weekend seeing buttons in the wrong place, military collars with hooks and eyes showing. I just sit there, hoping it's nothing to do with us.'

A theatrical costumier's is like a river: the stock from old companies, failed productions, flows into it. Much of it is so old that the costumes were actually worn in life. In an alcove on the fourth floor are the ball-gowns, the fox and velvet evening coats and the feather boas which once belonged to real people: the cleaners do not like working on the fourth floor.

Many of the uniforms are real, including those of the Tsar's Imperial Guard. Three members of staff do nothing but clean boots, blanco webbing and polish belts, batmen all their working lives. A whole floor is given over to uniforms: France, Revolutionary; France, Empire; France, Second Empire. They have to be very careful with uniforms or out of Camberley come the happy, furious letters. When *The Longest Day* was filmed in 1962 they clothed 5000 men in 57 different uniforms. They took the invasion of Europe in their stride. They even have an armoury locked away in the basement.

'Peasants (Yugoslavia); Peasants (Austria);' then abruptly, 'Rough,' shelves full of woollen jerkins and tights, many of them ragged. It seems that is the biggest money-spinner of all. The clothes for working-class mobs, peasants, all those groups who fill the backgrounds in films.

Lace, slashed sleeves, the silk of a Manchu Emperor, the silk of a panto emperor, Edwardian day, Edwardian night: you can make up a poem just by quoting the indices.

They have a research library to answer queries about difficult costumes. 'Ancient Babylonians, we can take them in our stride,' said Kate Izzard, the librarian. 'When it's hard is when we get asked about specific people. I was asked once what Stalin's mother would have worn. In the end I found an old lady in a black dress in a photograph.'

In one room they have their costume jewellery, the treasures of the Pharaohs and the Aztecs, the crowns of Europe. 'A girl came in once to hire the Coronation Crown to get married in. She looked lovely.'

The Last Human Cannonball

They had a sale once, in 1975, when they got rid of 10,000 items at £2 each. Before they opened Monty Berman got a telephone call saying there were 300 people in the street outside. Police were called and the public was given twenty minutes to rummage and twenty minutes to get out.

'And Trafalgar Square filled up with people in cloaks,' said Monty Berman dourly. Fifty-five years in the business have taken away any enthusiasm he may once have had for dressing up.

Berman and Nathan do guided tours, provided they are given sufficient warning. They do not advertise. People tend to linger.

The year they got the Queen's Award for Export it was in the company of firms such as Plessey, Reckitt and Colman and Rolls-Royce. It was the first time the Award had ever gone to an attic full of old clothes.

1978

THE WESTERN TOWN IN MYTH

～

There is a town in the badlands, or rather, in the white dust and scrubland thirty miles to the north of Almeria in southern Spain. It is not much of a town, being little more than two streets. No roads lead up to it, and none away. Nobody lives there. The town has no name. Yet if you went there it would be as though you had come home.

It is not a matter of everything being more or less where you thought it would be. It is exactly as it should have been, not smaller and shabbier as the things of childhood are, but as it always has been, just as it was. At the end of the street, where the town gave up the struggle, and the infinity of dust and scrub closed in again, was the corral. In front of it, irons cooling in the slight wind, was the blacksmith's shop. Half-way along the street was the sheriff's office, and next to it the squat brick bunker of the jail. On the one bend, appropriately where the way became broad, was the saloon, and opposite was the livery stable.

At one time, from the front row of small cinemas, I watched those streets almost every week. In 20 years and in what now must be 300 Westerns, they have not changed. The coaches rattle into town down that untidy street. Horses are hitched to the rails. The old men sit on benches on the verandahs and watch the world pass. The screens widened, colour came, but it was the same town into which the tall men stalked, even as Clint Eastwood stalked into this one in the spaghetti Westerns which were made here. The Western town has become a metaphor. Its topography, the saloon, the sheriff's office, the livery stables, are as predictable as the Stations of the Cross.

There has only been one parallel to the Western film. That was the Arthurian cycle, which, as Professor Eugene Vinaver, Sir Thomas Malory's editor, remarked, 'alone held the Middle Ages spellbound for three centuries'. It gave them a sense of style. This was the way the parfit gentil knight should behave, faced with danger, temptation or loss.

Five hundred years later the same preoccupation sustains the Western, however banal the script or the director. 'The Westerner is the last gentleman,' wrote the film critic, the late Robert Warshow, 'and the movies which tell his story over and again are probably the last art form in which the concept of honour retains its strength.'

Like the Arthurian cycle again, the Western film has an odd haziness about time and place. Unless there is a historical point to be made (or usually, obscured) the Western takes place at some time between the end of the Civil War and the coming of the railway. The scene is a small town, either amid the prairies of the midwest, or the deserts of the south. At the end of the street is the corral ...

Jack Schaeffer wrote the classic description in his novel, *Shane*: '... a stage and freighting line had picked the site for a relay post. That meant a place where you could get drinks as well as horses and before long the cowboys from the plains ... were drifting in of an evening. With us homesteaders coming now, one or two almost every season, the town was taking shape. Already there were several stores, a harness and blacksmith shop, and nearly a dozen houses. Just the year before the men had put together a one-room schoolhouse.'

The town, even in reality, was a transient place, with strangers coming out of the Great Plains and vanishing back into them. Sir Charles Dilke, the English politician, noted with a slight shiver that the permanent population of Virginia City consisted of people who had lived there for more than a month. The town was also bedraggled. In old photographs it looks as though it had been put up in a few weeks by men with other things on their minds. 'Its houses are built everywhere,' marvelled one traveller, 'and then the streets get to them as best they can ... not a flower, not a blade of grass anywhere.'

There is no grass or trees in the town in Spain. As the road goes north from Almeria all vegetation drops away. The rivers are all neatly signposted, but in summer no water at all flows in beds 300 yards across. Where the town is there is a line of white hills, nature's slag-heaps, whole ridges and canyons of dust.

The town was built in the 1960s for the Italian film director Sergio Leone who shot his Westerns here, *The Good, The Bad, and The Ugly*, *A Fistful of Dollars*. Other Western makers moved in from America. *Shalako*, starring Sean Connery, was made here. At one stage Almeria was almost the motion picture capital of the world, for Westerns. The advantages were obvious. Labour was cheap. The gypsies camped around Almeria could ride horses blindfolded and could double as Mexicans and Indians: they became a readymade pool of extras. And, of course, there was the weather.

So the town was left standing. The film makers came and went, hiring it by the week or month. But then recession hit the film industry and it became the turn of the makers of commercials, hiring the town for something over £200 a day. Perhaps two a year get made here now. Charles Llewelyn, who made the 'Bandit' chocolate biscuit commercials, found that even the gypsies had now got a sort of union together. 'We found we had to include the fare from Madrid to Almeria for their organiser.'

The town is a real town and not a conventional filmset, propped upright by poles. Many of the buildings have interiors and some are made of stone. It could house a small population.

In the films the hero usually gets to the town just before sunset. Before that he has crouched in many gullies and made the odd gallon of coffee, rocking back on his heels.

I got there in the morning. There was a rough sign at the road's edge, indicating a sort of trackway into the desert. It rounded a hill and there it was. No traveller came upon Constantinople with more enthusiasm. There was that huddle of flat roofs straight out of childhood, it was that legendary slum of Western films.

Outside the town there was a small hill with white tombstones. The town's begetters had not missed a trick. Boot Hill was near the town gallows. The caretaker's assistant, a small wary man, lifted the pole that barred entrance across a wooden bridge. He showed no interest. Strangers, as always, are common in a Western town. A small cowed dog ran for its life. That seemed promising.

The sun was behind me as I walked down the street. It cast a long shadow. The caretaker, an old fat man, was puffing as he dragged out the cases of Coca Cola for the tourists he hoped would come that day. He did not look up.

Suddenly a great delight at the predictability of everything came over me. I walked along the wooden sidewalk and my heels clattered, just as Gary Cooper's had clattered, and Burt Lancaster's. It was everything I could do not to peer at the rooftops, so much has that sound become imbued with menace when Death comes on Mexican heels. The irony about Westerns is that they often become more real than one's own life.

The Western Town in Myth

The first thing the man does in a Western film is to visit the livery stables. Here the dialogue is traditional. Its purpose is just to get him down off his horse. He asks the old stableman will he give it a rubdown and feed. No name is given. No fees are asked (money is hardly ever mentioned in Westerns, except when it becomes the thousands which are to be stolen).

Then he visits the hotel and books in. Usually the hotel is kept by a girl, often the heroine. It is the one restaurant in the town and, with its check tablecloths and traditional diet of steak and apple pie, is usually posed as the homely pioneer virtues in contrast to the saloon, with its fancy fittings of brass and imported furniture. The girl-who-keeps-the-restaurant/hotel is usually walking out with the local sheriff, a weak man. But once our man is in town nothing will ever be the same again.

I passed the livery stable, and walked across the street to the hotel. Alas, they were both closed.

The saloon was opposite – and locked. A bribe and it was unlocked. The batwing doors creaked and I was blinking in the darkness. The saloon was perfect: the tables, the long bar down which the barman slid the whiskies, that strange verandah on the first floor from which the bad men were always getting shot.

The clouds were gathering behind the sierras. They were dark about the water tower which the ranch hands either shoot full of holes during their spree or pull down completely. Behind the town they even had the sort of wagon a travelling fashion drummer or actor (the failed Shakespearian kind, beloved of director John Ford) would have used. The town's builders had not missed a trick.

I picked my way up Boot Hill. The prop men had had a field day here. There were great crumbling catafalques of wood got up to look like marble. The prop men had got their history right (many Westerners were first-generation immigrants: 'Draw, Seamus') but not, alas, their orthography. 'In memory of Patrick

Flanagan, Born Counti Roscommon, Ireland, December 25 1829 ... '
Now he, he would have been the man in the large house outside
the town. And Sandford J. Sandford would have been the old ham
actor fallen on evil days and whiskey. Roberst (*sic*) Smith would
have been the prop man in a hurry again.

The rain was falling now, a thin miserable drizzle drifting
across the town. Downpours you get in Westerns, when
Fonda/Stewart/Wayne puts on his oilskins, but what was happening now made me feel like Keats' hijacked knight coming to on his
cold hillside.

For I never yet saw a Western where it drizzled. The town,
abruptly, became a film set.

1977

THE REAL THING

◡

The saddest picture I ever saw hung in a saloon in Tomb-stone. I knew about Tombstone long, long before I ever went there, just as other men know about Athens and Florence and Rome. It was what the poet R. S. Thomas called a name which the spirit recalls from earlier journeys in the dark wood.

There had been many journeys. I grew up knowing far more about the geography of the American West than I did about that of my own country. I knew about mesquite and tumbleweed and coyotes, and Dodge and Corydon. But Tombstone was the centre. It was where the tall men walked against the sky.

The place was a disappointment. I had been startled to find another town, St David's, about ten miles away, which had been there all the time, though the comics and the films had never mentioned it. Tombstone was a sad, cold town on a ridge, exposed to the winds. It had changed little since Wyatt Earp's day.

I walked the route he had taken from the pub to the OK corral. In the films it takes forever. But the pub is next door to the Corral. It would have taken him, at most, a minute.

The Last Human Cannonball

The picture hung in a saloon Earp would have recognised, and had pride of place above the bar. It was a very large engraving of Marshal Blücher meeting the Duke of Wellington after Waterloo.

I stared at it and stared at it. I had been brought up to think of the West as an almost spiritual landscape, secure in the old traditions and values, a purer place. It was a version of pastoral for us children of the fifties. But as the bat-wing doors made their familiar crash in the wind I realised for the first time that it was none of these things.

They should have had a picture of a showgirl there, or of old Daniel Boone. Instead they had a picture of two heroes of the Old World they affected to despise so much, with its kings and its imperialism. In the end the West was just a long way from anywhere.

More lies have been told about its history than about any series of events which have not been religious. It began with the ghost writers turning out memoirs for the ruffians of the West. It is ending with Hollywood. No sophisticated propaganda machine contributed, for no such machine was necessary, so eagerly did the people of the world want to believe. But the myths of the West have left the most powerful nation on earth in a cradle of humbug.

No historical truths disturb the myth. It was even possible to accommodate the ugly American imperialism of the early nineteenth century which deprived a sovereign state, Mexico, of half its territory: that became a victory for freedom. In fact that conflict had been exacerbated by slavery. Mexico had abolished it; the southern American states had not. But then it has always been easy to lie about expansion across land. Expansion across sea is imperialism. Expansion across land is destiny.

The lies are everywhere in Western history; lies about the Indian wars, and even liberal lies about the Indians themselves, airily explaining away the outrages the tribes committed as a sort of wild poetry in action; lies about the Frontier; lies about its heroes.

In the history of mankind no more dubious collection of beings has ever been ushered into glory. Kit Carson, later to become a white-haired saint in buckskins, acted as scout in the 1840s to an American regular army invading Mexican California. The Mexican farmers, he said, would be no match for them. The Mexican farmers routed the American army. Much later, on his deathbed, Carson called for a quart of whiskey, two pounds of steak and five ounces of tobacco. It was his most heroic achievement. He ate the steak, drank the whiskey, smoked the tobacco and serenely entered the American pantheon.

Wild Bill Hickok shot three men – one from behind a curtain, one from behind a door, and one in the back as he ran away. Calamity Jane was a drunk and a whore. The one thing most people who met her remembered was the smell: she was once forbidden to enter an army fort because of it.

Earp, later to be played by a host of stars, amongst them Henry Fonda and Burt Lancaster, was a cardsharp, and after the gunfight at the OK Corral the citizens of Tombstone hung a large notice over the coffins of his victims, 'Murdered in the streets of Tombstone'. The killing there had been done with shotguns: in the West it was either that or being shot in the back, the fate of Hickok and Jesse James.

Jesse James, it seems, was not even that good at robbing banks. In sixteen years his gang collected $200,000. A Confederate lieutenant robbed three banks in 1864 and in fifteen minutes stole $170,000. Billy the Kid, in his one photograph, is a drooling idiot hung about with guns the way Marley's Ghost was hung about with chains. His last forlorn words, in Spanish, were 'Who's there?' He was one of the few not to be shot in the back.

Most startling of all, Bat Masterson, gambler, part-time lawman, friend of the Earp, later to be played by the great Randolph Scott, left the West to end his days as a sports writer on a New York paper. The equivalent of that would be Robin Hood living on to become a travel journalist.

The Last Human Cannonball

Dodge City, where Earp and Masterson dealt cards and kept the peace, had only fifteen murders in its ten years as the wildest cattle town of all. Tread softly for you tread on my dreams: they did not even kill each other.

Nor were they that wild. In 1882, in its heyday, with a resident population of 2000 Dodge had only thirteen pubs, or saloons. But near where I was born, the small Welsh town of Llandovery in 1847 had 48 pubs for a population of 1709, making one for every 36 inhabitants. But no cattle-drive ever hit Llandovery. What is more disturbing than the facts is the way Western life became a morality play. It embodies the virtues of the Frontier, and continues to affect the thinking – or for what passes as thinking – of American politicians. That joke about Barry Goldwater's response to nuclear attack, 'Waal, first we get the wagons in a circle,' came near the bone.

As in a morality play, there is a traditional cast. There is the school-teacher, played by Grace Kelly, whom the hero will marry but who does not understand why men should shoot each other in the cause of honour. There is the golden-hearted saloon girl (a singer, of course, not the whore of reality), played by someone like Faye Dunaway, who does understand, and, of course, has to die before the end. There is the man who owns the ranch/the town/the territory, always played by the great Lee J. Cobb, who eventually has to face up to the fact that his only son (Dan Duryea) is a psychopathic killer. And there is the man who keeps the local store, who dreams of peace and is a coward. Philip Larkin once wrote in a poem that this was the only man with whom he identified in Westerns.

Amongst all these, encased in virtue and simplicity, there moves the Western hero like a medieval knight in plate-armour: Cooper, Steward, Fonda, Lancaster.

Yes, of course, violence was necessary. It solved things. Virtue triumphant and the man with the thin black moustache dead.

[70]

The Real Thing

Violence is clean in the Western myth. I was brought up to believe that it was possible to shoot a man through his hair-line and knock him out bloodlessly. That was 'creasing', for Western violence has its own glossary. The comics had told me so, and the films. I also believed it was possible, even with the revolvers of the nineteenth century, to shoot a gun out of a man's hand. That was known as 'winging' him. Think on that. There must be thousands who still believe such tosh (and think on the late John Ford, in whose films fighting was a social gesture: you got up, wiped away the blood, and went off for a drink together, slapping Maureen O'Hara on the bum for her own good as you went).

One result of the Western myth is that we have lost sight of the men who were the real heroes of the West: the small farmers in their earth houses on the Great Plains; the last of the Mexican settlers in California, holding out against the might of the American army of invasion, complete with the drunk Carson; and the Mormons who exhibited more than anyone else grandeur and the lunacy of the human spirit. Many of those who lived through the Western experience came to believe in the myth – like Calamity Jane, exchanging copies of her ghosted memoirs for drink.

If there were villains they were the ghost writers in the sky, the dime novelists, as they were called, who persuaded such creatures they were heroes and launched them on a gullible urban public.

Some really believed in the West. One such was Will James, cowboy, artist and accomplished writer. In *The Last Cowboy Legend* Anthony Amaral tells his sad tale. James was a French Canadian by birth and spent most of his life concocting a fantasy Western past for himself. His real name was Joseph-Ernest-Nephtali Dufault, not a name for gunfights ('Draw, durn yer, Joseph-Ernest-Nephtali') and certainly not a name for the most famous Western writer of his day. So he erased his background, burnt letters and got his family to destroy photographs. The strain was such that he died a drunk in Hollywood.

Many of the Westerners died in Hollywood. They appeared in old age in films about themselves, though in minor roles. History does not relate what Emmet Dalton, failed bankrobber, or Wyatt Earp, failed faro dealer, or any of the other bemused old thugs thought as they saw their fictional selves ride into the sunset. It must have been one of the most absurd situations in all human history, but even the comedy of that did not overwhelm the myth.

America needs the West. Something has to knit the wastepaper basket of the Old World into a nation, and so it continues, perpetuating the humbug and the lies. And the harm.

But one man had his revenge on the West. I walked among the crosses on Boot Hill in Tombstone, mourning poor plump Ike Clanton, shot dead at the OK Corral. Dutch Annie was there, and George Johnson, 'hanged by mistake'. There were crosses to men murdered by Indians, or just found dead in mine-shafts. Boot Hill is a tourist attraction now and the last burial, said the custodian, had been in the 1890s. But then I saw it, a few feet away from the other crosses, 'Emmet Crook Nunally, Died 1946'.

The custodian looked a bit put out that I had seen that. Oh yes, he muttered, him. Sent his coffin cash on delivery, he did, with instructions that he was to be buried in Boot Hill.

The Tombstone authorities could find no address to send the coffin back to, so they were obliged to do just that.

So Emmet Crook Nunally entered the myth. Nobody knows anything about him. But if he did it for devilment he must be the greatest troublemaker of all on Boot Hill. I like to think of him as that: a Western hero.

1981

PART THREE
THE FLESH

THROBBING PAYNE

T he image was one of suffering humanity, aloof and noble. Thou thy worldly task hath done ... The El Greco hung over the grinning, romping faces in the photograph album. '*That* was the last time,' said Mrs Cynthia Payne. 'You've no idea of the mess we had to clean up.'

The photograph is of a living man. For five days of the week he is a bank manager in the south of England, but for one afternoon of his life he hung blissfully in a living-room in the London suburb of Streatham, covered with baby oil and the dust of several Hoover bags.

'"I want mud, Madam," he kept saying. And I told him straight: where the bloody hell did he think I was getting mud from? I wasn't traipsing round the seaside for him. It was then that I thought of the Hoover.'

The house is large and very neat. There are lace curtains on the windows of the front and Venetian blinds at the back. Inside, gentility, that old unkillable gentility of chapels and suburbia, is rampant.

The Last Human Cannonball

There are chandeliers and wall-lights, soft animal toys, eighteenth-century gallants and their ladies pirouetting on the walls, a velvet three-piece, little china ornaments everywhere. The respectability of it wells up around you like water in the hold of a doomed ship.

Yet four years ago, three weeks before Christmas, this house caught the imagination of the world. It did so on two counts. It might not quite have been the Naughtiest Place on Earth. It was certainly the Funniest.

On that day the Thin Blue Line of Streatham broke against the house, boots kicking in the door, and found fifty-three men and thirteen women inside. Most of the men were lined up in a queue that stretched from the kitchen into the hall and up the stairs. They were all clutching Luncheon Vouchers in their hands. All were over fifty, some of them old age pensioners.

It was the economics of it that caught the popular imagination. At a time when you got little change from £25 for dining in a West End restaurant, these men, who had paid £25 each for their Luncheon Vouchers, got as much drink as they could consume, as much food as they could eat, and then the sexual services of a young woman. It was for the last that they were politely queuing, munching their salmon sandwiches.

'Always red salmon,' said Mrs Payne. 'I gave them the best. The best Virginia ham. The best brown bread. The best wines. Didn't do no hot food, just a buffet. I mean, you can't, can you? Not when you're cooking for fifty, and you're arranging the sex as well.

'We had these two exhibitionists who used to do it all over the place, on the stairs, everywhere. It got people over their shyness. Anyway, they started doing it in the kitchen and this made an old friend of mine very cross. All the food was there. It wasn't hygienic.'

As a result of the police raid, only one person of the sixty-six was charged. Mrs Payne, a lady in her late forties, was sentenced to eighteen months' imprisonment for keeping a disorderly house and was immediately swept out of the news pages of newspapers and into the editorial columns. 'The hypocrisy of the law as it stands could not be better illustrated,' wrote the *Spectator*. There were leaders in *The Times*, *Guardian*, *Express* and *Mirror*.

There was an appeal and the sentence was cut to six months, of which in the end Mrs Payne served four. On her release there was a Rolls waiting for her (provided by an old friend), a bunch of roses held by a campaigning prostitute, her own aged Cairn terrier, and more pressmen than had gathered round Holloway since the last judicial execution.

Mrs Payne gave them the V-sign. V for Victory, she explained delicately, and V for Voucher. A small procession followed her back through the streets of London to the neat house with the net curtains in Streatham. Ulysses had returned to Ithaca.

Meeting Mrs Payne for the first time is like putting to sea in a small boat. The traditional landmarks of taboo and intimacy fall behind you, and suddenly there is just the water and a small woman talking. Mrs Payne does not stop talking.

She is a small, bird-like woman. With her large bust and her thin legs she looks like an insistent robin. In her dress buttoned to her throat, she could pass for the sort of woman who hands round the sandwiches after the chapel Band of Hope. She is a bright, attractive woman, given to peals of wild laughter.

'I do tend to go on. Well, I do, don't I? I'm highly excitable, I suppose. You find me funny, do you? Yes, everyone says that. But it will probably get on your nerves in the end.'

She is the daughter of a hairdresser in the south of England (she does not care to be more specific than that). Her mother died when she and her sister were small, and they were brought up by their father, with whom Cynthia did not get on. He found her irresponsible. She found him too strict. But the two had a bizarre reconciliation in the old man's last years, when he began attending her sex parties and the repressions of a lifetime went off like a

Roman candle. People, said Mrs Payne, often said to her that they wished they could have done as much for their fathers.

From an early age she was fascinated by sex. Not that she considered herself to be a particularly randy person, but she was, and remains, fascinated by the oddity of it. This brought her very soon to the wider shores of love.

'I was a waitress in Victoria and I used to rent my room in the evenings to this prostitute. It was a good business. I paid £4 a week for it, and she paid me £2 a night. I knew I'd soon have a down-payment for a house. I wanted my own backyard, you see.

'Anyway this girl, she specialised in kinks, and I'd found out that I could watch through a keyhole. She'd do this slave-mistress act and wear a great big hat like Garbo and have them crawling round on the floor. It was fascinating.

'And I began asking my friends round to watch, about six of us, there in the dark, trying not to laugh. One night my friend said she was going to sneeze, and I whispered, "Pam, you can't." She staggered to the window and we all leapt on her and put a cushion over her face.

'Course that was the end of it. I'd even made the keyhole bigger with a penknife, but the next time it was all dark. The bloody girl had put her chiffon scarf over it.'

Mrs Payne's own life had its dark side. She seems to have been something of a drifter and paid the price in the years before the pill: there were two illegitimate children, one of whom she had adopted, and three abortions, one in a lavatory in the Seven Sisters Road. The men were all unsatisfactory.

'Oh, yes, I believe in love. If you can get it, that is. I often wonder what would have happened if I'd been happily married. I don't know, but I think I'd still have held my parties.'

Her son now works in the City. He remains on good terms with Mrs Payne, whom he and his wife will soon make a grandmother. 'Tried to stop me? He could never stop me. Christ, he's had some of the best girls in the country through me.' On the boy's six-teenth birthday, worried about him, she treated him to a woman.

He was not put through public school, she said emphatically. She does not believe in public schools, having seen at first-hand their after-effect in her clients.

The road to the neat house had been a rocky one. There were flats and girls who didn't pay, and landlords who put the rents up. But in the end there was a small house and now, for eight years, there has been this one. Here she held her parties, to which the invitations were issued by word of mouth (one man, it turned out in court, heard about them in Bangkok, another whilst navvying on a motorway).

Mrs Payne has kept a photograph album of her parties the way other people do of their holidays ('I'll want to have something to look at when I'm old'). Here they parade: transvestites, transsex-uals, ladies in masks, ladies in black stockings, ladies in nothing at all. Most of the ladies were amateurs. 'Let's face it,' murmured Mrs Payne, 'if they'd been real pros they'd have been charging £50 a go. I think they liked the social occasion more than anything. It was a day out for them. And all expenses paid.'

Most of the men were in late middle age. The young, said Mrs Payne, were more likely to mess up the house, which, apart from a few cigarette burns, has come through unscathed. The older ones she even picked up from their homes ('One old boy said he was used to Meals on Wheels, but Crumpet on Wheels was a new thing to him'). There was a special rate for the impotent.

'You'll remember this interview when you're old,' she said suddenly, 'when nobody wants you. Many of the old boys who came here had lost their wives. They were lonely.

'And they'd sit here, having a drink, eating their sandwiches, watching pretty girls, knowing they'd never have to take them out, girls who'd never make any unpleasantness about their marriages. They were in paradise, my old boys.

'They'd come at two in the afternoon and they'd be nervous. So I'd usually put on a lesbian act for them or I'd have this lecturer putting on an exhibition with his girlfriend. He almost pulled my wash-basin out once. But it did put them all in the mood.

'And it was all so respectable. A solicitor friend once told me it was like a regimental dinner-dance without the dinner. They'd be there all in their suits and then one of them would go over to the girls, stepping over the naked bodies on the floor. "Excuse me, would you mind coming upstairs?" And this girl, pleased to be asked, would say, "Yes." You had to try and stop laughing, it was all so polite.'

One room had three beds and a stuffed cockatoo in it. That, said Mrs Payne, was the Group-Sex Room. As mistress of ceremonies it was her job to call, 'Anyone for group sex?' But you had to be very psychological with old boys, they could so easily be put off.

Upstairs was the Mirror Room. It had taken them weeks, said Mrs Payne, to get the angle of the mirror just right. Her one sadness was that the house had no cellar: it meant she could not fit up a Punishment Room.

The house is spotless, but then Mrs Payne is one of the last people in the western world with access to slaves. Respectable businessmen some of them, they do the housework wearing only a collar round their necks, and their reward, a great treat this, is to be allowed to eat out of a dog's bowl. Once, a retired police superintendent mended a friend's cooker. The friend, who keeps a shop, had to whip him in return; a customer, inquiring about the noise, was told that afternoon television had become *so* violent.

Mrs Payne has no guilt. Perhaps it was sad she said, but then life itself was sad. Her work, she ventured, might even have saved a few marriages that had grown stale. 'Men will always want sex, won't they? *Well, won't they?*'

She remains bitter about the judge who sentenced her, and

speculated briefly as to his sex-life. But then Mrs Payne speculates about everyone's sex life. On her arrest she rewarded the police with an account of their sexual shortcomings. She was never wrong, said Mrs Payne.

She is on the best of terms with her neighbours. One, a religious lady, had commented on the irony that the sex parties were usually held at the same time as her whist-drive (what had the police thought, all those ladies going in through one door and men through another?). Another, whose husband had left her for a younger woman, said she wished he had known about Mrs Payne's.

'I don't know why I enjoyed the parties so much,' said Mrs Payne. 'It wasn't as though I joined in, and at the end I always went out and had a good meal in a restaurant. One psychologist couldn't make me out at all. But I was always like this, outrageous. I always loved to see people get out of themselves.

'And some of the old boys looked so sad.' She went off into a peal of laughter. 'They didn't stay sad long.'

Once she admitted to some worry about her future. But it would be all right, wouldn't it? Wouldn't it? Inside her is a small and touching person whom nothing has changed.

When Garrick died, Dr Johnson wrote that his death had eclipsed the gaiety of nations. Mrs Payne's is a smaller geography, but they will not forget her in Streatham. The press called her Madam Sin; someone who knew her better called her Madam Baloney.

1982

THE ICON AND THE DAMBUSTER

◡⁓

Picture this moment. It is half past three on a spring morning on the Chelsea Embankment exactly forty years ago, and a young woman is directing traffic. Only, this being 1954, there is no traffic, which is as well, for although she is wearing the kepi, cape and white gloves of a French *gendarme*, she has nothing else on at all. Pamela Green, that nude icon of our memories, is being photographed again.

Uniform is a new departure for her, and a rare chance to escape from mythology. In the months leading up to her materialisation on the Embankment, she has been in turn Diana, Pandora, Venus and The Spirit of the Winds; she has held bows and arrows, peered into a large box, stood in a conch shell and, on one leg, in a stiff breeze. In the early 1950s, as she explains, there always had to be an excuse for being nude. So she is nervous standing there, cape blowing out behind her, but the photographer has assured her nobody is ever about at that time of night.

And then the car comes.

'What could I do? I stepped back and signalled it on like a real policeman, but suddenly there was this screech of brakes. I can hear it now. The car came to a complete stop in the middle of the road, but nobody got out. I looked back once and the driver wasn't even looking around, but just sat, staring straight ahead of him. He must have had a terrible shock.'

It is not known what became of the man, or whether anyone ever again believed anything he said. But Miss Pamela Green lives on the Isle of Wight now, where she is a member of the Women's Institute. Her husband is a former Dambuster, and they share their house with the 4000 photographs he has taken of her in the nude.

Some twenty-five years ago the negatives of her most famous poses went missing in the backwash from a studio bankruptcy, so Douglas Webb, a stills photographer on many British films made in the 1970s, set himself the long task of shooting them all again, sometimes on old film sets (such as the derelict Norfolk farmhouse where *The Go-Between* was made), sometimes on deserted beaches. It was inevitably a race against time but the results, he told her, could be their old age pension.

In 1989 he sold at Christie's the medal he had received for that night over Germany and announced that he hoped to use the cash for a book of pictures featuring his wife in her pomp, though the *Daily Telegraph* chose to refer to this as a 'publishing venture'.

She, living in a vast archive of her younger self, is able to refer to her body as a racehorse now out to grass, where once she ago-nised on whether it was too fat or too thin, and has just started to write memoirs which could turn out to be a classic of comedy. This is the story of the Icon and the Dambuster, and it is yet another reminder of what my old friend Jack Trevor Story used to say, that in this life it is only the mundane that we have to invent.

The two met in 1947. He was a former Fleet Street news agency man who did the odd glamour shot on the side and was on the lookout for models. She came into his studio, took her coat off as asked, and was curtly told, 'You'll do.' But as she put the coat on again he noticed her wind something round her neck and asked what this was. 'It's my school scarf.'

'Help,' said the Dambuster.

She was in fact an art student, aged seventeen, who had found that modelling clothes brought her four-and-six an hour but that modelling without clothes brought five shillings, and Pamela Green was a businesswoman. What she now calls 'the body' was about to enter the folklore of a nation.

I remember it well, as do many others, including Mr Frank Bough who, off camera during a television interview, confided to her that he had long been in love with her bottom.

'I saw the film *Peeping Tom* again and I was still impressed with the intensity of your scenes,' a fan wrote recently, having managed to trace her to the Isle of Wight. He used gold ink in honour of the occasion. 'Might I say that you were, as you are in all likelihood now, a most gorgeous woman.'

And she was. She was only five-foot four, and there was no geometry to her anywhere, just blonde hair and a sleepy young face which gave the impression that any connection with that magnificent body was purely fortuitous: Emma Hamilton had that look in Romney's paintings.

In the 1950s she was forever in *Lilliput*, in one issue of which there were 'Six Looks Through the Viewfinder at Miss Pamela Green'. Bill Brandt photographed her, as did Angus McBean, who recreated Botticelli's *Birth of Venus*, and she stood in a conch shell yet again.

With nude photography now as commonplace as special offers from the AA, it would be difficult for the young to appreciate just how famous she was. There were perhaps ten girls who appeared over and over again in magazines and on calendars, often under different names, so sleepy Pamela Green could put on a red wig and become Rita Landre, who wasn't sleepy at all.

It was this Rita Landre whom the director Michael Powell saw and cast for his *Peeping Tom*, just a small part in that classic of creepy eroticism, though an image of bouncing health in suspenders is the reason many now remember the film.

In the 1960s Pamela Green emerged from the mythology and shadows of the 1950s, and then there was the time of geology when, primeval if depilated, she lay on rocks in the photographs of Harrison Marks.

Women were not allowed to be shown with pubic hair then, though the photographer Jean Straker took a stand on this and fell foul of the law. No rebel, Pamela Green passed two shaven decades and this, she claimed, had its advantages for a platinum blonde.

Even then, she once appeared in court, charged with having 'depraved and corrupted' a schoolboy in faraway Alloa in Scotland with her short film *The Window Dresser*. The schoolboy did not appear in court but the film did and was watched three times by judge and jury, after which the judge dismissed the case.

What she remembers now is the extraordinary comedy of that time. Like pigeons there was the odd gangster around, but her Soho was a small, international village where everybody knew everybody else, and she topped up her tan on the roofs of Gerrard Street, applauded by men from the GPO.

She lived at home then with her mother in West Wycombe and the last train went at 10.30 p.m. Many of the photographs in *Pamela, A Portrait in 58 Studies*, were taken in her Mum's living room, though her public knew nothing of this.

But then they knew nothing about the making of the most famous British nudist film either. Harrison Marks got the Board of Film Censors to agree to *Naked As Nature Intended* – a film she calls 'Nani' – bought a camera, hired her and four other girls, and everything was ready, except the script. There never was a script.

'We all got in a van and headed west, and he filmed everything he saw: Stonehenge, the sea, the sky, the rocks again. He hired a boat, only one girl fell in the water and he filmed that, just as he filmed us drying her, but the Censor cut it on the grounds that women drying each other had to be up to no good. The result is that in the film a girl falls in and the boat sails on.

'The only line of dialogue we had was, 'Hello, do you come here often?' and the only action was the waving, the eternal bloody waving. Harrison Marks bought a beach ball for us, but the wind kept blowing it away and we made him run after it.'

The film, she said with awe, ran for a whole year. Another great success at the same time was Michael Winner's nudist film *Some Like It Cool*, on which her husband Doug Webb was the stills cameraman for the filming, which was done on an island in the Thames. During this he fell out with his director and made off in the one boat, leaving Winner and the nudes marooned like Ben Gunn.

Neither of them has kept in touch with anyone from those strange years, so it has startled her to find that her fans have not forgotten. As the result of an article I wrote last year on the long-dead British sex film industry, letters poured in and were delivered to 'Miss P. Green, ex-actress, Isle of Wight.'

A cult film magazine wrote about her, and letters came from the New World asking for photographs. 'Hello from Canada,' began one man breezily.

Some were sad. 'Hope you don't mind the familiarity, but it's hard to think of the lady I was madly in love with 35 years ago.'

Such letters bring it all back to them, and they remember the lunatics they once knew, like the male actor in *Naked As Nature Intended* who was so vain that he secretly applied complete make-up to his 'dangly bits' – and disappeared, along with his dangly bits, on the cutting-room floor.

Then, on the Isle of Wight, the Icon and the Dambuster realise it wasn't just a dream which they somehow shared.

1994

SQUIRE AMONG THE PIN-UPS

⟿

On a lawn in front of a large Victorian house in Sussex, three people sat taking tea. One of them had a notebook on his knee in which he scribbled from time to time. He was dressed fussily in a suit with collar and tie, and could have passed for the local curate. But anyone chancing upon the scene might have thought it a *tableau vivant* for some English *Déjeuner sur l'Herbe*. The other two were naked.

One was a woman, an attractive former model, though, a bizarre twist, missing her false teeth. The other was a man in his sixties. He was small and brown and looked over the top of a pair of half-moon spectacles like an absentminded troll. He was the host. In front of his baronial hall Jean Straker, sun-worshipper, crusader and photographer, poured out tea from an elegant silver teapot and answered my questions.

It is difficult for anyone who was not young and male some fifteen years or so ago to appreciate the position Straker held at that uneasy time. He had a photographic studio in Soho where, for a small entrance fee, you could complete your education. There you could take photographs, if inclined, and on permanent exhibition were pictures of naked young women. It was the fact that they were not bald below the waist which took Jean Straker in and out of the courts like John Wilkes. In his windows he affixed details of the cases the way a court doctor affixes details of his royal patient's health on the railings of palaces. But in the end his own health gave way and he retired here, to a mansion where the diamond millionaire Abe Bailey had kept great state: and on this vast Victorian pile Straker has set his own unmistakeable stamp.

You thought first of Miss Havisham's house in *Great Expectations*. But no writer of fiction, not even Dickens, would have dared dream up anything on this scale. At some point a great wave of objects had burst into the house to set like lava. It was three feet deep in chaos.

There was a decade of newspapers, crumbling and yellow, spilling long-forgotten crises and place-names. There were inkwells and statuettes and bits of clothing and old letters. There was a pair of sabres. There was box upon box of coins. In one corner, pouring out of cardboard boxes and rearing up over chairs, were 3000 ties, interwoven cables of colour and stripes. A child could disappear without trace here.

New rooms brought new chaos. The long table in the dining room was crowded with jams and chutneys and condiments, as though an army had been surprised here. It was the scale of the chaos which was so staggering, for it dwarfed even this Victorian baronial at its grandest and heaviest, lapping the oak balustrades of the hall.

Showing above it all, like guides to navigation, were the old pictures of the naked young women. One room was wholly given over to them, from floor to ceiling, so you felt you were entering a regimental square. The room, if you will excuse me, bristled.

On the lawn Jean Straker was defending the chaos. It was, he said, an exercise in pure logic. 'What's clutter, except things being where you put 'em?' Like jesting Pilate, he did not wait for an answer. 'Why should you employ people to put things where you haven't put 'em? What's the point of throwing away anything if you've liked it? I think it's good for your eyes to wander round, to see such shapes, such colours. You can't be lonely with all this about you.' He pointed to the garden, which was rearing up about the small lawn as though about to engulf it in a flood of brambles and rhododendrons.

Half to himself he went on, 'As a child I used to have a den where nobody came. Now the den's much bigger.'

He bought Ashurstwood Abbey in 1970, with 50 acres, for £33,000. He had sold his Soho studio at the height of the property boom. He has never counted the number of rooms in the Abbey, because he anticipated people would always be asking him that question: it is much easier and logical not to know the answer. He has the 3000 ties, though he himself has not worn one in ten years, because he believes they will acquire a value as social history.

Most of his schemes have a sort of El Dorado of profit glimmering somewhere, but they rarely achieve it. In his attic, in a bath raised on ropes, something shapeless and brown wallows in water. The smell is spectacular. Two years ago Straker thought he would start attempting to cure a cow's hide. He then forgot about it. The hide shimmers.

Ethelred Jean Straker (it is a name for litigation and P. G. Wodehouse) was born in London sixty-four years ago, the only child of a Russian émigré and his English wife. His father scraped a living as a linguist, the family was always just one step ahead of the bailiffs.

It was an exotic childhood. At one point they lived in Paris, where both adult Strakers appeared in the chorus line of the Folies Bergère. 'My earliest memories are of being surrounded by naked ladies in the dressing rooms. That was what made going to school in England so strange afterwards. All the mysteries were known to me. I had to keep quiet when the other boys talked about girls.'

The young Straker acquired logic early. 'I was more able than Mummy, and more able than Daddy, so I ran the family. Daddy's English wasn't very good, so I used to write all their letters from the age of seven on. It was only much later that I discovered children don't run families.'

He left school to work in a film publicity office. From this he stepped into freelance journalism, ghosting articles for some of the leading theatricals of his day. At the same time he was illustrating them with his own photographs.

During the war he settled wholly into photography doing photo-essays for the Ministry of Information. In 1945 he bought a studio in Soho Square in London and set up as a commercial photographer. He was very successful. 'But I kept getting into trouble with the customers and the advertising men. They would tell me exactly what to do, I was being treated as a plumber.'

So in 1950 he turned his studio into the Visual Arts Club. Here he lectured on photography, and even hired a French miniaturist to be his painting master. Straker never did anything by halves. The object of attention was the female nude. 'You can only teach art with the nude. It was studio photography in the old tradition, just as Rembrandt had done on canvas.'

The Club lasted twenty years. Ten years after he formed it Straker changed its name to the Academy of Visual Arts. At the same time he instituted a new discipline, Gynaecography. During his court appearances he had to keep explaining its etymology to magistrates: 'Gynaeco means of women; graphic means illustrative. Thus, illustrative of women.' What it meant in practice was that Straker and his 100 members took photographs of naked women. 'When I realised that people were taking me seriously I had to invent a new jargon.'

How much is idealism and how much tongue-in-cheek mischief in Straker is difficult to determine. There is no hint in his voice or expression. In an introduction to a collection of his photographs he writes: 'It is right that society shall protect itself against a degrading exploitation of its baser instincts, but it is equally important that its intellect shall remain unshackled and free to explore the vast territory of man's vision.' The rhetoric cracks when you consider that this is the right to publish photographs of women without their clothes.

Some people took him very seriously. An American university bought 112 prints. 'They were doing a research project into the semantic evaluation of verbal responses.'

Academy members included judges, parsons, scientists, engine-drivers. One member, an East Anglican parson, used to mention Straker in his sermons. Another, whose daughter modelled at the Academy, was tracked down by a Sunday newspaper. He told them loftily that God made mankind in His own image, and that Mr Straker was merely passing on that message.

It cost fifteen guineas a year to belong to his academy. Roger Newton joined when he was twenty-six and an engine-driver living in Ilford. 'It was more like a club than anything. You tended to behave as though you were in somebody's house. Nothing was organised.' A gifted artist, Newton came to paint the models. 'You'd pop in, and if one was free you went off to draw her.

'A lot of the members came to be provoked by naked women, but the odd thing was that an air of fusty Puritanism pervaded the place. There was nothing remotely naughty about it,' Newton shrugged, 'and of course it was very unkempt. Like everything that Jean has, it tended to decay.'

Myra Kime became a model there in 1968. She had never modelled professionally before. 'But it was a very hot September and I had a heavy suit on. I just wanted to take it off. I'd heard about this place in Soho, so I just went in, and did.'

'It was a lovely place. You came and went as you pleased. You'd chat to the members. Sometimes you'd even sing to them. But it breaks my heart passing there now, it's an office.'

He spent most of the decade, when the Soho club was well-known, talking. He addressed forums and seminars and university clubs. He gave evidence to commissions on censorship. He wrote letters to the papers. But mostly he explained things to magistrates.

His health, which had stood up to the almost non-stop litigation of the sixties, eventually gave out. He sold up, happily in a time of boom, and retired to Sussex. He has not taken any photographs since.

He shares the Abbey with his mother, a silent old lady in a sky blue dressing gown who occasionally materialises in the chaos. His wife, Elizabeth, occupies the gate-house and busies herself with a small goat herd.

'What do I do with myself?' echoed Straker. 'Oh, there's no lack of things to do. I cook. The logic is that if you've no income, like me, you use what you've got. If the apples are out you use 'em. If the blackberries are out you make jam. I'm a quite superb cook.' Occasionally some of his old models and former members of the Academy visit and talk of the old days.

He has settled easily into his new community, his visitors politely indifferent to the fact that he may receive them in the nude. He has even become secretary and founder of the East Grinstead Current Affairs Society. This year's programmes included an address on 'Being a town mayor: a joke or a job?' by the mayor of East Grinstead. The town librarian talked about his job. A businessman speculated on the future of the independent trader in East Grinstead. But Straker addressed them on 'Obscenity: is it law, logic or licence?' He soldiers on in exile.

1978

A LIFE IN PICTURES

~

Her finest hour. 'I was posing for the life class at the Sir John Cass College at the City of London Polytechnic and when it was over the tutor came up to me. "Yvonne," he said, "Oscar wants you to pose for him in Italy." I was stunned. I had heard of Oscar, but he was an abstract painter. "Oscar's got this house in Italy and he'll pay all your expenses." Apparently he'd come in one day and ... "Well, it's your back, Yvonne. Oscar finds it magnificent. You do understand, don't you? *You could be his last chance to get back to the figurative.*" So I went.

'Me and the body,' said Yvonne Vinall. 'And no need for a suitcase.'

The body came into her life seventeen years ago, like an uncle from America, when she began posing for artists. It is all around us now, from skirting board to ceiling, and the only bits of wall visible are those square places where the body is temporarily on loan to an art gallery: the body crouched, sprawled, taut, the body languorous, the body prim, in oils and watercolour, crayon and pencil, charcoal and chalk, so your eyes ricochet constantly between its painted slopes and hollows and its live tenant beside you. Small and grave, straight-backed as a headmistress, Mrs Yvonne Vinall, aged fifty-eight and a grandmother, sits in a council flat in Tunbridge Wells, in a room which is a little cave of … 'Me,' says Mrs Vinall.

Me, as seen by seventy strangers, some wistfully, some brutally, a few with longing, most with the distant interest of a landscape painter: Me, the other side of the looking glass. The room bristles with breasts, buttocks and explosions of hair.

'It's an odd thing, but sometimes the only way I can recognise Yvonne is by her bum,' said her husband Chris, a retired shipping manager. 'And the older these artists are, the younger they make her. See that one?' Mrs Vinall, rosy and round and nude, is stretched like a kitten before a fire. 'Chap's well into his eighties.'

The paintings, drawings, lithographs and busts (for there are also three severed heads of Mrs Vinall) have all been presented by the artists. Some of them, like Edward Ardizzone, were famous; others, like the Hon. Rupert Bathurst, a boy at Eton, were not. In the remorseless rising tide of Me there is a solitary sandcastle, a portrait of Mr Vinall.

Her most bizarre moment was 'the first time I posed at Eton College. It was for the younger boys and I must admit I had great reservations. I thought it would be all nudge, nudge, but there was nothing like that.' As the art master at another public school said, the biggest problem the boys face with Mrs Vinall is headaches from concentrating too much.

Mrs Vinall is just five feet tall. ('I know that from sculpture. It's wonderful what you find out about yourself when the callipers come round.') She is not, as she puts it, a voluptuous woman; the curves may be slipping a little, but hers is still a neat, strong body. Not that any of this worries her: the years merely add a new drama to the hollows and the slopes.

A Life in Pictures

She lectures on her work, taking part of her large archive with her so that the pictures fill a guard's van. 'I have become well-known to British Rail,' reflected Mrs Vinall. And in the last ten years she has bounded out of the studios to take the body where no body ever went before. She is the first woman to pose nude in the boarding schools of England: Eton, Harrow, Westminster and Highgate. In the long history of painting and of English education there has never been anything like Mrs Vinall of Tunbridge Wells.

It was a curious experience meeting her, for it made me feel incredibly old, my school days part of the eighteenth century. Gone were the days when we would all stare worriedly at the air-brushed nudes in *Health And Efficiency* and speculate on the sinister haze below each waist. My friend Geraint Morgan, more advanced than the rest of us, joined the local art school because he had heard there were life classes. He was fourteen, it was the small Welsh town of Carmarthen, and, as you might expect, they made him paint flowers, week after week of flowers. The only thing was, the *real* life class was just a wooden partition away. So Geraint took his penknife to the art school.

And the day came, as in a POW escape film, when the hole was big enough. Geraint put his eye to it and saw … nothing. There was a curtain the other side. He put his finger through, felt it and began to move the curtain, not knowing it ran the length of the partition. Grimly he began to wiggle his finger.

It was ten minutes before the shouting started on the other side, and he didn't know that the curtain had been wrenched aside to reveal the finger which went on wriggling in air until someone grabbed it. Of course, they wouldn't even let him loose on the stamens after that and Geraint is now a polytechnic lecturer. But this was long ago, long before the coming of Mrs Vinall.

'It was after my son started school and I was looking for a hobby. I took up painting and one day my tutor asked if I had thought of modelling. I thought it was something to do with clay but he said no, that people sat still for hours and got drawn. He told me I had this inner quality of peace. Good Lord, I said. I was also quite attractive to look at. Quite attractive? Thanks a bunch, I said.

'I asked what sort of clothes did he think I would wear? That was the point, he said. Nothing at all. Now, I'd been brought up in a house where my mother sometimes walked around with very little on, but still …

'I can still remember that first class. There were fifteen there, some of them quite old and some – hmmm – very young indeed. I was introduced and they were told I hadn't done anything like this before. Then, as in a dream, I heard the tutor's voice. "'Right, Yvonne, would you mind popping into the changing room and putting on the robe you'll find there?"

'Suddenly, I found myself undressing. When I came out I was asked to take up a pose. I'd done ballet when I was young and this wasn't difficult, the muscles were still there. But then, very slowly, I found I was really enjoying myself.'

Mrs Vinall smiled. 'You've no idea how peaceful it is. All you hear is the sound of a pencil being sharpened, or the scrape of a knife on canvas. You find yourself moving away from yourself. It's quite extraordinary and the outside world doesn't exist any more. Only when it's over do you become *you* again, the movable object. You go out into the world and the sound really hits you.'

When that first class was over the participants stood up and applauded her. This startled the tutor and when he asked them why, they said she was the best model they had ever had. It was all art schools at first. Some were fun, others were bleak places without proper changing rooms or lockers. But by word of mouth the fame of the small, motionless lady was spreading, and Mrs Vinall went for an interview at the Royal Academy.

It was now that she began to learn the perils of her new trade. The sculptor John Rivera asked her to model the mother in his family group, now on the south bank at Battersea Bridge. When she got to his studio there was just a podium, above which was a trapeze bar attached to the ceiling and swinging.

'He said, "That's for you." He wanted the mother to have the baby in her outstretched arms and to be running at the same time. You couldn't keep that pose even with a doll, so he wanted me to hold on to the trapeze. Even then my back was arched and the strain went from my heels to my back, across to my shoulders and arms.

'My whole body went on full alert. Some of these artists have no idea of what they are asking you to do.'

Statues she once had passed by without a glance began to appear in a new light ('all that human suffering'). She marvelled at the young woman in Sloane Square in the half-crouch ('That's a hell of a pose'), and in Piccadilly stared with awe at the long-ago unknown who had had to balance on one leg, bow in hand.

It has never been highly paid work. At first she was getting 95p an hour; now, with expenses extra, she can get £5.40. Her latest project is to be sponsored to tour schools for the deaf. 'I wouldn't do it if I didn't like it. I really enjoy being with people who are part of the art world.'

She waved a hand at the pictures. 'I like feeling that I've had something to do with all this.'

It was her idea to go into the schools. With life classes on the curriculum for A-levels and GCSEs, she wrote to the headmasters. For some reason this fascinated me. 'What did you say, "Can I be naked in your school?"' I asked.

'No, I didn't put it quite like that,' said Mrs Vinall tolerantly. 'I have acquired a business mind I know how to promote myself. And you must remember that things have changed quite a lot since your time.'

'No one fainted?'

'No one fainted,' said Mrs Vinall.

The Last Human Cannonball

At Highgate, the director of art actually wrote to the parents first; nobody objected and one father even went so far as to sponsor Mrs Vinall for the first term. Her age, she said, had been a great help to her and also to the pupils. If there was an element of shock it was from the staff. 'I was doing a life class and there was the usual silence when one of the teachers burst in. "Aaaaaah," he said, just like that, then, "I'll come back later."'

She has never made a secret of what she does. 'Off to the studios again?' her neighbours ask. On trains (Mrs Vinall does not drive) she usually tells people that she is in the art world, and they assume she runs a gallery. But if they enquire further, she tells them. 'Believe me, I can stop all conversation in a crowded train.'

The only shock she has had in her new relationship with Me was when she appeared five years ago in a television documentary.

'I had to hide my face in my hands, I looked so *unreal*. There was this lady walking and talking. You see, I was suddenly not part of someone else's imagination.'

I saw that documentary. In one scene Mrs Vinall, dressed in a fur coat and with what appeared to be half a raven trailing from her head, was trying out all the perfumes in a local shop. 'Ah yes,' she said finally, 'this is *me*.'

In the little cave of Me ('a visual diary of my moods and memoirs'), she sighed. 'So many memories,' she said, 'so many moments, so many rooms.' Ever helpful, I pointed out that there were no pictures, as yet, on the ceiling. That was because they had fallen off, said Mrs Vinall.

1992

THAT'S NO LADY

◦~◦

On a sofa in a windowless bar on the edge of a light industrial estate, a young woman is being photographed. She is fetchingly, if bizarrely, dressed in a pearl choker, long black evening gloves, black stockings and high heels, but in nothing else at all, as though in her preparation for the ball the Fairy Godmother had paused for a tea break, leaving Cinderella stunned on the sofa.

Only this young woman, a civil servant, is not in the least stunned. Neither is her boyfriend, a Lloyd's insurance broker, who, from the twilight behind the flashbulbs, keeps giving little waves to encourage her in what, to the two of them, is clearly a ritual, which in its way it is. The civil servant is twenty-two and the photo session is part of her prize as runner-up in the 'Readers' Wives' of the Year Competition.

At this point some of you will be convinced that I am at last certifiable, but by no means all. Readers' Wives. Drop these syllables into conversation and some people will look blank, but there will always be a pair of eyes, or two or three, which will light up in recognition, as if in the Roman Empire you had drawn the sign of the fish in air. It has nothing to do with age or sex or class; someone will know that you are talking about the secret icons of the late twentieth century.

Photographs of Readers' Wives appear monthly in at least three of what are called 'adult magazines', possibly on account of the fact that you need to be at least six feet tall to reach them on the top shelves of newsagents. Some 300 to 400 of these women appear each year – so many that the magazines are obliged to print special supplements. With each post the photographs come, taken by husbands and boyfriends, and in all of them the women have nothing on.

Some are al fresco, posing beside a hay bale or stretched out on the gleaming bonnet of a car (never more than a year or two old), but most are photographed indoors, on Dralon chesterfields, sheepskin rugs and increasingly on duvets, but never now beside an open fire, for beyond the white shoulders Old England has changed, and never before have we had this confirmed by being allowed into so many homes.

Ross Gilfillan, editor-in-chief of *Fiesta*, Britain's largest-circulation adult magazine, claims after eight years in the job to know more about interior decoration than Sir Terence Conran. 'You realise something has happened to you when you find yourself staring at the furniture in the photographs which have been sent in. I have to restrain myself from writing back, "Please, that carpet doesn't match those curtains", for my world has become one of colours and soft furnishings. I make a deliberate effort now to spot what is lying on top of them.'

Like the SAS, the women are anonymous, for the names Andromeda of Blakesley, Alice of Hertford and Lisa of Docklands have been wished on them by sub-editors, obliged to flesh out the caption material; the effect of this coupling of Christian name with geography makes the captions read like some roster of the Middle Ages.

That's No Lady

A man once phoned one of these magazines to accuse its editor of publishing a photograph of his naked wife. He knew it was his wife, he said, because he recognised the wallpaper; he was not sure of anything else but he was sure of the wallpaper. What made the story so poignant was that the woman was indeed his wife, with a photographer for a boyfriend.

Readers' Wives first appeared in *Fiesta* twenty-one years ago, and, as with America, there are at least two claimants for the discovery, only as Ross Gilfillan pointed out, they probably discovered themselves.

'What really happened was that desks kept getting covered in these grainy black and white photographs which people sent in. One day in desperation someone published some of them.' Then in the late 1970s, with the sales of Polaroid cameras, the floodgates opened, for no one needed to fear that Boots would ring up the police ever again. The magazine had stumbled on an extraordinary fact: that out there in the streets and housing estates and villages of England there was an inexhaustible pool of women who wanted to be seen in the nude by millions of strangers.

Fiesta alone has a circulation of 250,000, but it is estimated that each copy is read by at least five people and it has a much longer shelf-life than that of any other magazine before its final disappearance. In a bluebell wood, I once found two copies stuffed down a badger sett.

Mr X, a twice-married builder, has sent photographs of both his wives to the magazine. He took over 2500 of the first one, so many that in the end the bottom of the drawer he kept them in gave way; they are now divorced. 'If you bought a new car and were proud of that you would take photographs of it. I am proud of my wife,' he said, polishing his car vigorously. 'This is not a dress rehearsal for life, this is life.'

But why the women do it is a mystery. It is not as though they are all dazzlingly beautiful, though some are; every month there are some who could have been painted by Raphael or, the more earthy of them, by Rubens, and this in spite of the hard flashlight which makes them all red-eyed as ferrets. But some are not beautiful at all, neither age nor weight being a barrier to the rendezvous with the family Polaroid.

This fact prompted that anthem of the 1980s, '*Readers' Wives, my candlewick Madonnas ...*' which is as much as I dare quote here. Never played in public or publicised, the song made it into the charts, something that has not happened before or since. The singer, who also wrote the song, did so under a pseudonym, Ivor Biggun. Yet his song, and another on the same subject recorded by the rock'n'roll star Dave Edmunds, are male fantasies. What of the wives of England who have not spoken yet?

Their identities have been revealed from time to time, usually when somebody tipped off a local paper that Georgina of Blisworth was in real life Mrs Jones of Carmarthen. This happened some years ago in a small town where I used to live, when a lady working in a bread shop was recognised as having been photographed dressed only in a red corset. The morning that news broke they sold out of bread before ten o'clock but next day the lady no longer worked in the bread shop. So it is not surprising that the wives until now have not spoken.

But all that changed when a film by accomplished young documentary maker appeared on Channel Four. Suzanna White, who made the much acclaimed *Volvo City* about the Hassidic Jews of north London, had been trying to make a film about Readers' Wives for five years.

'Somebody showed me a copy of *Fiesta* and I was astounded. This was a slice of British life I knew nothing about, with all those sofas and curtains. But you've no idea of the trouble I encountered. I was going to do it for Ed Mirzoeff on *40 Minutes*, but then he went and there was a woman there who didn't like the idea at all.'

The film involved White in two years of research, and what

bewildered her most was the feeling that she seemed to have stumbled on a secret tribe that did not share society's guilt. 'It was all so domestic. I kept talking to them about obscenity but I couldn't get through at all. To them it was no more shocking than getting their photos into the local paper. I found nothing in the least kinky about any of them.'

They ranged in age from early twenties to late sixties, and in jobs from a dinner lady to a civil servant. Their motives varied greatly. Some saw it as a little moment of glamour before time blew their looks away; some had had these blown away long before but didn't care. One woman, unhappily married until the age of forty-seven, when she discovered sex, needed to share the discovery. And then there was Emma, she of the pearl choker and the black gloves and nothing else: Emma the civil servant.

Emma is not her real name, and her father is a senior civil servant. She is very tall, and blonde, 'Forget Me Not' in a circle of leaves tattooed on one hip in honour of a long-gone boyfriend. For being runner-up she had won £750 and was getting another £200 for the day's shoot. 'Not bad for doing absolutely nothing and being the centre of attention,' said Emma.

It all began when her boyfriend took photographs of her in a bluebell wood – but it was at her insistence that he entered these for the competition ('He took a lot of persuading'). Emma, you begin to suspect, is one of those girls best classified under 'Trouble'. *Fiesta* to her is 'quite amusing because of its silliness', so it was a laugh to enter, and Emma likes a laugh.

And there they were, she and her boyfriend, restaging the photography among the bluebells for the TV documentary. 'Only this time two people came by and reacted in a typically English way. They walked past very quickly without any expression of any kind on their faces.'

It was a known fact, a former editor of *Escort* once told me, that there was nowhere in Britain, neither peat bog nor mountain, in which anyone could take their clothes off for longer than ten minutes without encountering a jogger, a cyclist or a man with a dog. Clothed you could, but not unclothed.

In the photo session for the magazine Emma had managed to intellectualise her embarrassment away. 'I may not like being told "Hold yer boobs, love", but it does allow me to feel very detached from my body. Everything would be quite different if a friend walked in.'

Teased that she seemed to regard her body as a library book borrowed for the day, she agreed it was something like that. But there was another dimension: she was badly injured in a car crash two years ago and she had found posing a sort of therapy. 'Hey, it's me, people still want to look at me.' She did not think she would regret posing, but then she did not think she would do it again, either. No, she was not in the least bit interested in any of the other Readers' Wives, with the exception of the winner.

'They have to be very strange for me to be interested in them now,' said Ross Gilfillan. 'There was this grandmother who kept sending us photographs of herself, in one of which, taken at midnight in her garden, she was covered in mud and biscuits.

'So she came along for a photo session here and we put her in a bath of tinned tomatoes.' We were in *Fiesta*'s boardroom, an elegant place with replica Regency furniture and leatherbound copies of the magazine which, when opened, showed a fat lady grinning out of the tomatoes. 'And what do you do with the tomatoes afterwards?' said Mr Gilfillan, sounding 3000 years old.

The Readers' Wives are fêted when they come in for their shoots, get put up at hotels and ferried to and from the studios where their day starts in make-up. Many later send girlish letters of thanks. They get just £20 for each photograph published (the competitions of course yield more); it is clear that, whatever they do it for, it is not for the money.

'This is a picture of my wife, Sarah, taken in the local woods when it was too hot to wear clothes.' In spite of this, Sarah is an unblinking mask of make-up and is wearing black stockings and suspenders. 'Please return these, they're precious to me ...'

On the noticeboard are pinned the letters of two women, and their photographs: one very young and worried that a boyfriend might get his own back by sending 'intimate photographs'; the other telling how her husband's luggage was stolen and some 'pictures' went with it. Publication of photographs requires signed statements from photographers and models, also from witnesses.

Some glimpses into their lives are depressing. One set of photographs sent in to *Escort* came from a couple who had only been able to afford paint for half a room. They had moved all the furniture into this half and the wife had somehow managed to fit herself in among all the chairs. Others are just bizarre. 'It's worse when you first come here,' said a secretary at *Fiesta*. 'This Wife turned up with her husband, I think he was a stockbroker, and they had this very posh car. Only they'd brought their baby as well, who cried all day.'

The magazine has tried a page called 'One For The Ladies', in which men snapped by their wives appear, but this has never taken off. In one of the photographs, John of London, a scowling bearded man in his forties, glistening with suntan oil like an oven-ready turkey, sits naked astride the gun barrel of a tank.

'Yes, I remember that,' said Ross Gilfillan wearily. 'He was a soldier. We get many photographs from soldiers. I think we may even have got some taken during the Falklands War.' In his own office, Mr Gilfillan has just one pin-up: Marilyn Monroe, fully clothed, reading *Ulysses*.

This is still the centre of that reckless world, of 'Perhaps you could call me Wendy Witch from Wigan', of women in feather boas and one, like Miss Havisham, in a tattered wedding dress, worried women photographed at bus stops or in empty offices, women not worried at all, tanned, pale, women who look like navvies, and some who are startlingly lovely.

And some would be extraordinary enough to excite the awe of old Falstaff. 'A mad fellow met me on the way and told me I had unloaded the gibbets and recruited the dead bodies. No eye hath seen such scarecrows ...' Yet someone must love them enough to have spread their dreams like carpets before all these strangers.

1994

THE SECRETS OF CUPBOARD 55

～⁓

There is a point in the British Museum, beyond the last display cabinet, where a man might think he had entered a Victorian lunatic asylum. Here, where the public does not go, the corridors are long and silent, the oak doors locked, and members of staff glide by with bunches of keys at their waists. And here, in Medieval and Later Antiquities, is Cupboard 55.

There are no numerals on the door, it is just one in a long line of cupboards, and nothing at all to show that it contains the collection of antiquities and objects of worship lovingly assembled by a former mayor of Bedford. When Dr Alfred Witt, a surgeon turned banker, presented this to the Museum in 1865 he did so 'with the hope that some small room may be appointed for its reception'.

For, after all, this is what most collectors dream about at the end of their busy lives, the public filing past, suitably awed at one man's energy and scholarship. Only there never was a Witt Room. No sooner had his collection been received than the Museum turned the key on it.

The Last Human Cannonball

'This was their way of making sure the British Empire did not collapse,' said Dr Richard Gaimster, who is responsible for the cupboard known to Museum staff as the Secretum. 'They believed that would have happened had the female sex and young people been exposed to the sort of material it contained.'

The irony is that of those who now apply to have the cupboard unlocked, ninety per cent are women. But what is even more of an irony is that it is Dr Gaimster, 134 years on, who is resisting calls to have its contents dispersed to other parts of the Museum.

Dr Witt's obsessive interest was in what he called 'Symbols of the Early Worship of Mankind', but not in just any symbol, for the Mayor was a specialist. He collected across the centuries and the continents every representation of the phallus, which is a posh way of saying the erect penis, he could get his hands on. Assyrian dicks. Egyptian dicks. Greek and Roman dicks. Medieval dicks. Dicks with wings. Dicks with eyes. Dicks with hawks' heads. Boxes upon boxes in Cupboard 55 contain wax dicks, lead dicks, dicks in the form of signet rings, lamps, brooches ...

The Mayor of Bedford collected them in the interests of scholarship, convinced – as were many of his contemporaries – that these were the icons of all primitive religions, and he was in the habit of lecturing on them on Sunday mornings to selected audiences. The single-mindedness of his quest was awesome, as are the dimensions of some of the objects that his quest unearthed.

'Rather remote from the average archaeological collection, don't you think?' said John Cherry, Keeper of Medieval and Later Antiquities, turning the key on Cupboard 55. 'But at least they are all together here.'

Which is precisely where other members of the Museum staff do not wish to see them remain. 'It runs contrary to the disciplines of archaeology,' said Catherine Johns, author of *Sex or Symbol, Erotic Images of Greece and Rome*. 'When you take these objects out of time and lump them together you relate them not to the culture which produced them but to the culture of Victorian England.

'It seemed so strange to the Victorians that other cultures should have such different attitudes to sex, that they were fascinated and shocked at the same time. This is the reason they put these objects together: it enabled them to see them as rude and improper.

'But the phallus, on horse trappings, say, was just a symbol of good luck. In Roman times it had no more to do with sex than the four-leafed clover has to do with botany in our own. I can't say how different people would have reacted to them, whether some Roman women thought them smart or others refused to have them in the house, but so many have survived as lamps and pottery there must have been a lot around.

'And of course their shock level was so very different. When I was younger and prettier, these metal-detector chaps, usually rough diamonds, would bring some things in, and would say very slowly, looking at me, "And I've found one of these." They were hoping to see me blush, so when I'd say, "Ah yes, a first-century phallic amulet," they'd look very confused. But your shock level is undermined by familiarity, as it would have been in antiquity.

'I'm not an erotic specialist, my speciality is Roman silverware, but because of that and because of the book I wrote twenty years ago this is a part that has been thrust upon me,' said Miss Johns, robustly oblivious to double meanings. 'But I feel very strongly that these things should be dispersed to the relevant departments of the Museum, so you see the Roman objects in the context of Roman culture. You shouldn't see them through the filter of your own time.'

Some have actually been dispersed, most of them between the Wars, but the remainder, roughly half of the Mayor of Bedford's original collection, remains under lock and key in Cupboard 55, where Dr Gaimster (there is, you will have gathered, no need for me to make any of this up) is determined they will stay.

'When I first saw them ten years ago I thought, "Wow." To me this is a time-capsule of Victorian collecting attitudes, and has more to do with the nineteenth century than with antiquity. What is of value here is not individual objects, but information about the Victorian mind.

'Feminists come to photograph a steel chastity belt which was part of the Witt collection. No such thing dating from the Middle Ages has been found anywhere in the world, but Victorians believed in them and this is one of their confections. I must get thirty requests a year to see it. I'd love to see the collection go on show, but as a collection. I will resist any attempts to see it dispersed.'

What makes all this even funnier is that last month the Warren Cup, a silver Roman goblet bought by the Museum for £1.8 million, and carved with explicit scenes of buggery, went on show. The Romans, who had no word for homosexuality, may have had a different attitude to this (believing, like the sailor in *Fanny Hill*, that it was a matter of 'any port in a storm'), but it does leave Cupboard 55 high and dry on the beach of changing public taste. Even a few years ago, the Museum's director admitted, the Cup would also have been kept in a locked cupboard.

The same is true of the British Library's notorious Private Case of pornography, which contains little you could not buy now in any motorway service station. I was shown round it some years ago, and remember it as a series of three locked rooms of ascending degree, rather like the three dogs in the fairy-tale, with eyes like saucers, like plates, then like millstones. But it was the millstones that confused me. Here, next to a lavishly photographed, three-volume German study of penile fashions in New Guinea, was the *AA Book of the Road*. It was the danger of theft, I was told, that now determined which books were forbidden.

In 1953 the Library handed over to the Museum some late eigthteenth-century condoms which had been found used as bookmarks in a 1783 *Guide to Health, Beauty, Riches and Honour*. Made of sheep intestines with delicate pink drawstrings, they too add to the period charm of Cupboard 55, to which they were promptly consigned. But his condoms, said Dr Gaimster proudly, had now appeared in every recent history of contraception.

Here too, bound in morocco leather, are the whimsical reflections of early collectors on phallic worship – which one of them, an MP called Payne Knight, was convinced survived on an island off the west coast of Ireland. The inhabitants of Inishkea, he insisted, worshipped a large stone phallus wrapped in flannel. These boys saw such things everywhere. T. H. White, 150 years later, thought the stone a pillow used by an ascetic monk.

Still, you have to admire their nerve. Witt was collecting at a time when a man called Thomas Wirgman entered English legal history as the only defendant ever convicted of 'publishing' an obscene tooth-pick case. And all these years later the collection itself has still to appear in the Museum catalogue, being entered only in longhand in the sort of ledger Bob Cratchit might have used ('Lamp in the form of dwarf with large phallus, on the wick of which he is blowing').

Yet the Secretum survives in a week when three men pleaded guilty to publishing obscene material, only, to their bewilderment, to be told by the judge that he had seen far worse on television. Their videos, like the contents of Cupboard 55, were already a time capsule.

1999

STARK RAVING

~⌒

I have this nightmare. In it I am dancing slowly and sedately with a woman I hardly know. Her husband is a Guards' officer and she is talking about garrison life – polite, inconsequential chatter. But I am not listening, I am holding her with the care of someone new to bomb disposal, for the woman is naked. And I am naked. And all around us other naked couples are moving, just as sedately in the twilight. As we circle (for here no couples collide) I am conscious only of the fact that I would like very much to be elsewhere.

Naked women I discovered somewhat late in life, but I discovered them under certain rules. For a start, their nakedness required a great deal of persuasion, also privacy. But in my nightmare there are no rules. Only it is no nightmare.

This actually happened some twenty years ago. I had written an article about the remarkable development in the Languedoc, where funds made available by the French government had resulted in the world's first nudist city at Cap d'Agde. This was not a camp, this was a place with blocks of flats and streets and supermarkets, where any contact with what had been reality disappeared the moment I stood in a queue of buttocks waiting to change Deutschmarks in a nudist bank. The most prosperous shops, curiously enough, were the boutiques, where stark naked women sat around waiting to try on clothes.

I had been supposed to stay for a week, but left after three days. The first hour was extraordinary – all my teenage fantasies come to life – but after that there was just a jaded interest in callisthenics, in seeing what moved. Distantly I watched as girls played tennis, and a man rode a scooter over rough ground. But then on my second afternoon I walked out of the place and saw the most erotic thing: a girl came down the street towards me *in a dress*. I spent the rest of my time reading.

Still, it got me interested in nudism, a movement which the Nazis, with a world war turning against them, found time to legalise. I visited a village in a wood where an attempt had been made to recreate the Garden of Eden, and where a woman, born and raised there, told me of her shock the first time she saw pavements and street lights.

As a result I was interviewed by a woman who was writing a book on the subject. Until then I had been struck by its decorousness (Camus called nudists 'those Protestants of the flesh'). Some camps forbade drink, others meat, and even in Cap d'Agde there was little socialising once the sun went down. But she told me of a place in England where there was a weekly nudist disco. This took place indoors, at night, and there was a bar. Urban nudism was odd enough; indoor nudism with booze and darkness was off the spectrum, but curiosity makes fools of us all.

I had told my then girlfriend that my guide was physically unattractive. In fact she was a good-looking redhead in her early thirties, married with one child, who talked about Christmas parties at Balmoral as we drove to the disco. I felt as nervous as a boy on the eve of his first day at school.

The Last Human Cannonball

It was held in what seemed to be a log cabin, and we undressed in a cloakroom as cold as any school changing-room. I kept stealing worried glances at my guide, who looked magnificent as she talked about the difficulties of finding a good nanny. Together we padded shivering into the dance room.

Picture a room the size of a scout hut but with a small bar, behind which stood a naked man. The lights were low. There was music playing, and about ten couples waltzing clumsily – for it is impossible to dance with a partner if you are not wearing heels, which is why the dances of the Middle Ages tended to be in a ring.

But after a few double whiskies there we were, shuffling with the best of them. The music was so loud that in order to hear anything the other was saying we had to stand very close and, this room being hot, I began to appreciate one advantage of clothes: couples wearing them tend not to stick together.

I think we were there for half an hour, after which I persuaded her to leave. She laughed most of the way home. But the earth is flat, whatever Columbus found, and a man must recognise the moment he reaches its known rim.

1998

THE JOYS OF SEX FOR MRS X

~

C all her Mrs X. You could of course call her Cleo Cordell, for that is the name under which her second book, *Senses Bejewelled*, appears next Thursday. But then you could call her by any name you like except one. When you write her sort of books (and look like her) the name you were born with has to be jettisoned as abruptly as the booster rockets of a space probe.

That falls away, back to the part-time job in the public library and to the house on a Northampton housing estate. The rest streaks on: *The Captive Flesh* appeared last September, *Velvet Claws* is out in June and *Juliet Rising* in the autumn. And that is just the beginning, for in the next two years she will write five books. 'I am speeding up,' she said, for this is what happens to a space probe.

So call her Mrs X, for that best conveys the extraordinary phenomenon of a woman once a housewife and the mother of two teenage sons and now, at a rate of 4000 words a day, every day, locked into a programme at the end of which, unknown to her neighbours, she will have written not one or two books, but a complete erotic library of her own.

Mrs X appears under the Black Lace imprint which, introduced last July by Virgin, set out to publish for the first time a library of erotica written by women for women. That the publishers felt they themselves were moving into uncharted space is shown by the anxious questionnaire at the end of each Black Lace book ('Would your ideal heroine be Contemporary/Bisexual/Naïve/Introverted/Kinky/Anything Else?' – I love the 'Anything Else'), and by the fact they felt obliged to advertise for new writers in the newspaper.

So all over England word processors were switched on as these writers gamely tried to fulfil their contracts; only their hearts were not in it. 'He put it in and moved it about' or, supremely, 'His face was a mask while his balls were on fire.' The result was that some Black Lace books crash-dived into unintentional comedy. But then there was Mrs X.

'Put it this way,' said Mrs X. 'If you're going to write this stuff, you either worry about relatives reading over your shoulder or you go for it. I went for it.'

A beautiful woman, her hair done in a Japanese style with two skewers through it, is writing rapidly in her front window. 'Then he found that something strange began to happen. His resistance receded. He began to welcome each stroke of the whip, each new stardust of pain ...' Mrs X has gone for it.

Her first two novels are set in harems. But these are not the harems of history, the glum barns where women died of boredom (it was said of the last Sultan of Turkey, Abdul the Damned, with his harem of 1000 women, that his one idea of enjoyment was to have Sherlock Holmes read to him in translation by his butler). In the harems of Mrs X's imagination there is never a dull moment. One quick shipwreck and she has them all there: two enslaved Frenchwomen, a bisexual Greek and a devilish Pasha; her books have the obsessiveness of true pornography. Mrs X does not muck about. 'Who wants to hear about women making Sainsbury lists in their heads, as half England does?' asked Mrs X and did not stay for an answer.

Her husband is a video technician. 'I had to look up some of the things she was writing about,' he said. 'When I told my friends this, all they did was nod their heads and say, "Ah well".'

Mrs X is forty-two and after trying to write professionally for ten years had sold just one short story to *Woman's Realm*. Her two long novels, one set in the Iron Age and the other in a parallel universe, remained in manuscript. Once she was part of a local writing circle, but resigned because there were too many poets in it, who insisted on talking about themselves.

Mrs X then set up a group with two girlfriends. One is a former nurse called Christine Green, which is her real name – she writes crime fiction and her characters merely get murdered. The other, a young mother of four, is now Roxanne Carr (not her real name) in the Black Lace list. 'I don't know how she fits it all in,' said Mrs X.

Fitting things in is, of course, a major problem in her line of work and at first they used to read each other's chapters to see if all the arms and legs were in the right places. But then the other two became alarmed at her new aptitude and even tried to remonstrate with her.

'I told them that when it comes to sexual fantasy, the sky's the limit. These books are erotic rollercoasters, that's all. You would need medical attention if you tried some of these things. But I do draw the line at some. Like what? Like coercion. I always introduce the phrase "Of course you can leave now ...", only in my book nobody does.'

She chooses her locations with care. 'If you find yourself in a harem, you know you're not there to do the washing.' She knew the reality of harem life was grim ('most of the women never went near the Sultan. They just hung about in baggy trousers and caught colds'), but background reading did provide some plums, like the compulsory depilation of all body hair. Mrs X got a whole chapter out of that and came to love research.

An interview with her publishers in London and a chance visit to a strange corsetry shop which, it turned out, did not restrict its custom to women, yielded some of the odder moments in *Senses Bejewelled*. But then a biography of the Victorian explorer Mary Kingsley provided the plot of her third book ('Of course, I had to add some stuff – all she ever collected was plants').

The Black Lace titles are all written by women; the one man who did manage to get in on the act was caught out. The publishers now check on all their authors. 'I wonder if they did random sex tests,' mused Mr X.

At one time his wife thought she could distinguish between erotica written by men from that written by women but now, writing the stuff herself, she is not sure. Like John Cleland in *Fanny Hill* she vaulted the first hurdle, the naming of parts, by eschewing all four-letter words and attempting her own delicate coinages based on metaphor.

The result is that at times, with all the 'secret buds' and 'petals', you feel you are reading a gardening catalogue. But Mrs X's heart, unlike those of her colleagues, is clearly in the work. 'In the dim interior the bodies looked carved from porcelain ...'

She has no embarrassments, quoting her mentor, the American writer Ann Rice who, in her retelling of the fairytale, has the prince quietly rape Sleeping Beauty before awakening her with a kiss. 'Writing to arouse the reader,' said Miss Rice, 'is a noble-enough art.' Nor is Mrs X tiring of the Great Game, even though there are days when rain falls on Northampton and she cannot bear to conjure up the fountains and the silken athletic girls.

'But if I thought about the reality of things I couldn't write. You must think of the erotic as a genre, just as much of one as the Western and the crime novel. We all know the West wasn't really like that and amateurs don't solve crimes.'

For her, the invitation to write for Black Lace was, she admits, a godsend. Besides, as the sacking of long-serving editors at Mills & Boon showed, women's popular fiction is going to be more erotic in future, if only to sell. Her own two straight novels, she said glumly, were still going the rounds of publishers.

Meanwhile, both her mother and mother-in-law have been squared. Each has been given a framed edition of the first book's cover and advised they would not like the contents at all. She is safe with her two teenage sons, who do not read books of any kind.

And now, as she admits, she is having the time of her life. She has appeared on television alongside Ken Follett and Claire Rayner, she is the only one of the Black Lace authors to allow herself to be interviewed and photographed, and, as she grows in confidence, claims to have reduced her bonk-to-plot ratio. 'I am capable of writing an entire chapter without any form of sex in it,' said Mrs X proudly. One day she hopes to extend this to two or even three chapters.

But all that is ahead of her and Mrs X, four books under her jewelled belt, still finds herself pausing from time to time at the word processor.

'Oh yes, I do get turned on by some of it, but I write in my front window and it doesn't do to wriggle in one's front window,' she said, oblivious to the fact that the grass beyond this ran wild long ago.

1994

PART FOUR
AND THE DEVIL

TALK OF THE DEVIL

~

He was the busiest man who ever lived. This has been claimed of others, like Robespierre who directed the Terror of the French Revolution, but such men had ambitions and whole worlds to change. He had none. His attitude to his fellow-men was as simple as that of the eighteenth-century highwayman Jack Sheppard, who, awaiting execution, reflected, 'Those I met, I robbed.' And no man worked harder at his trade than Colonel Francis Charteris.

He was still busy on his deathbed in 1732. Death being a setback even he had to recognise, the Colonel offered £30,000 in cash to anyone who could disprove the existence of Hell (this at a time when a farmer could make a good living on £100 a year). But the offer, he went on hurriedly, did not include Heaven; he was indifferent to that. The Colonel was a practical man.

And afterwards that energy lingered, for wherever the Colonel was, in life or death, there was chaos. He died in a raging thunderstorm, and at his burial in Grey Friars Church in Edinburgh, the people of the neighbourhood interrupted the ceremony, trying to pull the body from the coffin, and when that failed they threw dead dogs in and offal on top of them. All the Hollywood burials of Count Dracula have been exercises in restraint beside the passing of the Colonel.

In the one reliable likeness we have of him, Plate One of Hogarth's *The Harlot's Progress*, the Colonel stands in the background, which is as he would have liked it, for, despite his travels and the many aliases, every single action of his adult life landed him squarely in the foreground of public notoriety.

Hogarth's engraving shows the yard of a London pub called The Bell, in which the early eighteenth-century equivalent of a long-distance coach, a travelling wagon with a canvas roof, has just stopped. A young country girl, ripe for ruin, has alighted, and an older woman is comforting her. The latter, with her lace and chins and beauty spots, is the recruiting procuress, the girl the Harlot to be. In the background, watching from the pub door, in shadow like a spider, is the man who is to be the agent of the ruin.

Not a man of fashion, and not young, the Colonel is shown as a large, lounging, untidy figure, loose-mouthed, his expression far away, one hand in his pocket, the other resting on a cane. But there is a suggestion of power in the way another man, a small fluttering figure, peers round his arm as though awaiting his next command. For the Colonel had the perfect cover for his raids on humanity: he was a gentleman.

England in the eighteenth century, a time of privilege, predators and corruption (the paymaster of Marlborough's armies fiddled so much money in just five years that in the end they had to make him a duke), but, for the poor, of a terrible legal code, chaotically applied (a soldier of George II received 30,000 lashes in 16 years, 'yet the man is hearty and well, and in no way concerned'). A time of powdered wigs and dirty linen, of white bosoms and bad teeth ... the game reserve of Colonel Francis Charteris.

The respectable Victorian intellectuals who compiled the *Dictionary of National Biography* intended to include 30,000 memoirs of the great and good, but they found themselves pushed to one side by a few people who may be said to have included themselves by their sheer awfulness. Here in a sunless gallery are the creatures of tyrants, the traitors, the arch-criminals, and, at the far end, curtained off, the object of the *DNB*'s fascinated horror. Draw those curtains and, in the sudden flash of lightning, you will see the faraway expression and the loose mouth of a man without a single saving grace.

Of a Lowland Scots landed family, Charteris started off as a soldier, his father having bought him a commission in the Duke of Marlborough's army. But wars were not to the Colonel's taste. He was thrown out of one regiment for cheek, out of a second for theft, and finally out of the whole Allied army by the Duke himself when he proved more of a threat to morale than all the French.

In winter quarters he had fleeced his fellow officers at cards, then lent them their money back at 100 per cent interest, a combination of gambling with usury which was to be the foundation of his vast fortune. But the Duke, faced with nothing less than a bankrupt officer corps, intervened and the Colonel was court-martialled.

It is known that his father tried to buy him another commission (the Colonel's military career tells you a lot about the British army 300 years ago), but this time the officers refused to enrol him. Yet by 1711 he was an officer again, and an officer who had made an interesting legal discovery: men who chose to enlist in the army were safe from their civilian creditors.

The Colonel enlisted every bankrupt he could find, they were duly grateful, and the money rolled in. But this time he made a mistake unique in his career: he had an accomplice, a sergeant, and they fell out. He thrashed the sergeant, the sergeant sang like a canary, and the Colonel received the grandest, and rarest, court martial of all. On 1 March 1711, he was arrested and cashiered at the bar of the House of Commons by the Speaker himself.

During the Jacobite Rebellion of 1715 he offered his services to the Crown, which refused them. He then offered them to the rebels, *who also refused them*. In a time of national emergency, when anyone with military experience was welcome, neither side felt able to cope with the Colonel. He settled into the life of a professional gambler and money-lender, for, whatever else he was, the Colonel was a self-made man.

Using a mirror, he won £3000 at cards from the Duchess of Queensberry, which so horrified the Duke that he introduced a Bill into Parliament prohibiting gambling over a certain sum. It was the only time in the Colonel's life when it may be said he was responsible for something good.

There was the odd setback. Found to be playing with loaded dice, he was grabbed by the company who stripped him naked and made him stand in a corner. Here he proceeded to behave so obscenely (the details are vague) that everyone rushed out into the night. He was fined £80 for biting off a miller's nose in Edinburgh, and threw £90 on to the magistrates' desk, inviting them to have a drink on him. He was fined a further £50 for contempt.

He defrauded bankers, butchers and innkeepers, for they were all one to him, and this, with the gambling and the usury, enabled him to buy several estates, one of which, Hornby Castle in Lancashire, housed his sexual research and development staff, a harem presided over by an elderly woman named Mary Clapham who, with the Colonel's creature John Gourley (the small man in the Hogarth print), kept the place stocked with poor girls, for Charteris was indifferent to rank.

Honesty fascinated him, for he could not understand it. Of the Lord Advocate of Scotland, he observed that his honesty was so whimsical the Colonel rated it forty-five per cent above that of Don Quixote. He seems to have materialised among mankind like a creature from another world, and how he managed to live so long in this one is a wonder. He fought duels, though he never seems to have understood the rules, taking advantage of the elaborate preliminaries to stab one man in the arm. 'If a gentleman once takes but a little to the practical art of the sword, courage becomes habitual,' observed the Colonel airily.

Several homes meant he had to travel between them, and at York, falling ill with pleurisy, he was taken in by a clergyman. Unfortunately the clergyman had a daughter. He also had two much younger children who, playing with fire, set the house alight. A crowd which gathered to watch the blaze saw the invalid and the daughter, both in their underclothes, jump from the same window. The vicar tried to bring an action against the Colonel, but was dissuaded on the grounds that his daughter had already seen too much action with the Colonel.

About this time he made the acquaintance of Thomas Woolston, a notorious theologian who had denied the Virgin Birth and the Resurrection (the Government was later to indict him for blasphemy). The Colonel had him to supper, and in a wide-ranging discussion, *in the course of which the two consumed seven bottles of port*, was so taken with Woolston that he offered to set him up with a harem of his own. There was an innocence about the Colonel at times.

When his guest declined the offer he declared he would make him his private chaplain as soon as a vacancy occurred, though there is no record of any incumbent. Woolston, who had denied so much, found it necessary to take out a newspaper advertisement denying he had ever met the Colonel.

He is known to have married at least once, a Miss Swinton ('who hath scarce met with any other comfort since her marriage than that of universal commiseration'). She was the daughter of a Scottish judge, and their daughter Janet married the fourth Earl of Wemyss. But there were other children.

At one point, very ill and thinking his time had come, the Colonel declared he would build a charity school and fill it with his illegitimate children, of whom there must have been enough to make the project worthwhile. The only problem was, he no longer remembered who they were, but announced he would put advertisements in the papers. He also thought he would provide for the women he had ruined; he reckoned twenty-four almshouses should do the trick, and hired an architect. Then the Colonel recovered.

But in the end the women got their own back. One of the few times we know exactly where the Colonel was, and what he was doing, was 10 November 1729, when he was in his house at Hanover Square; fifteen days later he was in Newgate jail, trying to bribe the warders to exchange his fetters for lighter ones. At the age of seventy, according to his daughter (but fifty-five, according to the *DNB*), the Colonel had been charged with rape.

A young Lancashire girl in domestic service, Anne Bond, had become ill, and, as must have been common, had been sacked by her employer. Thrown out of her lodgings, she met an old woman who said she would find her a job with a Captain Harvey. On the third day, hearing someone ask for Colonel Charteris, she realised his true identity, and tried to escape but was stopped. On 10 November he raped her as she was lighting a fire. He then offered her money and fine clothes, but when she refused them he threw her out.

The eighteenth century was an ugly time. There was no police force, so Anne Bond was advised to apply to a grand jury at the quarter sessions, and, because the Colonel was a gentleman, was told only to charge him with attempted rape. But a member of the jury stood up and said that the Colonel had attempted to rape his sister. The Colonel was charged with rape, found guilty and sentenced to death.

There was a tremendous sense of shock in fashionable London. His daughter wrote a thoughtful letter to Jonathan Swift, 'If a man must do wrong he should aim a little higher than the enjoyment of a kitchen maid he finds obstinately virtuous.' For there was something worse than a rapist, and that was a democratic rapist.

> '*Brought to the bar, and sentenced from,*
> *Only for ravishing a country wench?*
> *Shall men of honour meet no*
> *more respect?*'

Society and politics came to his aid. His son-in-law, the Earl of Wemyss, appealed to the King, who, with the Jacobite threat still hanging over him, wanted no trouble with the Scottish nobility. On 10 April 1730, George II announced at a meeting of the Privy Council that the Colonel was to be released on £8300 bail. In addition, he was to pay £800 to Anne Bond. The Colonel's last rape had been expensive.

Just after his release he was pulled from his coach in Chelsea and beaten up by a mob. This, following his experiences in Newgate, prompted a breakdown in health, and he withdrew to his northern estates.

There were flashes of the old spirit, as when on his deathbed he asked his daughter how much he should pay the clergyman, the Colonel being convinced that all men had their price. On being told that such payments were not customary, he said happily, 'Then let's have another flourish from him.' Nobody took up his generous offer to disprove Hell.

He had fascinated his contemporaries. Swift wrote an epitaph, 'Here Francis Charteris lies – be civil./ The rest God knows –

perhaps the Devil.' But it was not his evil that fascinated them, it was the consistency of that evil. 'He was the only person of his time who could cheat without the mask of honesty ...'

The Colonel left everything to his daughter, and the earls of Wemyss gratefully changed their family name to Charteris, as members of the contemporary aristocracy might in similar circumstances have changed theirs to Kray. Sir Martin Charteris, the Queen's Private Secretary, was a direct descendant of a man the *Dictionary of National Biography* refers to simply as 'the greatest scoundrel of his age'.

2001

COMEDY OF ERRORS

~

I t was not an eventful day, 10 December 1925. All the *Annual Register of Events*, that bible of reference libraries, records is that a new headmaster was appointed to Harrow School. It does not mention that all over the country that morning men gazed at their newspapers with a wild surmise. In libraries dry hearts which had never known such excitement pounded. In sale-rooms well-dressed men sank back and saw large sums of money begin to form in the air above them like the Horsemen of the Apocalypse.

In a world where a few years later two words, Shakespeare's signature, were to be spoken of as being worth a sum in six figures, there was something yet that went beyond avarice or imagina-tion, or even dreams. No sonnet, no stage direction, survives in Shakespeare's handwriting. The only evidence that he could write at all is fourteen words, six signatures in three different spellings, all on legal documents. One signature is prefaced by the words 'By Me'.

Yet on Wednesday, 10 December 1925, Hunter Rogers, a

labourer, of The Dell, Langley, near Slough, announced that he had discovered Shakespeare's manuscripts. Not just a poem or a scene: Mr Rogers had the lot.

There was no melodrama. No grave was opened. No team of scholars stood blinking sheepishly in the flash-bulbs. It would be difficult to squeeze any kind of drama out of a house called The Dell. But you would not need to. In Buckinghamshire a man had stood up and said he had all Shakespeare's manuscripts.

Now just to give you an idea of the passions that must have been unleashed that morning, let me recall an article I wrote about Shakespeare in January 1973, in the *Sunday Telegraph* magazine. Shakespeare is buried in Holy Trinity, Stratford. There is a grave in the altar steps and a bust in the wall above, of him as a plump Rotarian, bald and with the familiar stubby Imperial beard, seemingly at his accounts. The article concerned an American cipher expert's conviction that the manuscripts were hidden behind the bust. The clues, he believed, were in the inscription.

After the article had been published the letters did not stop coming for three months. There was even an American businessman who engineered a trip across the Atlantic to get me to sidle into Holy Trinity with him, some kind of electronic detection device concealed about us. But you occasionally get such things in journalism. It is when the world of action intrudes that you step back. That October the bust was pulled out of the wall.

It is a mystery how it was done. A locked church was entered and left, and three hundredweight of stone pulled down. The vergers today still talk of it with awe, for the only clue was an open window near the nave roof, about eighty feet up. It was cat burglary of an order which no writer of fiction would dare unload on his readers. But there was no cavity, and there were no manuscripts. There were no charges, either, for nobody was caught for breaking in. You can only speculate as to the sentence the Stratford bench would have handed down – the only market town in

England with a Hilton hotel does not appreciate anyone nosing around its financial props.

But you begin to appreciate what the *Morning Post* meant when it breathed, in December 1925, that if Rogers was telling the truth he would go down in history 'as a discoverer of treasure trove compared with whom Aladdin was an amateur'.

The *Post* rather grandly sent what it described as 'a Representative' down to Langley; and, hedging its bets (for there was the chance that it might not be a joke), it sent with him 'one of the greatest authorities on Shakespeare … in the country'. It was that time of blessed anonymity, before news-readers were named.

The two men received a series of shocks. The first was Rogers himself. 'He proved to be a man verging on illiteracy, and indeed apologised in advance for any flaws in his explanation which might arise through his want of education.' But the manuscripts were not there. They had all, said Rogers humbly, been sent to America. He thought he might get £20,000 for four of the plays.

But if the manuscripts were not there a great deal of other stuff was. One room was piled high with furniture and old books and manuscripts. All, said Rogers, had belonged to Shakespeare. There was a sixteenth-century 'Breeches Bible' inscribed 'William Shakespeare – my loving mother'. There was a 1557 Prayer Book and a copy of the 1571 Roger Ascham's *The Schoolmaster*. Inside this there was a rough sketch of a troupe of actors with the word 'ME' scribbled under one. Beside the sketch were the disjointed words, 'These foles at Oxforde … this obserd'. There was also the signature 'William Shakespeare'.

There was a great deal more. There was a desk with 'Hathaway' cut into the wood. There were two iron candlesticks with 'WS' carved on the wooden bases; and there was a large butcher's knife. (This last is still very odd. John Aubrey, who claimed to have met some of Shakespeare's old neighbours, wrote that in his youth the playwright had followed this trade: '… when he killed a

Calfe he would do it in a high style, and make a Speeche.' The oddity is that in 1925 Aubrey's manuscripts were mouldering in the Bodleian, and had not been published.)

You can sense the confusion in the Representative's mind. He recorded object after object, and still the terrible inventory went on. Added to this was the attitude of the expert, who said worriedly, yes, everything was certainly very old, candlesticks and all, and probably did date from the late sixteenth century. That he, too, was shaken is revealed by his comment: 'Whether any of the signatures are genuine can be decided only by prolonged study.'

But there was something else which added to the Representative's confusion. Reading between the lines, you know that he felt sure that morning he was about to unmask a fake (the expert was just riding shotgun). For the Representative had done his homework. He had found out that only a few years earlier Rogers, then a gardener in Cobham, Surrey, had found two old masters by the eighteenth-century painter Hoppner and a letter from Constable in the false bottom of an old chest of drawers. Newspapers at the time had marvelled at the coincidence, because Rogers had announced that he was a direct descendant of Hoppner. They mentioned in passing that the sale of the paintings had raised him to affluence (and, probably, to The Dell).

The finding of the Shakespeare material, Rogers told the Representative, had also come about through family connections. One of his ancestors had married into the Hall family, that same family into which Shakespeare's daughter had married.

But the manuscripts he had come by in a much more romantic way. They had been buried by one of his ancestors in the early part of the nineteenth century in the grounds of Compton Wyniates, the great Tudor manor under a Cotswold hill near Banbury. His ancestor had done this, said Rogers solemnly, to prevent their falling into the hands of notorious forgers like William Ireland, who was still about (the late eighteenth century was the Golden Age of literary forgery).

The Representative knew it was all too good to be true. And yet ... and yet ... His account on 10 December 1925, took up two and a half columns, some 2500 words. He was a baffled man, and with each paragraph the bafflement mounted.

Two days later the *Morning Post* sent a Special Correspondent to Langley. This was most probably another man, for there is a new jauntiness in the writing (it was he who compared Rogers to Aladdin). Some news editor must have felt that someone had to get to the bottom of the story, for by now another figure had appeared on the scene.

Captain William Jaggard had announced that there had never been 'a more important assembly of Shakespeariana'. Jaggard was a formidable figure. A governor of the Shakespeare Memorial Trust, he had spent twenty-two years compiling his monumental 'Shakespeare Bibliography'. A bookseller and publisher in Stratford, he too was involved in a family matter, for he claimed direct descent from the Jaggard who printed the First Folio. Between them Rogers and Jaggard gave the impression that the late sixteenth/early seventeenth century was just an afternoon ago.

The Special Correspondent sought him out in Stratford, where he displayed other articles he had bought from Rogers. They included the *Apologie of the Earl of Essex*, the Earl's defence at his trial, *but written in Shakespeare's own handwriting*. The Special Correspondent noted with glee that one of Jaggard's assistants was sporting an odd walking stick. It had been Nelson's favourite stick, he was told, and Rogers had thrown it in as a gift when the deal was accomplished.

The *Morning Post* was beginning to get its nerve back now. *Further inquiries had revealed that the virtually illiterate labourer had discovered in all six Hoppners, two Correggios and a Constable.*

A Reading solicitor had come forward and announced that

Rogers had shown him Queen Elizabeth's quill pen, a book in which Oliver Cromwell had written his name, and some music inscribed 'Horatio to Nelson'. But that was just the beginning. Suddenly the relics were coming out of the woodwork.

Enter the Provost of Eton. A few years earlier Rogers had presented the Provost with a mathematical exercise book which, he declared, had belonged to the Duke of Wellington while a boy at Eton. The Provost had duly presented it to the school library. Some months later Rogers had turned up again and given the Provost a lock of Lady Hamilton's hair. This, too, was accepted.

On 14 December the Special Correspondent was back at The Dell. This time Rogers and he motored up to Compton Wyniates. Rogers showed him the spot where he claimed he had dug up the manuscripts at night in the company of an unnamed American and a Mr Morten of Slough. He had been acting on an old map which had remained in his family.

He said that the three men had erected a triangular screen of canvas to hide the light they were using from the Marquess of Northampton's gamekeepers. Two feet down they had come on a slab of stone with 'William Shakespeare' chipped into it. Beneath this were the caskets containing the manuscripts.

The Special Correspondent had arranged for the Marquess's head gardener to be present. The gardener said flatly that it was impossible for anything to have been buried there. In 1909 he himself had built up that piece of ground to dispose of earth that had come from a sunken fence. Nothing could have been buried there in 1818 because that ground did not exist in 1818.

Roger, records the Special Correspondent, was unmoved. That is the lovely thing about the story: Rogers throughout preserved the poise of a Shakespearian villain. And then he crowned everything by producing another map. On this, a few yards from the house of the Marquess's beautifully kept lawn, was a cross. That, he declared, marked the spot where Shakespeare's own library had been buried. The Special Correspondent, who must have felt that he was moving in for the kill, makes no comment. No one even hints at the possibility of digging up the lawn. Back at The Dell, Rogers, in an expansive mood, produced a box full of plaster. This, he said, had fallen off the walls of Shakespeare's birthplace.

In his front room he pointed to a table he said had been made out of floorboards the Bard had once trod. In his outhouse he had lead guttering from the birthplace, and buried under his own pathway was a box containing three hundredweight of 'other bits of the birthplace'. The Special Correspondent did not even allow himself the reflection that it was a marvel the birthplace still stood.

But Rogers must have sensed something in his manner, for he said abruptly that he was sick of all these suspicions. He had decided to go to America, and had put in his will that if he should die there the entire collection was to be destroyed by his solicitor.

Hunter Rogers did go to America. The *Morning Post* kept a beady eye on him, and on 20 April 1926, its New York correspondent wired a single paragraph to the effect that Rogers, disgusted with his reception there, was proposing to hand over his collection to the Shakespeare Trust at Stratford.

He was to make the papers once more, this time on 22 March 1927, tucked away in a short law report in *The Times*. Captain Jaggard sued Rogers for the £800 he had paid him for Shakespeare's Bible, some legal documents signed by Shakespeare, and Essex's *Apologie* that the Bard had transcribed in his one appearance as a court reporter.

The Judge found for Jaggard, and added with the note of bewilderment which characterised almost every comment on the matter: 'The only thing which has caused me the slightest difficulty is in wondering how in the world the defendant managed to impose upon a gentleman of the obvious intelligence and experience of the plaintiff.'

Gerald Jaggard, the Captain's son, who still lives in Stratford, remembers the case. More than fifty years later he is still baffled by it. 'Rogers was half illiterate, a labourer of some kind. It was quite extraordinary how he managed to get across people.' Mr Jaggard believes that Rogers died not long after the case.

Certainly he disappeared abruptly from the newspapers which had once hung on his words. I have been able to find no obituary and no photograph of this remarkable man.

Like Rogers, Jaggard, too, seems to have belonged more to Shakespeare's art than real life. In 1936 he was in the papers again, this time with evidence from handwriting experts in London, Paris and Geneva. He had come upon three volumes of Holinshed in which he had found handwritten entries in the margin 'in a hand strangely familiar'.

What had emerged, he declared, was nothing less than Shakespeare's own working copy of Holinshed's history. There were his initials in the margin: WS. There was the odd piece of doggerel.

But there was also, announced Jaggard proudly, a veterinary recipe: 'Blacke soap, pigge meale and honny, mingled together, good for a horses leg swollen.'

Jaggard lived on until 1947. At his death *The Times* recorded: 'To unlock the treasures of his beloved shire for the benefit of others was his simple joy.' There was no hint of irony and no mention of Rogers, who had helped him unlock them with a vengeance.

1978

CRIPPEN BROKE THE NEWS TO THEM

ᕲ

Not a place that is easy to find; she would have liked that. Yesterday it was a village, tomorrow it will be an overspill town, but today it is the despair of postmen, so quickly are new streets being added.

Here, on this West Country estate, the bungalows are so identical that the planners threw in the odd ornamental well to give character to some gardens. A man could retire here and cut his small lawn and think of nothing in particular, until, that is, the morning when the letter comes.

Bob Smith, aged seventy, had retired here with his wife Doris, and it was here that he learned that his old Mum, such a trial in her old age, Mum who wrote up recipes in her neat longhand, who cooked Christmas cakes and chocolate rolls, and drew railway engines for him when he was a boy, old Mum who never wore her teeth except to go out, was once the most famous young woman in the world. It was here that the writer Jonathan Goodman came to tell him that she was Ethel le Neve, mistress to the murderer Dr Crippen.

No murder has ever caught the popular imagination so completely. It was not the crime – that was ordinary enough, the remains of the American quack pedlar's wife being found in the earth under his cellar. It was the fact that for the first and last time the public was in on the nemesis gathering over two fugitives.

Crippen, a small, frail, balding man, and his pretty young mistress were fleeing to a new life in America on board the SS *Montrose*. But the captain had recognised them and in the first use of wireless for police purposes had telegraphed the news back. The fugitives did not know this.

As the *Daily Mirror* of 27 July 1910 wrote: 'Only a Robert Browning, in some imaginative monologue, could do justice to the situation as it must be now on board the SS *Montrose*: only Robert Browning with his strange gift for peering into the minds of others and for identifying himself with the feelings of people totally unlike himself, could represent to us what must be the sensations of the hunted Crippen and his companion, caged in the floating ship in mid-ocean.'

The tension mounted (the captain being retained by English and Canadian papers to give day-by-day reports, while at the same time cold-bloodedly entertaining the oblivious pair at his table). And across the Atlantic went the faster liner *Laurentic*, bearing the hunter, Chief Inspector Walter Dew.

It had everything, this situation. There was the beauty of the twenty-seven-year-old London typist, the titillation of the fact that she was dressed in boy's clothing, and, much later, the evidence of the mutual devotion that existed between the couple.

There was even humour. The late Mrs Crippen, a music-hall entertainer, had been guaranteed, according to Marie Lloyd, to empty any theatre in which she appeared. She had been notoriously unfaithful to her husband, the homoeopathic doctor turned postal quack, dispensing his pile ointments and toothache cures to the credulous. Miss le Neve, born Ethel Neave, had been his secretary.

Mrs Crippen disappeared in February 1910. People began to ask questions and the doctor put it about that she had returned to America where she died suddenly. As a result Inspector Dew came calling on the house in Holloway and was told quite a different story. She had gone off with a man, said Crippen, and he had invented the other tale to stop scandal. Dew accepted this and it was only Crippen's abrupt disappearance which prompted his return and his subsequent spotting of the loose brick in the cellar floor.

The tension mounted. Millions of people read in their papers of the telegraph message from the *Montrose*. Bookies did a roaring trade on whether the *Laurentic* would reach Quebec first.

And then it was over. Dew, dressed in pilot's clothing, boarded the *Montrose*, went up to a Mr Robinson, and said, 'Good morning, Dr Crippen.' When they entered the cabin where Master Robinson was reading a novel called *Audrey's Recompense*, Miss le Neve fainted.

'Mum was a great reader,' said Bob Smith.

Crippen was tried at the Old Bailey and found guilty of murder. Ethel le Neve was tried as an accessory but, Crippen refusing to give evidence against her, was acquitted.

The letters he wrote to her from the condemned cell are haunting ('One Sunday, how early I came for you – six years ago last summer it was – and we had a whole day together, which meant so much to us then ...'). On the morning of his execution she sailed to North America again, under a new name, Miss Allen.

It was known that she returned a year later, and subsequently married a man called Smith. It was also known that she had died in south London in 1967. And that was all.

Enter Jonathan Goodman, the crime writer, who was researching a new book, *The Crippen File*. Goodman, whose experience of such matters had taught him that answers often lie in the most obvious places, went to the new Somerset House to look up the death certificates of all the Mrs Smiths who had died in south London in 1967. It took him less than an hour. On the certificate was the name of a son and his address in the West Country. He checked with the telephone directory and found that Bob Smith still lived there. And so to the bungalow went a carefully written letter ('your mother ... inadvertently mixed up in the murder of Mrs Crippen ...').

Bob Smith remembered turning to his wife Doris: 'Some loony has written to me.' He knew little about Crippen, except that he had been caught by wireless. But they replied to Goodman, using his stamped, addressed envelope. ('A little trick,' said Goodman. 'People feel they can't waste 17p.'). And there followed the strangest meeting.

Now put yourselves in their place. Bob Smith, aged seventy, retired joiner, and his sister Nina Campbell, aged sixty-four, a widow and a retired secretary; the children of Stanley and Ethel Smith of Croydon. Suddenly they were faced with the possibility that their parents had kept from them a secret as huge as an airship hangar, that their mother had been someone most recently played by Samantha Eggar in a film. That Mrs Smith might have run the Croydon KGB was nothing compared with this. Goodman was similarly taken aback. 'I knew there couldn't be a mistake, but Ethel just stops in 1910 and this wholly new person appears. I mean, Ethel had run Crippen's business for him, she was a sort of executive. And then there's this mum, the housewife who always put a new apron on after she'd done the housework, this terribly ordinary human being. They just seemed two separate people.'

But slowly the children began to remember things which had puzzled them. There was the fact that Mum had once said she had been to Canada, and talked to them about the railways and the Rockies; they had been small then and it had not occurred to them to ask what she had been doing there.

And then there was the matter of Mum's name on their parent's marriage certificate. Ethel Harvey. They had always assumed that she had been married before, but had never asked ('You could never discuss anything personal with her'). Harvey was Crippen's middle name, which in one of his last letters he begged her to assume.

And there were the strange little bits of knowledge which Mum occasionally exhibited, as when she told them of how the cutlery was arranged at banquets. Ethel le Neve, who had dined at the captain's table, would know such things but not the Mrs Smith whose children could not remember her ever dining out with her husband, who had died first, in 1960.

But the things which finally convinced them were Goodman's photograph of their grandfather, and the specimens of Ethel's handwriting which he had found. It was then that a single sentence spoken recently by an aunt in her nineties sprang into headlines: 'There was always some mystery about your mother.'

They began to realise how little they knew about her. 'I didn't know that she had worked at the office where Pop was a book-keeper,' said Bob, 'and where I later worked as a joiner.' Even when Nina took up shorthand and typing her mother never once let on that she, too, had been a trained secretary.

'I knew everything about Dad,' said Bob Smith. 'I knew the orphanage he was brought up in, when he served his apprentice-ship, what regiment he was in during the war. But I knew very little about Mum.'

All they have left of her is the notebook in which she copied out her recipes, and the group photographs taken at the time of Nina's marriage. A neat, small, middle-aged woman looks unsmilingly at the camera. She had observed spitefully before the marriage that there had already been one rogue mixed up with the family.

But what astonished the brother and sister most was the number of people who had kept the secret. Mum had four brothers and a sister, most of whom they saw from time to time. She also had a father who had lived with them (and who had disgraced himself by selling her story to a magazine in 1910). And there was the gentle figure of their father, whom they had never heard quarrel with their mother. All these people they thought they knew, had kept it from them.

'But say we'd been told,' said Bob Smith. 'Say she'd told us when we were eight or so, we'd have been bound to let it out. And kids can be cruel. Think what we'd have been called. And then when she was older she might have worried that it would have turned us against her.'

Both admire their parents now, and marvel at the strain they must have been under leading this odd double life. They feel they would rather not have known but it has left them with an awe for the people they knew as Pop and Mum.

It has also led them to speculate on the strange last meeting with the old lady when, in hospital on the day of her death, she refused even to speak to them, but lay with her lips clenched tight, as though preparing to leave with her secret safe.

They talked much about the mysteries that people can lock inside themselves. People said you had to live with someone to know them, muttered Doris Smith; this really knocked that on the head.

Bob Smith wondered how easy it was to get into Scotland Yard's Black Museum. He had read that the Princess of Wales had been shown a picture of the woman who was his mother, dressed in boy's clothing on the *Montrose*.

'I wonder if I could get in there, seeing as I'm an interested party, as it were. I'd promise to keep it secret.'

'You could tell them that runs in the family.'
Bob Smith began to laugh. 'I could at that.'

1985

Mrs Hitler's Diaries

~

On 20 January 1939, the London *Evening Standard* carried the photograph of a thick-set, extremely tough-looking woman who, suitably disguised, might have passed unnoticed in the front row of any Welsh rugby team. The accompanying story was no more than a caption. It began, 'Mrs Hitler Answers a Rate Summons'.

Mrs Brigid Hitler, it went on, the Irish-born sister-in-law of the German Führer, had appeared at Highgate police court to answer a summons for non-payment of rates amounting to £9 13s 10d. She offered to pay this in six weeks and her offer was accepted by the court. Afterwards she told reporters that she had just been offered a job as a hostess in a New York night club.

Dear God, a hostess ... A bouncer perhaps, for Mrs Hitler is carrying a hand-bag like a Thompson sub-machine gun. But Mrs Hitler? The truly extraordinary thing is that the *Standard* did not think the story worth more than a photo-caption. It did not even mention the fact that her twenty-eight-year-old son, William Patrick, Adolf Hitler's nephew, born in Toxteth, Liverpool, was living with her at the time.

Whether she did pay her rates is not known, for two months later the curious couple emigrated to America, the press of which had always been more interested in them, *LOOK* magazine publishing an article by Mr Hitler entitled 'Why I Hate My Uncle'.

In 1944 William Patrick Hitler joined the US Navy, his recruiting officer being a man called Hess. For many of you, I suspect, that will be the last straw. No writer of fiction would dare invent such a cast, a nephew born in Toxteth (and, for it gets worse, a member of the 11th Toxteth Boy Scout Troop), an Irish sister-in-law, and a recruiting officer called Hess.

But then that is the trouble with the monumental moments of history: you tend to simplify them because they mean so much to you and to everyone else. You forget the footnotes and the attendant oddities. For example, and at the risk of destroying any vestiges of credibility that I have left, did you know that Herod of the Bible died in the South of France? He had retired there with Herodias, and, possibly, Salome.

So when you hear that Hitler had a brother living in Liverpool, where, as a very young man, he may have visited him before the First World War, you throw up your hands in disbelief, for Hitler's was a German tragedy enacted on locations by now familiar from newsreels and re-enactment. How do you fit Toxteth into the sinister events of Nuremberg and the Bunker?

Even the fact that Hitler may have been someone's uncle seems incredible.

Which, curiously enough, is how he wanted it. A Man of Destiny can have no private past, or present (which was why the existence of Eva Braun, his mistress for twenty years, was kept from the German people). He has to be remote from all human weakness, in Hitler's case loudly trumpeting the fact that he took no salary as Führer (and forgetting that he was a multimillionaire from the royalties of *Mein Kampf*, a copy of which the State presented to every newly wed German couple). Such a man could have no skeletons, and the trouble with Hitler was that he had a cupboard full.

Put yourself in his place for a moment. It is 1933, you have just been made Chancellor of Germany, when off the train they trundle, an Irish woman who looks like a rugby forward and a nephew called William Patrick Hitler.

And, if that were not enough, they have come to see your brother, the husband of one and the father of the other, who, married to a German woman, is now quietly keeping a pub in Berlin. The only thing is that your brother, having forgotten to get a divorce, is thus a bigamist who has also forgotten to pay any form of maintenance for ten years. What would you do? Exactly. You, too, would say, 'Thank God for the Gestapo.'

What follows is based on a typescript, 225 pages long and ending mysteriously in mid-sentence, which turned up in a manuscript collection bequeathed to the New York Public Library. They are the memoirs of Brigid Hitler, and were first published in 1979 by Duckworth. It is not known why she wrote them or why they were not published before that, for their existence only became generally known in the early 1970s.

Brigid Dowling was seventeen when she met Alois Hitler at the Dublin Horse Show in 1909. He was a dandy, his moustache waxed like that of the Kaiser, and a bounder who claimed to be on a European tour studying the 'hotel business'; he was actually a waiter at the Shelbourne Hotel, to which he had been sent by a London employment agency.

He was also the half-brother of the future Führer. His father, a customs official, had married twice and he was the son of the first marriage. An additional complication, from Adolf's point of view, was that his father had been born illegitimate, at a time when Adolf's grandmother was working in a Jewish household. The fact that he may have had Jewish blood was also in the cupboard, along with the skeletons. As he was later to tell William Patrick Hitler, that spectre at the feast, 'These people must not know where and from what family I come.'

Alois and Brigid eloped to Toxteth, where William Patrick was born, and where Alois was in turn a restaurateur, hotel owner, bankrupt, and razor blade salesman, before disappearing.

There can be no doubt about any of this, for the *Liverpool Post* published the reminiscences of men who were boys with William Patrick. One was called Arthur Bryan of Crosby, who, at the beginning of the Second World War, suddenly ran into another old school friend.

'... And he said to me: "Remember Willie Hitler?" That's when I remembered that Willie had always talked about this uncle of his who, he said, was a general in Germany.'

It is a wonderful story. All Europe is going up in flames around them as these two boneheads, for whom the 1930s had passed like a summer evening, realise for the first time who Willie's uncle is.

Adolf Hitler's trip to Liverpool is more doubtful, his only other visits to the West being in the company of the entire German Army, and, though a garrulous man, he never mentioned it to anyone. But Mrs Hitler had no doubts. She and her husband, she wrote, met him off the train at Lime Street Station, 'A shabby young man,' who immediately had a row with his elder brother.

Her account is very convincing for she throws in some odd details, like Hitler's admiration for Tower Bridge and the fact that he was convinced that he had heard the Bavarian National Anthem being sung on the Mersey (the music is the same as for 'God Save The King'). But she didn't like him, she found him 'weak and spineless' (which comes as a bit of a shock) and couldn't wait to see him go after six months. If only she had been a bit nicer to him, she wrote gravely, he might have stayed in England and become a barber or a carpenter. She stops short of blaming herself for the Second World War, but it is a moment of pure black comedy.

They had managed to make contact with Alois (through the Lord Mayor of Hamburg) when, in 1929, William Patrick visited his father. He was then eighteen, and met his uncle for the first time, having earlier attended one of his Party rallies. In a letter home to his mother he gave an example of Adolf's attempts at small-talk. 'And you, you English boy, what is your opinion on the Jewish question? What are they doing about it in England?' Uncle Adolf, it seems, was doing his best to be nice.

Where the solids hit the fan was on his return to England, when William Patrick and his mother gave their first interview to the English press, in this case to two London evening papers, the *Standard* and the *News*. Mrs Hitler comments ingenuously that they did this to correct the facts about the leader of the Nazis, who, she grieves, at that stage did not even have an entry in *Who's Who*.

The response was a telegram from Germany addressed to William Patrick. 'FATHER DYING STOP COME BERLIN AT ONCE.' Mrs Hitler does not give a date for this but it seems to be in the early 1930s, when Uncle Adolf was poised to assume power. Alois was, of course, not dying, but, as he told his boy, he was terrified that he might soon be, for it was Hitler himself who had ordered the telegram sent.

William Patrick was taken to Hitler, and the full force of the temper which was to cow the entire German General Staff was directed at the English teenager. 'Who gave you permission to appoint yourself an authority on my private affairs ...? Anyone can now say who I am, where I was born, what my family does for a living. They mustn't learn about this stupid bigamy, I can't have it ... I have been so careful. I am only a step away from attaining the top ... I might even become Chancellor. And now there is a "nephew" to tell them all the miserable little details they want to know. They'll hound me.'

And with that, screaming at an SA officer who had come into

the room, Hitler lurched out, shouting that he was about to shoot himself. It is amazing that no one has ever thought to make a film of this, for it is pure farce, a Hitler Family Reunion. But then, nobody wants to be reminded of what an absurd figure Hitler was, it is so much easier to accept him as an embodiment of evil. But, to cap it all, Hitler's sister Angela, who was also there, asked William Patrick what the title of the article had been? 'My Uncle Adolf'.

There followed an amazing interlude during which she and Alois tried to persuade William Patrick he was no relation at all, that Alois, his father, had been adopted. When Adolf came back they tried this out on him and he agreed, telling the bewildered teenager to call a press conference on his return to England and to say it all had been a big mistake. So ended the Family Reunion.

William Patrick and his mother did their best and issued a statement, but this made things worse. Both lost their jobs, their employers thinking them unreliable, so they decided to emigrate to America. The difficulty was their nationality, Alois being an Austrian citizen but, when Mrs Hitler applied for an Austrian passport, research in Vienna showed there was no question of adoption. Hitler and her former husband *were* brothers.

William Patrick took it badly. He had been lied to, so, with the indignation of the young, he wrote to Uncle Adolf, telling him what he thought of him. But events had moved on. Adolf was no longer a leader in waiting: four months earlier, in January 1933, he had been made Chancellor of Germany. In Berlin he pressed the panic button.

The telegram was again from Alois, but this time it was addressed to his dearest wife. He told her to put off all ideas of going to America and to come to Germany. 'GO TO THE GERMAN EMBASSY IN LONDON STOP THEY WILL PROVIDE YOU WITH FUNDS FOR THE TRIP STOP BRING WILLIE WITH YOU STOP.'

In fact, Willie went alone, Mrs Hitler feeling uneasy about the trip. And Willie vanished. Not a phone-call, not a letter. After two weeks Mrs Hitler went to the German Embassy in London where she gave a stunned official her name. He phoned Berlin and fifteen minutes later William Patrick was on the phone, followed by his father; both assured her that everything was all right. But she was unconvinced.

In the year which followed she read in the papers of the start of the Nazi terror, of priests being arrested and Jews beaten up. The result was that when, in answer to her frantic letters, Alois wrote again, inviting her over, and promising funds through the German Embassy, she accepted. So Mrs Hitler went to Germany to see her boy.

William Patrick met her at the station and, as he kissed her, whispered into her ear that she should not have come. He was a frightened man. Yes, they had got him a job, but it was a poorly paid job in a bank and, when he tried to see his uncle, Hitler's SS guards had practically thrown him out of the Chancellery. He wrote his uncle a letter and this time the SS called on him, accusing him of blackmail.

Things, he told her, were terrible in Germany, he was effectively himself a prisoner, his request for an English visit having been turned down. The corruption extended to the top, Hitler himself having a secret bank account under, of all names, Birkenshaw. The Führer's immediate circle, he went on, was made up of gangsters. People disappeared, and Hitler himself might have had a hand in the mysterious death of his niece Geli with whom the Führer had been known to be in love.

His own position was precarious. William Patrick explained that he had been picked up one night by a storm-troop patrol, incredulous at seeing the name on his papers, and, briefly put in a concentration camp, he was released only after the intervention of the British Embassy. William Patrick's one aim, he told his mother, was to get out of Germany.

But father Alois was prospering, having opened a pub in Berlin. It was just that he, too, was terrified of Hitler, especially of the possibility that his brother might at any moment take away his licence. Nervously he asked her how long she intended to stay, and she, primed by her son, said she intended to live the rest of her life there.

The next morning Rudolf Hess's adjutant called on her, inviting her to call on the Reichminister. Hess congratulated her on her decision to stay in Germany and recommended her to take out German nationality, for it had been a little embarrassing for the Führer to have English relatives, he confided. Mrs Hitler was invited to Berchtesgaden. The car which called was Hitler's own, her guide her own sister-in-law Angela. It was to be her first meeting with the man whom she had twenty years earlier thought 'weak and spineless'.

Her first sight of him was the following morning. Hitler was dressed in short leather knickers, his knees bare, and was wearing a green cap. Photographs exist of him in this extraordinary Bavarian rig, and he looks like a garden gnome. But Mrs Hitler was struck more by how sleek and plump he was. 'I thought suddenly of a *petit-bourgeois* who had won first prize in the sweepstakes and come into possession of everything he'd formerly lacked.'

The Führer said gallantly, 'The years have passed over your head without touching you.' And she, trying to think of something uncontroversial to say, asked, 'Why haven't you married?' It must have been a wonderful moment.

He laughed it off. He was married to the women of Germany, he said, some of whom could not bear to wash their hands for a week after having shaken his. She and William Patrick had lunch with him, and she noted how he bolted his vegetarian diet, one of the reasons, his biographers noted, for his uncontrollable breaking of wind (after a meeting with Hitler the former Crown Princess of Germany called loudly for all the windows to be opened). When he relaxed, thought Mrs Hitler, his lack of breeding came through.

There is little on his conversation, except that at one point he expressed an admiration for Cromwell and at another said that Catholicism's days in Germany were over. He asked her to call on his other sister Paula in Austria and urge her to come to Germany. Paula, according to Brigid's account, told her that she had no intention of putting herself in the power of a madman. Encouraged, Mrs Hitler told of her secret plan to get William Patrick out of Germany.

Here the narrative becomes confused. Mrs Hitler does not say how she got out of Germany but some years later mentions that William Patrick called on her in London. He was by now working for Opel cars and had managed to get away from the company's annual Norwegian holiday. He would stay a week, he said, but would then have to get back.

This ties in with a story of his visit in the *Daily Express* in November 1937, under the headline 'HITLER'S ENGLISH NEPHEW IS HERE'. He told the paper guardedly that he had no authority to make political statements, and had no wish to embarrass his uncle.

The narrative ends in 1938, when William Patrick turns up again, this time for good. He had, he said, been smuggled out of Germany. But before that he had been arrested by the SS, alerted by the fact that he had given notice on his flat, and this is where his mother's story ends, with him being taken off to a police station. The last sentence, ending in a comma, is, 'Nevertheless, I decided to try him,' ...

What happened next is almost as mysterious. William Patrick emigrated to America with his mother in 1939. What became of her is not known though in 1941, aged forty-nine, she joined the British War Relief Society in New York. In a rich Irish brogue she acknowledged it was a bit ridiculous but said: 'My name is Hitler and I'll work just as hard as anybody, notwithstanding.' She was hoping, she said, to have her marriage annulled and to become an American citizen. With that she disappeared from public view.

In his biography of Hitler, published in 1976, John Toland says that William Patrick was by that time living in New York. In his sixties, he had changed his name and refused to discuss his uncle. He had a son, whom, remarkably, he had called Adolf.

Alois survived the War, having also changed his name, in his case to Hiller. In the early 1950s he is said to have sold photographs of Adolf to tourists, having first, true to form, signed these himself.

All three found sanctuary in the footnotes from which they had so improbably emerged.

1997

THE LAST WITCHCRAFT TRIAL
IN ENGLAND

~

I n the history of mankind there occur moments, but they are
very rare, when you feel the sunlight breaking through. This
is such a moment. It happened two centuries ago but time is
of no matter, for even now we can bask in the humanity and the
commonsense of one man.

An old woman stands in an English courtroom accused of
witchcraft. There were many like her, illiterate, so confused by
days of interrogation they were prepared to admit to anything and
yet at the same time to take a perverse pride in their notoriety.
She has just been accused of flying.

'Is this true, you say you can fly?' asks the Judge, giving her the
opportunity to deny it. But his question has the opposite effect.

'Yes, I can.'

What is he to do? Out of her own mouth she has condemned
herself to the gallows. And then it comes, that wonderful
moment.

'So you may, if you will,' says the Judge. 'There is no law
against flying.'

The Last Witchcraft Trial in England

His name was Sir John Powell. Swift, who met him, called him, 'the merriest old gentleman I ever saw, spoke pleasing things, and chuckled till he cried ...' And it is that laughter which comes down the centuries to help us. Stop beside his memorial in Gloucester Cathedral, for this was a man we would all love to have known, who in 1712 laughed the Middle Ages out of England.

At the Spring Assizes in Hertford, a woman named Jane Wenham, aged seventy and very poor, appeared charged with witchcraft in the village of Walkern. But the law, which had prosecuted so enthusiastically throughout the seventeenth century, had become uncomfortable over such matters. The only indictment the lawyers would draw up was for conversing with the Devil in the shape of a cat, a charge at once specific and absurd.

That such a trial was by then a nine-day wonder is revealed by the presence of the country gentry in great numbers. There were so many fashionable ladies in court that old Judge Powell, then sixty-seven, airily told the jury, 'You must not look out for witches amongst old women, but among the young.'

But there were others there grimly intent on a conviction. The Revd Francis Bragge, curate of Biggleswade, who was present, later wrote in a pamphlet reprinted four times in a month after the trial, 'If a continued course of Idleness and Thieving for many years, if the character of a Whore and the Practice of Common Swearing and Cursing, will denominate a good woman, we are willing to allow Jane Wenham that name ... But the truth of the business is that her nearest relatives think she deserves to die, and that upon other Accounts than Witchcraft.'

The clergy came out of this very badly. Three of them, including Bragge, had interrogated her for days, and a prominent local justice, Sir Henry Chauncey, whose son enthusiastically tortured her, had drawn up the warrant for her arrest.

So, on one side is a confused old lady (her one statement of

defence was that she was a 'clear woman', whatever that means),
who, because of what she had been through, had admitted her
guilt. On the other was the county society of Hertfordshire. In the
middle was the Judge.

The first witness was a maid servant at Walkern Rectory, Anne
Thorne, who claimed to have been afflicted with fits by the
accused, and immediately threw one in the witness box. Judge
Powell, watching this, said he had not heard of an afflicted person
actually having a fit during a witch trial before.

A vicar offered to intervene, saying that prayer had helped in
the past. The Judge asked, what sort of prayers? Parts of the
Common Prayer. The Judge said he had heard of Roman Catholic
exorcisms but was not aware of any such in the liturgy of the
Church of England. He said he was proud to find such virtue in
English prayers.

So the pattern of the trial was set, witness after witness presenting their wild testimony, and the Judge muttering urbanely in
attempt to bring an element of commonsense into the proceed-
ings. And all the time the maid servant Thorne kept throwing fit
after fit in court.

It had started that February, and at one level Jane Wenham
may be said to have brought it on herself. She obtained a warrant
for defamation against a local farmer who had called her a witch,
saying she had cast a spell on his labourer.

Let us examine this charge in detail, for it reveals how poor
these people were and what they were prepared to believe. On
New Year's Day Jane met the labourer carrying straw and asked
him for some. He refused but she helped herself anyway, so she
was a tough old thing.

But afterwards the man found himself unaccountably forced to
run three miles to a dunghill and there to stuff straw from this
inside his shirt. He had thereafter been unable to work.

The matter was referred by Sir Henry Chauncey to the vicar of

Walkern, who told Jane not to quarrel with her neighbours and awarded her one shilling compensation from the farmer. So far, so good, except that now the vicar's servant Anne Thorne also claimed she had been bewitched, Jane having gone away, muttering she would have justice elsewhere.

Anne Thorne began to behave very oddly. She was lame yet she was seen to leap a five-barred gate 'like a greyhound', and to run at eight miles an hour, which was then fast for a stage-coach. Anne Thorne had, in fact, turned into a cross-country athlete, wading streams, leaping more gates, and running all over the place. She also started having fits.

Jane Wenham was dragged to the vicarage and confronted with the girl who immediately attacked her, raking her forehead with her nails. There was a sound, said a witness, as if panelling were being scratched, but no blood. Young Chauncey, the disagreeable son of the squire, later stuck pins up to the head in her arms and claimed these had not drawn blood either.

The clergy now got involved, the vicar's wife asking Jane to repeat the Lord's Prayer, which she did but got some lines wrong, saying, 'Lead us not into no temptation,' instead of, 'Lead us not into temptation.' This was held to be highly significant.

Others now came forward. A man called Adams, later murdered by a highwayman on his way home from Hertford market in 1728, said he had told her off for stealing his turnips when she was starving. As a result, four of his sheep had died and others *had stood on their heads*.

Anne Thorne was meanwhile seeing cats everywhere, cats which scratched at her door at night, one of which had the face of Jane Wenham. Young Chauncey, who was developing a taste for violence, killed the next cat he heard scratching at the door.

Thorne was also finding pins all over herself, and her pillow, when opened, was found to contain feathers caked together so tightly no one could pull them apart. The Rev Bragge found these cakes were circular, with hairs, cats' hairs, in the centre, and gave evidence to this effect in court.

Judge Powell showed some interest in the feathers and asked if he might see some but was told they had all been burnt. 'What a pity,' he said. 'I should like to have seen an enchanted feather.' Young Chauncey then offered to show him any number of the pins he had taken from Anne Thorne. The Judge said wearily there was no need, that they were all crooked pins.

The vicars, for these had gathered like crows in Walkern, interrogated Jane day after day until she offered to submit to the old tests for witchcraft, the water ordeal, whereby if a woman floated she was guilty, but innocent if she sank, though dead. Sir Henry Chauncey, who was now involved, said this was illegal and he would not allow it, though he did allow his son his little ways with the pins, it being thought there was no feeling in a witch's body.

As a result, Jane Wenham did admit to being a witch, saying she had been one for sixteen years with three other women in Walkern, all of whom were arrested. She also threw in that she had killed her first husband. The old lady, who from various accounts seems to have spent most of her time trying to stay alive and not starve, seems from this account to have had an industrious life.

The Judge had an even more industrious one. Thrown off the bench in the reign of James II when, as in Hitler's Germany, the judiciary was relentlessly drawn into politics, he had been restored after the Glorious Revolution. Since then he had presided over some of the most famous cases of his day, but, in old age (he was to die a year later) he now found himself listening to this catalogue of rubbish in Hertford. But there was worse to come.

His summing-up was very short; all who heard it were agreed on that, especially the clergy who took such exception to his conduct throughout. Judge Powell told the jury that he was leaving it to them to determine whether they had heard enough to warrant taking away someone's life. They were out for an hour and a half.

When they came back Sir John asked them pointedly whether they found Jane Wenham guilty upon the indictment of conversing with the Devil in a shape of a cat. Their foreman had no doubts. 'We find her guilty of THAT,' he said with emphasis.

So there was nothing for the Judge to do, he being as much a victim of the system as Jane, but to reach for his black cap and proclaim sentence of death upon her. No comment of his is recorded, but behind the scenes he immediately petitioned Queen Anne for a full pardon, which was granted, and she was released.

There followed an extraordinary war of pamphlets, with the Revd Bragge rushing into print to attack Jane Wenham, witchcraft and the Judge. This touched a nerve and someone wrote, 'A Full Confutation of Witchcraft ... proving that Witchcraft is Priestcraft.' That it prompted a crisis in the Church itself is shown by the fact that one of the royal chaplains made it his business to seek out Jane in retirement.

She had come out of it well, a Colonel Plumer giving her a cottage on his estate in Hertford. Here the chaplain, Dr Hutchinson, met and recorded his impressions.

'She is a pious, sober woman (who) so far from being unable to say the Lord's Prayer, made me hear both the Lord's Prayer and the Creed, and other very good prayers indeed, and she spoke them with an undissembled devotion, though with such little errors of expression as those who cannot read are subject to.

'I verily believe that there is no one who reads this but may think in their own minds that such a storm as she met with might have fallen upon them, if it had been their misfortune to have been born poor, and to have met with such accidents as she did, in such a barbarous parish as she lived in ...'

It was the last time anyone was condemned for witchcraft in England, though in Hertfordshire forty years later a mob near Tring lynched an old woman by putting her to the water torture. The ringleader was executed but it took two troops of Horse Guards to overawe the people and get him to the gallows. After that it became safer to be old, and poor, and a woman, in Hertfordshire.

1996

PART FIVE

HEROES ACKNOWLEDGED AND UNACKNOWLEDGED

Not quite the essence: a tragic english hero

~⌐

Around breakfast time on Sunday morning, 11 July 1920, a barber from Bristol disappeared into the Niagara Falls. His name was Charles Stephens and he was in a barrel at the time. But this was no young daredevil, Stephens was fifty-eight and the father of eleven. And it was a terrible end. All that was ever found of him was an arm with the tattoo, 'Forget me not Anne', from which he was identified.

But if Anne and Bristol did not forget, the world did. In its roll-call of the fifteen lunatics who have gone over the Falls the Niagara Parks Commission, in a bleak 'Results' column, records only, 'Died'. The barber became a statistic.

Except that in Wiltshire Mrs Diana Ralph remembered something her grandfather had told her. George Francis, fostered in Bristol, used to talk about his foster-mother's sad references to her late brother Charles. But he did so in such a fragmentary way ('Stephens in a barrel – ooh arr, I knew 'ee'), usually during the TV advertisements, that Mrs Ralph grew up thinking one of the family had been taken by the fairies, though she was a bit confused about what part the barrel had played. The fact that her grandfather rolled about with laughter whenever he mentioned the name did not help.

What follows is based on her research in the libraries and newspaper files of Bristol as a childhood mystery was finally cleared up. It is also an attempt to rescue Charles Stephens, variously known in his lifetime as 'The Demon Barber' and 'The Professor', from the black humour his resurrection will attract, and to portray him as a tragic hero. In this it will fail.

Every photograph that survives sabotages the attempt from the start. It is hard to keep a straight face just looking at that small, surprised face, the mild eyes and a moustache so vast and straggling it could have been borrowed from a carwash, except there were no carwashes in his time. Stephens looks as though he was born to fall off ladders and into waterfalls, being a dead ringer for the old silent comedian Chester Conklin.

He must have been aware of this for one of his last acts at Niagara was to shave off that moustache and to dye his hair black. He had a date with destiny, also with a film crew waiting on the bank, and he did not want to enact a scene from the Keystone Cops. This, unfortunately, is what he had always done.

He once parachuted from a balloon over Bristol, only being Stephens he landed on a railway line minutes before an express was due. He rescued a would-be suicide from another line but did so by so narrow a margin that the woman's skirt and underclothing were snatched away by the train. He jumped, or fell, from the Forth Bridge. He only had to see a lion's cage to jump inside, 'whenever the opportunity presented itself,' as a local paper delicately put it.

But none of this, and this is where his story becomes extraordinary, was for money. There was a wistful commercialism at the very end, for Stephens hoped to make something out of going over the Falls in a barrel, but as for the rest, as his daughter Annie, then eighty, confirmed, it was done for the sheer hell of it. 'He was a lovely and very kind man who thought the world of his family, but found life a little humdrum …'

As nobody in a white coat ever reported on him the only possible explanation for his behaviour lies in a strange story. At the age of five Charles Stephens died. A doctor pronounced him dead and he was three days in an open coffin before the doctor, who presumably had some doubts, popped in and found those mild eyes looking out of the coffin at him. After that, it was said, physical fear of any kind became a stranger to him, boredom an old friend.

A circus had only to appear in Bristol for the Barber to call, offering to shave customers in their lions' cage. He kissed lions, put his head in their mouths, and it was probably only good taste which prevented him from shaving them as well; for he was proud of his shaving and boasted that he could shave a man with three strokes of his cutthroat razor. But in the one eye-witness account which survives, the shaving took seven minutes and to the victim these seemed like seven years.

The football team, Bristol Rovers, was as usual in a bad way financially and desperately needed some publicity. The Barber, also as usual, was willing and the team's young assistant trainer was persuaded to go into the cage with him. George Endicott in his eighties remembered his horror when he saw that the tamer was a woman, a revolver in one hand and a truncheon in the other.

'I thought the lion would be sitting or sleeping. Instead she kept rapping it on the nose to make it stand on its back legs. Talk about the smallest room in the house; that cage was the smallest place I'd ever been in all my life.

'And this woman kept telling the Barber to hurry up, that the lion was getting restless. Yet all the time she kept hitting it on the nose. When he had finished the Barber made a bolt for the cage door, followed by me with the lion tamer at my heels. The lion was a close fourth.'

Endicott won a £5 bet just for being there, but when he took the hat round for Stephens afterwards the entire collection amounted to only 18s 2d. That is one of the saddest features in the story, the accountancy of it. Football teams benefited, and circuses, also Sam Parker, who ran the Coach and Horses in Victoria Street, Bristol, for people turned up in their hundreds to meet a man shaved by the Demon Barber in yet another cage. The 18s 2d is almost the only recorded amount that Stephens himself ever made. Almost, but not quite ...

The lions came and went, and there was a woman sharpshooter who shot a lump of sugar off that small head on which a tuft of hair stuck up, again just as on the heads of some of the silent film comedians. Odd for a barber though, as Mrs Ralph said. There was also a circus swordsman who put an apple on the throat of the prone Stephens, then sliced it through with a sweep of his sword.

And then there was the First World War which made life a little less humdrum. How the Barber got into the war is a mystery, for he was well over fifty, but the Western Front opened like the lions' cages and of course he emerged unscathed.

About this time a family group photograph was taken. He is shown with a line of glamorous daughters behind him (being lathered by one of the girls was a great draw in the barber's shop), his two sons to one side. All are immaculately dressed, and even Stephens for once does not look like a silent-film comedian. He is seated in the centre, wearing a wing-collar, his hair slicked down, the perfect paterfamilias.

Yet this man had for eleven years been preparing to go over Niagara in a barrel. This had been done twice before, once by a woman, Annie Taylor, and once by a man called Bobby Leach; both were badly hurt but survived.

It was after the Great War that he redoubled his efforts, a black tedium having probably settled on the razors and the brushes. This time he tried the Canadian side, writing to one H. F. Carter, master of the steamship *Maid of the Mist*, which travelled the calm stretch between the foot of the Falls and the whirlpool rapids in which the great Captain Webb lost his life.

Carter wrote back, 'I should like to discourage you from the attempt … first, because there is a great chance of losing your life, and next, there is no money in it … At least that is the experience of those who have done it.'

But Stephens was convinced otherwise. In the one interview which survives he said he hoped to make a lot of money by it. A film would be made, a Toronto newspaper editor, whom he had contacted, having arranged for a camera crew to be there. He would then parachute from a plane, be photographed doing that, and with these films, he declared, he would travel the lecture halls of the world.

'This is not bravado, nor is it the result of a silly bet. I shall succeed … I am going out to do the biggest thing of my life.'

He saved up £140, £20 of which he spent on the barrel which he had made in Bristol. This did not look like any barrel you have ever seen, being 6ft 2 inches long (Stephens was 5ft 9 inches), tapering from 32 inches in diameter at the middle to 29 inches at either end. It looked more like a cigar tube than a barrel.

It was made of oak, Russian oak according to most accounts, had ten hoops for strengthening and it weighed six hundred-weight; the oak alone was two inches thick. This weight was a controversial feature for with ballast, Stephens reasoned, it would stay vertical and fall through the water, not be sent spinning over. He himself was to be strapped inside so as to experience a minimum of concussion. There was a breathing apparatus, enough to give him eight hours of air, also a dim battery-operated light. The barrel, in short, though painted a colourful black and white, would have induced such claustrophobia as to drive most people out of their minds in a minute.

His family pleaded with him not to go, and they all went with him and the barrel to Temple Meads station where he was due to catch the Liverpool train.

Doubts there never were, not even when he saw the 300-foot drop and, what was worse, heard the roar. When a river man who had spent his life near the Falls advised him to send the barrel over first he refused. This is the sadness of the accountancy again, for Stephens could not have afforded another barrel.

Jauntily he wrote back to the men who had made it, Heffer and Son, of The Cooperage, Milk Street, Bristol. 'Canada is dry and I don't like it here and the sooner the feat has been done I shall come to dear old England now. I hope all the boys in your workshop is [sic] quite well I am sending my good wishes to you all there.'

To his family he wrote, 'Dear children and the family on both sides, don't let anyone run me down should you hear them. I am not wishing you all goodbye, but only so long till Sunday morning. What a day that will be for me. This is from your loving husband Charlie. Keep a good heart up, I have got one anyhow for the feat.'

It was in his wild handwriting and there were many kisses at the end. But you will note the terrible irony in some of the phrases, for by the time this got to Bristol his family already knew what had happened.

The barrel, its top screwed down, was towed more than a mile into midstream by a motor boat, after which the tow-line was cut. Twenty-six minutes passed, the barrel floating slowly at first, gathering speed as the current caught it, then almost lazily it went over. The watchers saw its black and white sides for a moment and after that they did not see it. It was just after 8.30 in the morning.

They had gathered early, fearing the authorities might intervene. 'Goodbye, good luck,' said the little group of cameramen and watchers. 'We'll meet you below the Falls safe and sound.'

And he, his hair dyed, his moustache shaved off, said, 'I'll be there with a smile.'

The watchers waited. It had taken Bobby Leach thirty-nine minutes to go over and be picked up. Thirty-nine minutes went by. It had taken Annie Taylor forty-nine minutes. Forty-nine minutes went by. After that, time passed very slowly.

The first thing they saw was around 12 o'clock when something black emerged from the foot of the Falls and was borne downstream. It was part of the barrel and it was when they saw this that they realised there was no hope. The barrel had gone through the water, borne down by its weight and had shattered on the rocks. The next day they found the arm with the tattoo on it.

I made contact, incredibly, with Charles Stephens' last surviving child, Viola Cogan, the small child in the family group photograph, now eighty-seven and still living in Bristol. She remembers that the family heard the news of his death not by telegram or phone but by news-boys calling out on the street.

Six years ago Mrs Cogan, who herself rode a motor-bike until she was seventy-eight, visited Niagara, the first member of the family to do so.

'It looked wonderful until I remembered he had gone over that in a barrel. It was terrifying then, and I felt so sorry for him.'

She remembers that her mother had to pay £21 for the burial of the arm with 'Forget me not Anne' upon it. But most accounts add that the camera crew paid a fee of £20, which was more than he had got for all his stunts put together. It is little things like that you remember in the end about Charlie Stephens.

1997

JACK GREILLER'S SWIM

This chapter has its origins in a stunned memorandum which ricocheted between the departments at the headquarters of Saga in Folkestone, the organisation specialising in holidays for the elderly. The writer, Robert Sissons, who had just returned from the Myths and Majesty of Peru Guided Tour, clearly felt the need to tell someone, anyone, of something that had occurred in the course of this. But then so would I. Or you. Or any man. Listen …

'While staying at the Explorama Inn on the shore of the Amazon, where earlier we had successfully fished for piranha, one of my group, Mr Jack Greiller, expressed a wish to swim the Amazon.

'The manager of the Explorama was reluctant to let him do this, but Mr Greiller insisted he was a very strong swimmer and had previously swum the Nile at Aswan.

'Mr Greiller accordingly did his swim …'

This is dramatic writing at its best. It would not have been so had Mr Sissons tried to inject excitement into it and scattered exclamation marks all over the place. As it is, the build-up of short, flat statements gives the impression of a man who feels he is at the edge of the known world and, with the last sentence, has stepped into the unknown.

For there he was, not at the bank of the Amazon but on its 'shore': this is a river like no other. It is, moreover, a river that contains fish which, after the Bond films, are in all our folklores, fish that can strip a man to his wristwatch in minutes. And there was Mr Sissons leading a holiday group when one of them mentioned that he would like to swim the Amazon.

Not a determination, you will note, more of a whim. 'Mr Greiller expressed a wish…' It is something to fill a long November afternoon in a rain forest. But the man on the ground, the manager of the inn, who had seen the river pouring by each day, was horrified. For who was this English *kamikaze*?

Mr Sissons' bold narrative suggests he himself is now someone for whom life after that amazing day holds little meaning. 'Mr Greiller accordingly did his swim …' You can imagine Mr Sissons on subsequent tours, twitching slightly, as he stares into the faces of other Saga travellers who might express similar wishes.

'What mountain is that?'

'Didn't you know? That's Everest.'

'I see. Now am I right in thinking that we've got nothing planned for this afternoon?'

It is now a month later and I am sitting with Jack Greiller in his Ruislip bungalow. We are, of course, talking about the Amazon, which should be far away, for this is a late afternoon in an English winter, only it isn't far away at all and I have almost come to believe that it is flowing through Mr Greiller's drawing room, just as Mrs Anthony Eden, the former Prime Minister's wife, came to believe that the Suez Canal flowed through hers.

Electric motors are one of his interests and they are much in evidence. Inside, they power the curtains in the room where we are sitting. In his garden, the motors draw back the canopy on the swimming pool he has built himself; they also power the pumps that create its waves. Another interest is cooking. The weekend before we met he was sixty-six and for his birthday party created a six-course banquet.

'Yes, I am very fit,' says Mr Greiller. 'I keep fit by being busy.'

As we talk, people keep ringing up and Mr Greiller keeps quoting the prices of his electric converters. He is, he tells me, retired.

He is a tall man, wide in the shoulders and so upright he leans slightly backwards from the waist like a regimental sergeant major in his prime; there appears to be no fat on him. Time has staked some small claim, for there is white hair now, and spectacles, but Mr Greiller comes out of a chair as though he has some inbuilt ejector mechanism in his bottom. He is, in short, just the sort of man who, having nothing better to do, would swim the Amazon.

It was the last day of the tour. They had been to Lima, had seen the cities of the Incas, and were staying in an inn on the edge of the rain forest which could be reached only by air or a four-day journey by boat.

In front of this was the Amazon, 2300 miles from its estuary, a river so big the tree trunks being carried downstream in its current looked like chewed pencils, and so muddy that if a man held his hand just under the water he would lose sight of it. In midstream it was said to be 100 feet deep.

He knew there were piranhas in it, for he had caught some, but piranhas, Mr Greiller reasoned, only attacked when there was blood in the water. Like most of us he was aware of the terrible folklore of the river but, having seen Indian children playing in the shallows, he did not think there would be anacondas lurking. That other fish, tinier than piranhas, which can swim into a man ('up any orifice,' said Mr Greiller delicately), he discounted. He only did the breast-stroke so his mouth was never under water. So

Jack Greiller's Swim

Mr Greiller stared at the Amazon and began to think.

He had come to swimming late, being thirty-eight when he learnt, but he then built up his strength so quickly that at one stage he was swimming a mile a week. He had also succeeded in swimming the length of an Olympic pool underwater. 'Why? I don't know really, just to see if I could, I suppose.'

For similar reasons he had swum the Nile in Aswan twelve years ago, at a point where it was three-quarters of a mile across. Why? The sun was shining and it was a beautiful day, said Mr Greiller. And now he was on the shore of the Amazon.

He calculated that it was about one-and-a-quarter miles across, and the water early in the morning was as smooth as a mill-pond. If a man had a boat in attendance, could he not swim it then?

'No,' said the local tour guide, a Peruvian. 'The current is too fast and there are whirlpools ...'

Oh dear, thought Mr Greiller, he did not sound keen on the idea at all. So he worked on Mr Sissons, telling him about the Nile and about his swimming ability, and Mr Sissons approached the Peruvians. He came back shaking his head.

That was their penultimate day. On the last day of all Mr Greiller fished for piranha which he later ate ('a bit bony') and had given up all idea of swimming, much to his wife Jean's relief. But then, over lunch, the Peruvian tour guide said, could he be ready by two o'clock? That was only a quarter of an hour away and, needing time to digest, Mr Greiller suggested two-fifteen.

He was there, waiting in his costume, with a tail of curious tourists, including his wife, when the guide came to say that the manager of the Explorama refused to take responsibility for the attempt. There was a lot of arguing and at three o'clock they phoned the headquarters of the Peruvian tour company.

At three-ten they were back at the river's edge with a hastily typed document in Spanish which Mr Greiller could not understand, but its import was clear. It was what is known in the trade as a blood-chit, taking all responsibility for what might happen, and Mr Greiller signed.

He already had a rough plan for the attempt. There was an island about three-quarters of a mile out, in the lee of which he hoped to shelter, regaining his strength, before making for the far bank. What he did not know was that there were two islands, with a channel between, the current of which would catch him and take him three miles downstream.

The current was a problem. He could not have swum against it and had he swum with it there was no telling where he might have ended up. He had to swim across as far as he could, at right angles to the flow, and all the time there were logs and whole trees floating down at speeds of around ten miles an hour.

But he started strongly, the men in the boat rowing at this stage. In fact, everything went well, even when he encountered the second current between the islands. He just let this carry him downstream and round the second island.

He twice had cramp and had to slow up in the hopes that it would go away, which it did. The real trouble came ten minutes before the end when the rains came, so abruptly and in such volume that the people waiting on the bank lost sight of him. But what was more terrifying was that, now in the last of the three streams, he was just 100 yards from the bank and *suddenly he lost sight of it.*

'With one's head virtually at water level splashing rain caused a mist of about a foot's thickness on the surface, and I realised that I was now being carried down the river very fast. I knew then that I had to make a last all-out effort.'

He was about ten feet out when he found himself among reeds and, thinking himself in no more than two or three feet of water, decided to grab hold of them and stand. He was in fact still in eight feet of water and almost drowned, threshing out and touching the boat, the occupants of which grabbed him and pulled him out. He had been in the water for almost an hour. This time, with visibility down to twenty feet, they started the engine and made for the other bank.

Only one photograph exists of the swim: it was the last of thirty-six exposures on the family camera. A tiny head, no bigger than a tennis ball, shows up in the brown water.

Mrs Greiller's reaction to her husband's swim was remarkable. Sheltering from the downpour in a hut, she looked out as her husband landed from the boat and came up the steps from the river. 'Jack, would you please go up to our room and get an umbrella for me, will you?'

The Saga travellers were equally nonchalant. Some bought him drinks in the bar, as they had promised, but there was packing to be done and piranhas to eat; this seemed more interesting than the fact that the fish had not eaten Mr Greiller. But the local people were impressed to the point of amazement. They knew, as Jack Greiller knew, that had the rains come a few minutes earlier he would not have done it, and it rains 250 days of the year there.

In Ruislip Mrs Greiller says she was not apprehensive when her husband announced his wish to swim the Amazon. 'I've lived with him for a long time.'

The Amazon, says Mr Greiller, is beyond the imagination of most people. It is not that they wouldn't believe him, they would just not understand.

But one man does. He works in Folkestone and, like any witness to history, had to set it down. 'Mr Greiller accordingly did his swim ...'

1996

ALL ABOUT ME: THE MAKING OF
A MAN OF TASTE

⌒

A few years ago David Hicks approached me with a view to seeing if I would make a suitable biographer. We met and I found him fascinating, having previously encountered such an ego only in fiction, so that when I came to write a specimen chapter I made it a dramatic monologue, for the man never stopped talking about himself. It was prefaced with two quotations, one from Hicks ('I enjoy being me'), the other from Earl Mountbatten's diary for 13 September 1959 ('walked with Pammy barefoot on the lawn for one hour hearing about David Hicks. As a result had blood blisters on both feet. Very painful').

Here is the chapter. The scene is Mr Hicks's apartment in Albany, Piccadilly.

'I'm so glad you could come. It is nice here, don't you agree? You come into this building, you have this impression of great dignity, then you come up here and it's the perfect antidote to today. I'm excited by tomorrow and I did love yesterday, but today's different. You have to work at today.

All About Me: The Making of a Man of Taste

Of course people in my profession would recognise this room as being *me*. They'd see the geometric patterns, the festooned curtains. But do you know why these are festooned? It's because the people opposite haven't replaced their windows properly; I've had to cut out the view. I'm an extraordinary mixture of – well, perhaps not genius – but quick thinking and practicality. When I'm in a tight corner aesthetically I'm at my best, I have to fight to get out. Would you like to see their windows? No, I couldn't do that to anybody. They're such dreadful suburban things.

But what's really *me* are the colours, the *vibrating* colours. Before I came along people said that colours clashed. "The carpet's magenta, the chairs scarlet. Is my wife going to like that?" Your wife, I tell them, will find it *exciting*.

Some colours I don't like to see together, like peacock blue and orange, but even then it depends on how they're used. There are so few definites in life and so many "I should prefer not" situations. Don't you agree? I knew you would. I hate everything which matches up, it's so suburban. Is there anything worse than suburban? Not in this world.

A company in Yorkshire once asked me to select and name thirty-nine colours for a new range of fabrics. I did so and I told Mountbatten this. He said, "I simply don't understand. Are you trying to tell me that hard-headed Yorkshire businessmen are paying you to name colours?" Yes, I said. "But there are only so many colours." I said no, there were millions. Of course, he had no taste, Germans never do. The only thing that ever interested him about my family was that my grandfather had been born in the reign of George III.

It's very new, my profession. It only became a profession after the Second World War, and I'm the one who did it. Before this century, apart from William Morris and the Adam brothers, it just used to be an architect who also did a bit of interior design. Then in the 1930s it was people like Somerset Maugham's wife, after a chat over tea – "you have such a pretty house. *Do* help me with mine."

People have to be told, "Pencils massed in a container both look decorative and are useful. *But they must all be the same colour and be sharpened.*" I put pencilled marks on mantelpieces where the objects must go. After the dusting they must be put back.

I've lived here since 1977. I was at a party and someone said, "Now you've got a shop in Jermyn Street you could come and live here." So I asked the chap who arranged such things if he couldn't *squeeze* me in. He was very apologetic, said there was a waiting list of twenty-five years, so I went back to the office but then the phone rang. "You won't believe how lucky you are, young man. I've just seen some people who are moving out and they asked, did I know anyone nice?" He had suggested Lord Snowdon and David Hicks but they thought Lord Snowdon sounded a bit *complicated*. So here I am.

I've written nine books, you know. I may only have been responsible for very few words in them but, my God, those words were carefully chosen. The whole place was painted pale green when I came. *Awful*. All my life I have fought that colour.

In the Army it was a sort of creamy green, all my barrack rooms were like that. And when I started to work on grand people's houses it was *eau de nil*. All right once in a while, but people did whole houses out in it. Broadlands was like that when I married. I remonstrated, but in a very tactful way. "Tell me, what do you have in *mind*? Are you keeping this furniture and those curtains?" Very slowly I would *destroy* the whole room.

This is basically two interconnecting rooms, a living room and a bedroom. I keep the door open between them so the carpet had to go through. A patterned carpet.

I do hope you realise I am solely responsible for the revival of patterned carpets in England. There wouldn't be any if it weren't for me. Twenty-seven years ago I found a company that would do carpets to *my* design. Now half the carpets sold are patterned. I designed this one. Gives the room a cosiness, a pattern. You agree, of course.

The only things I liked here were the Louis XVI marble fire-places, well, not quite, just late nineteenth-century copies. I loved the depth of the shelf, you can set out so many things on them. Vases, Etruscan red and black. Mercury, head of, seventeenth century. Pewter plates, seventeenth century, a pair. Some Lowestoft china. A Christmas card from the governor of the Himalayas, another from an interior decorating lady with a dog on the front. There you have the range of the Hicks's acquaintance.

My life after thirty years is completely entwined with that of the Mountbattens. You may not like my in-laws but you must admit they were fascinating.

You will notice the matching mirrors in this room and the bed-room. That gives an illusion of space. But note that the mirror here is the width of the entire chimney breast, not just of the man-telpiece. To have it the width of the mantelpiece would make it look *squalid*.

The portraits? Oh, family portraits, eight oval seventeenth-century pictures. I've hung them against this rich red background, you have to have a *serious* background for pictures like these. Notice how they hang on silk damask ribbons. But see, the ribbons hide the wiring.

There are twenty-eight sources of light in this room, and you can't see a single bulb. I have this rule: *I never want to see the bulb*. There are picture lights and lights in bookcases. There are two in the bed, for who knows when I might want to sleep at the other end? No centre lights. Yes, you are learning, that would be *suburban*. I lived in rooms with central lights when I was small, but when my mother and I moved to a timbered cottage in 1945 I decided then that it was an end to them. It is such a gradual evolution, the making of a man of taste.

And no television, I hope you noticed that. It is hidden away under the table. I can't *bear* them to be up anywhere in a room. I hate those legs, they're so wobbly, and people will put the *Radio Times* on the thing. Even when it's on I like it to be on the floor. That way it's like being in the dress circle.

I love my bedroom. What, you've never seen a bed in the centre of a room? Have you never been to Malmaison? Dear me. I just love canopy beds, they give one a feeling of luxury and protection. It's a wonderful bed, an important bed, it's a bed to die in and to receive one's doctors. It has to be in the centre of the room.

I suppose you think my ego is terrific. Some people do, you know. I have to be careful: I am very famous and clever, and I am also married to a very rich lady. So I mustn't brag. Mind you, I've known some bad times. School was bad, and the Army. Being marched through Bury St Edmunds with a lot of smelly young men my own age was the lowest point of my life. Then there was the time I first met the Queen and after dinner went into their little cinema. I was sitting next to the Queen as the film started and I fell fast asleep.

Sometimes I sit here and I remember the good moments. When I was sixteen I took the train south from Paris to Avignon, and in the morning I found myself looking out at this Van Gogh world, the corn and the blue, blue sky. Not that long ago I went that way again, in a very expensive car with white leather seats, but it didn't work; I'd had too much to drink.

Things are so neat here, don't you think? I spend a lot of time here on my own. I shall keep things like this.'

And that was the end of the book.

1995

THE JUMPING JACK FLASH
WHO NEVER WAS

〜

J agger was late. He was three-quarters of an hour late, was Jagger. It is a name you cannot help repeating. You can see it bleak on a brass plate: Jagger, Clutterbuck and Jagger. A name of fogs and evil, a name Dickens would have loved; but not a name for the twentieth century at all, and certainly not for its ultimate pop star, old Jumping Jack Flash himself. Jagger was an hour late.

We were in the Rolling Stones' London office, a slightly shabby place occupying the top two floors of a house in a Chelsea cul-de-sac. It could have been the office of a not-too-successful solicitor, except for the pictures of the founding fathers on the stairs, the old black rhythm-and-blues singers on whom all rock stars model themselves; it was these men who made possible the white millionaires.

The office, despite the secretaries and the morning papers, did not seem busy. On the doorstep there had been a long pause after I pressed the entryphone. It has been the Stones' office for seven years.

The books on the shelves would have bewildered the fans. The *British Middle Market Directory*, *The Bankers' Almanac and Year-book, 1967*. Was this what the Golden Ones pored over when the shouting stopped? All of them – or just Jagger?

You could tell when Mick got out of a taxi, said a friend once: it took such a long time. He always had to get a receipt from the driver. It was Jagger, at the end of the notorious 1969 American tour, after the frenzy at Altamont when a man was killed, who flew off with the loot to the numbered Swiss bank account. Jagger was an hour-and-a-quarter late.

But it had taken a year to set this up. There had been talk of a meeting in France, then in New York; and even now there had been a fortnight of telephone-calls. It is par for the course. John Mortimer sought him in London, then in Frankfurt, before being admitted to the Presence in Madrid (and then Jagger watched the World Cup on television throughout the interview).

But then what is left, when in your early twenties you become rich beyond the dreams of avarice? Whimsy? Jagger fascinated Cecil Beaton, who saw in him 'one of those calf-like creatures who seem never to have been young: like the Mona Lisa he knows everything, has seen everything, and has never lost his arrogance. Then he knows he is doomed to be a has-been by the age of twenty-six.'

Only it did not work out like that.

His business advisers have pages of telephone numbers for this forty-two-year-old father of four. Each gets changed every four weeks, as the fans find it. The Stones toured last in 1982, when they made £1m a concert and moved across Europe and America like medieval emperors, with retinues of 150 at a time, including accountants (there are always accountants).

Jagger was probably the third most famous Briton, said his publicity man Alan Edwards, who has to cope with the press queries.

The Jumping Jack Flash Who Never Was

Was Jagger going to Princess Di's party? Was he about to marry Jerry Hall, the Texan mother of his two youngest children? Everyone connected with him immediately became international news; first his former wife Bianca, then Miss Hall (pictures of whom in the nude were in *Playboy* in the office waiting room, a startling introduction to a senior partner's mistress). Jagger was an hour-and-a-half late.

Alan Edwards began talking about his other responsibilities. Was Bill Wyman going out with a thirteen-year-old girl? The press was interested in Wyman.

Bill Wyman, né Perks, of Penge and now of Norfolk, bass guitarist for the Stones, who rarely smoked or drank, and was in bed with a cup of tea by eleven o'clock every night on tour, was a man with one gloomy ambition: to enter the record books. He had slept with 364 women 20 years before, when the other Stones stopped counting. On tour he would ring down to the hotel porter, ordering batches of teenage groupies ('No, not that one, the one wiv blonde 'air, not that 'orror'). His wife finally left him, telling the press she was not prepared to share the tiny Mr Wyman with 'thousands of strange women'.

Then there was Charlie Watts, drummer ('a great guy, but from a promotion point of view he doesn't exist'). Charlie Watts had given just one interview in the national press, to the *Daily Telegraph*, and he talked about cricket. Charlie Watts of Devon, where he lives with his sheepdogs and his collection of old cars, has a different suit for each car. But the one thing he does not have is a driving licence; in his various suits he sits happily in his stationary cars, a man at peace with the world.

The third Stone, Ronnie Wood, rhythm guitarist, is a replacement brought in for Mick Taylor, who quit, and was himself a replacement for Brian Jones, found dead in his swimming pool. Ronnie Wood of New York and Los Angeles.

But the Stones, as far as the fans and the press are concerned, are really just two, one of them Keith Richards, the music man behind the group, a night owl who refuses to enter a recording studio until he has heard midnight strike.

Keith Richards, who obsessed the group's most recent Boswell, Stanley Booth ('the world's only bluegum white man, poisonous as a rattlesnake ...'); there is more of this, much more. According to Booth, Richards had known more exotic substances than any pharmacist in a school of tropical medicine ('I decided that if Keith and I kept dipping into the same bag there would be no book and we would both be dead'). Keith Richard, undead, is now of Jamaica.

And then Jagger, the Pied Piper for a permissive age, the owner of famous lips (three foot of them, worked into a piece of material, hung over the office settee – 'raw giblets', as someone once called them); the prancing skeletal figure for whom the millions bayed.

Jagger the gym teacher's son, who descended from the heavens in a helicopter to talk in a garden to the Editor of *The Times*, the Bishop of Woolwich and a former Labour Home Secretary. It was the silliest event of a silly decade and was filmed for television after Jagger's release from jail on a drugs charge in 1967. Malcolm Muggeridge has a photograph of the event which he keeps like an icon: 'Look at them, practically the whole of the Establishment, all of them listening to old Jaggs, and old Jaggs can hardly speak.'

In the photograph old Jaggs is putting out his large tongue at the cameramen, before the helicopter comes again to take him up like Elisha, watched by the three awed figures.

Jagger, who returned and is still there at forty-two, the manager of the Stones in all but name; Jagger, the strangest thing in the late twentieth century, the ageing pop star.

Below us in the street there was suddenly the clatter of a taxi engine and Alan Edwards crossed to the window. 'Thank God,' he said, 'Mick's here.' A man in a loose leather coat seemed to be involved in complicated negotiation with the taxi driver: Jagger, two hours late.

'Been waitin' long?'

I had seen him on television a few months before, when he looked as though he might have been at school with Tollund Man. In the flesh, or what there was of it, he looked ill, huddled against the cold, a tall man, more haggard than any jockey, the lines in his face stitched in creases.

But the first impression was misleading. Physically he is extremely fit and, contrary to rumour, still in possession of his marbles. He can remember everything, except Sir William Rees-Mogg in the garden.

'I'd just got out of jail remember, and the next thing I'm in this helicopter. Haven' had time to wash me hair or anything, and I'm in this little chiffon number. I remember there was a bishop. There's always a bishop somewhere. Who d'you say had the photograph? Muggeridge? He's a funny one. He wasn't there, was he?'

The lips are smaller than you expect. But then you expect something the size of a white shark's mouth. Country cords; white socks and black suede shoes little more than slippers; a jacket chequered so you could have played draughts on him; a blue shirt, a pullover, long, untidy hair. He was in London to see some old friends – and a few plays 'n that. The south London accent came and went, disappearing as he relaxed, to emerge again only for the odd sneer. He is a sharp man. He had also used the time to pop over to France to see his house there ('Small château, is what I wanted. I got four kids now').

There were three houses ('any more, and they become a bit of a burden'). There was a house in Mustique. And another in New York ('little terraced house'). The house in Cheyne Walk in Chelsea went in the Bianca settlement. He now either rented a house or stayed in a hotel when he came to Britain, where his two elder daughters, aged fourteen and fifteen, were at boarding school. Both girls had come to the christening. Christening?

Yeah, he had just had James Leroy, aged three months, christened at the church nearest his rented house ('Jes' in case they need it later! I was christened, and me parents').

So he was leading a family life? 'Wiv Jerry?' he echoed, surprised. Well, it was somewhat family-orientated, said Jagger the old London School of Economics man, but then they both worked.

We talked about Beaton. 'Funny old boy, he was obsessed by age. He was in this 'plane during the war and saw his reflection in a window. He saw these lines. He wasn't worried about the Germans, just about the lines in his face. Said I was arrogant, did he? These old gays, they love you being arrogant.'

He was not worried by age himself? 'Nah,' said Jagger. 'We're blazin' a new trail now. When I was young there were no pop stars over thirty: it was a quick in-and-out thing. But once you're in the American market, that's so big they never get fed up with you. Main record-buying public's over thirty anyway. It's them who've got the Audi Quattro 'n' the cassettes 'n' that.' Jagger is interested in motor cars.

'Retire?' His face exploded into even more wrinkles. 'Nah, you don't retire in this business. There's always summin you can do. Perhaps you should grow old a little gracefully. But I've noticed they do have a certain respect for me, some of these young pop stars. I'm inviting derision, but I've seen it in their eyes the last few years. Least they don't want to kick me knee-caps in. Nah, they don't call me Mr Jagger. I've never met anyone who called me that, 'cept you.'

At one point he showed some irritation. I asked had he given his pension any thought. 'You mus' be jokin',' Jagger said with some emphasis. 'Look,' he went on, 'I think we've talked enough about old age.'

In the street people stared at him, puzzled for a moment, and then smiled; and suddenly there were girls in office windows. Yeah, he liked being a pop star. It was better than working for the government, which was what he might have been doing, had he stayed on at the LSE. That bloke who resigned, under-secretary or something, he was on £20,000 – £20,000 was a lunch bill, said Jagger in the restaurant.

'Nah, I'm not interested in money. I just wanted always to have enough. The people around me were always saving up for Morris Cowleys, or lawnmowers.' He was not sure what he did with his money, though he seemed to spend a lot. He was not a collector. He did not own boats or planes, not even a dog.

He had a lot of cars. He was not sure how many. They were all up in north London, but none of them had been able to start when he wanted to go to the pictures the other night. He had had to borrow a Renault. He did not even go in for investments, he went on. You were lucky to clear ten per cent on investments, and even then you had to worry about them all the time.

He liked city life. In New York he went out at least three nights a week, dancing and that. Yeah, people did come up to him. The worst thing was the way they talked across you, like mothers with a sick child ('Is he who I think he is?'). Generally he told them to sod off, said Jagger.

'Went to India a couple of weeks ago with me brother, and the only people who knew me there were these middle-class Indians who have MTV.' MTV? 'He doesn't know what MTV is,' said Jagger to his publicity man. He knows something about everything, Jagger, but he seemed to know a great deal about MTV. It is a twenty-four-hour pop music video station. It probably figures large in his accountancy.

'Anyway, I'm in the desert near Pakistan, and these girls from Bombay started "Yaaaaah-ing" all over the place, just like it used to be in the sixties.

'I was in this little village in Peru, near Cuzco, when this little

boy, he was about nine, came up. I thought, he's after money.
But no, he had a picture of me – in Peru, right up in the bloody
Andes.

'It's an odd thing. One minute you're hiring people to do your
publicity for you; next minute you're buying a farm in Wales to
hide from it. Most people who go in for this business, they've got
no idea of what's going to happen. North Africa, that's where you
don't get it. Russia? Don' know 'bout that. I don't think Russia's
much fun.'

What was it like playing in front of hundreds of thousands of
people, all staring at you? Scary, said Jagger; your knees turned to
water. Was he being serious? Nah, said Jagger. You haven't got the
time. Anyway the audience can smell it when someone's not got
confidence. And a gig's the same wherever you are: in some small
hall, or in Hyde Park. You can't hear them in the open air, but in
those big domes in America, that's where it gets a bit noisy.

He is a very wary man. Ask him about Mrs Thatcher and it
suddenly is not a matter of two men chatting round a table: there
have been too many interviews for him not to know what a comment would look like in print. C'mon, said Jagger.

No, he had never been hurt by anything written about him.
You had to be accurate and well-informed to hurt. And the Jumping Jack Flash of the Sixties never existed; or if he did it was only
in the minds of the men who wrote about him. Most of them were
drug fiends anyway, said Jagger.

'I know some people thought we were a threat to everything.
But me, all I ever wanted to do was sing and make a lot of money
as well. When you come to think of it, there's not been a lot of
threats, apart from us and the Sex Pistols. Been a pretty lean time
on the old threat market.'

Yes, he thought of himself as a responsible man. He made
plans up to eighteen months ahead. He was planning now for the
launch of the new Stones album, *Dirty Work*. He had had a very

busy year ('Some years you don't feel like doing anything, but I'm a creative person, I like doing things').

And he rarely acted on whimsy, except for that Indian holiday with his brother, a manufacturer of electric guitars, and even that had taken a couple of days to organise. His brother had responsibilities, said Jagger.

He was a good father, or he tried to be. He watched his parents, and other people, and then it was up to the kids themselves. He had spent a lot of time thinking about schools for his daughters. On the christening, asked whether he was a Christian, he paused, running the headlines through his mind, then said ... 'By culture.'

He is a quick man, not a warm man – but not unfriendly, either. A man who does not miss a trick. Apart from the business of a pension he seemed only taken aback once. Would he let his daughters go out with a pop star? 'Would I mind?' echoed Jagger. 'No, I wouldn't mind.' It would depend on the band they were with, said his publicity man quickly.

Most of his friends were in the business, he said. Doors might have opened for him, and he wanted them to, but all he had ever wanted to meet were the old blues singers whose pictures lined his office stairs.

Did he see the other members of the Stones? If they were in the same country, said Jagger. He was going to see Charlie Watts, who had left the sheepdogs and the cars, play that night with a jazz group. So what were they now, an old firm much dispersed?

'You said it,' said Jagger.

1986

BEAUTY

~~~

Seven years ago, she was a schoolgirl. Now she is 'the world's most beautiful woman' and, all day, they have come and gone in the windowless bunker under the Dorchester Hotel – reporters, cameramen, sound recordists – in a schedule as rigid as that of a space shot. At 7pm, Miss Claudia Schiffer is to be launched at the stratosphere in Concorde, but the schedule is unravelling, just as in a space shot.

They're running forty-five minutes late, says the PR man, scurrying up and down and looking at his watch like the White Rabbit, for it is still vivid, that terrible night when Diana Ross missed Concorde, the subsequent scheduled flight was cancelled and Miss Ross found herself alone in the Heathrow VIP lounge, with no one to guard her and, even worse, no one to interview her. For celebs, there is just one circle of hell below that, and it is complete oblivion.

Under the Dorchester Hotel, the press and the television crews have assembled to sit at Miss Schiffer's size seven feet and hear her views on ... What? What does one ask the 'most beautiful woman in the world?' Had he had the chance, what would Homer have asked Helen of Troy about? Diet, exercise, men?

I am locked into the schedules, between the photographers who are assembling their portable studios; each has been allowed five minutes and their power cables are everywhere. In the world of Claudia Schiffer, there are many power cables. It is made even more surreal by the fact that all this is taking place in a nightclub during the day, and I am staring distractedly at the threadbare sofas and hunting prints.

But the White Rabbit is back, telling me to be on standby, for the *Standard* photographer is starting his five minutes, and a very tall, very thin young woman, endearingly knock-kneed, is being led to a chair like a child at the dentist's. And then things begin to happen very quickly.

A tough-looking man runs out of the shadows and with his hands, no comb, begins to throw strands of her long blonde hair about and arrange it around her face. When Miss Schiffer is being interviewed, nobody cares; she is left to herself. But as soon as a camera appears, so do people I have not seen before, like the young woman with a brush who begins to dust that face. Words, and those who live by them, are interlopers in the world of Claudia Schiffer.

Which is curious, seeing that we are in the bunker because of a book. *Claudia Schiffer: Memories*. Gordon Bennett! The woman is just twenty-four years old.

Thankfully, there are not many memories and, apart from the dedication, the book has been written by others, though she does throw in the odd memory of photo locations and one little boy at school. But the dedication is long, and includes 'the photographers and the fashion designers who gave me the chance to share their dreams ...' while her father and mother 'gave me the gift of life'. There is no mention of her fiancé, the magician David Copperfield.

Her hair and face-dusting people have moved away. I have

time to watch her. Is she beautiful? Oh yes, but no more beautiful than half a dozen girls I have seen on my way to the Dorchester Hotel. Just much taller.

Miss Schiffer's is a healthy, tough little face (if you turn to page 62 of her book you'll see more than a passing resemblance to the boxer Terry Downes). Big cheekbones, lips naturally apart, round chin. When she sits down, she is a small woman, but when she stands, she goes up and up like a lift; the height (5ft 11in) is disproportionate to the weight, 126lb. And with her jacket shut, there is no sign of the famous bust which distinguishes her in the world of flat-chested supermodels.

But in reality, you've very little time to notice the details of her appearance for, with the soft explosion of the flashgun, her face goes into action. It smiles, grins, winces, flirts; no two expressions are alike and all are independent of the photographer's instructions. The flashgun is going like a machine-gun but the expressions keep pace. I have never seen anything like it.

'And now *with* the book,' says Miss Schiffer, placing it in front of herself.

'Could we have one without the book?'

'No, you have had them *without*. Now we're having them *with*.'

There is little hint of an accent, the vowels being more Transatlantic than anything, but the emphases are amusing. There may be some who are not sure what they're doing in a bunker on the hottest afternoon of the year, but there is one among us who has no doubts. Miss Schiffer is here to flog her book.

Asked by Paula Yates once what she would take with her to a desert island, she said this: 'I'd buy the entire Revlon skin-care range and, if I couldn't take that, I'd settle for their tawny beige blusher. It's just so brilliant, I can't tell you.'

Charming, you might think, the sort of thing a young girl might say, until you remember that this particular young girl has a £3.5 million contract with Revlon. She reminded readers of

Hello! magazine that her fiancé and 'soul-mate' David Copperfield was the eighth best-paid entertainer in the world.

And now it is my turn to meet this self-made millionairess
young enough to be my daughter (*Forbes Magazine* estimates her
current income at £3.33 million a year). I shake a soft, cool hand
and desperately try to think of something to ask her. Such beings
should be glimpsed from hiding, not interviewed.

The circumstances of her 'discovery' are too well known; the
lawyer's daughter from the small German town of Rheinberg,
spotted by a stranger in a nightclub and invited to Paris, whither
she went a fortnight later, the face on the magazine covers becoming the body on the catwalk, becoming ...

I ask her about Rheinberg, which I seem to remember housed
the Diet of the Holy Roman Empire. Am I wrong? For a moment
she stares at me as though I am off my rocker, then starts to tell
me about old statues, and it is clear we are talking about two different Roman empires. But who cares?

She has been up since 6 a.m. in the Dorchester Hotel, and it is
her second day in Britain. Tomorrow she will be in Seattle, inter-
viewing someone ('I can't tell you who') for her new television
show, the day after in Leipzig, the day after that in Paris, and then
New York. Days of jet-lag and planes, of being met by strangers
and by men who will toss her hair about before the cameras start.

She has just come from Prague, where she was for a whole nine
days. 'That was hard, it was exercise all day long, fifteen hours a
day and nothing else at all. I was making my own exercise video.'
But she remembers that at one point she was taken to see the
Danube, and afterwards went to bed, just as yesterday, after the
interviews, she went to bed. The nightly phone call home like ET.
And bed. David Copperfield, asked by a tactful journalist whether
he slept with his fiancé, said there was little room in her bed
because of the number of fluffy toys she carried around with her.

Presumably these are in the sixteen suitcases which I earlier heard one of the PR team mention as she frantically tried to arrange a second car for the airport.

Bed is one of the few things Claudia Schiffer talks about with real enthusiasm, a small and private place without power cables or hands throwing her hair about. The other thing is food, only she talks about food with nostalgia.

'It affects me in the sense that I get tired when I eat. The digestive system takes a lot of energy, so I don't eat meat now, even though I'm German ...' She shrugs prettily. 'When I sit through a long meal, it tires me out, and I used to love meat. I don't smoke, I don't drink, I eat fruit and light salad. But when I finished those nine days in Prague, know what I did? I ate a whole bar of chocolate.'

Does food make her put on weight? Oh yes, she is not like those models who are unaffected by what they eat. Why once, she leans forward confidentially, she put on three whole pounds; 129 pounds! And it suddenly occurs to me that somewhere in Miss Schiffer there might be a sense of humour.

But Miss Schiffer wants to talk about her business activities, the book, which was her idea (oh no), her new career in television, her career in restaurants (she and Naomi Campbell are opening a 'fashion theme' restaurant in New York). Miss Schiffer is fluent and bland and forceful. No, she and Miss Campbell are not close friends, they are ... colleagues. She has no close friends among the super models. It happens.

No, she does not remember how many interviews there have been in the two London days. No, she does not mind them, they are ... promotion. Have any questions surprised her? No. They have all been asked before.

So finally I dig up that buried figure, the schoolgirl just a fingertip away who thought seven years ago that she would be a lawyer when she grew up.

Her father, she says, thought so, too. The girl who worried about her height, being head and shoulders above the boys in her class and watched her small confident class-mates with their boyfriends.

She remembers, on the rare occasion when she had a boyfriend, how these girls would laugh. 'Oh God, look at him.' Even in her dreams, she had not thought how such a thing as her height might one day turn to her advantage. She does not know what has become of the small confident girls.

'It is strange how all that no longer matters, but I still smile when someone tells me I am beautiful. I like it, though I smile most when it is said by someone I know.

'When I see photographs of myself, I never think of myself as beautiful. I look at the clothes, the lighting, the make-up.'

As she talks, she moves her hand and something flashes; yes, it is the engagement ring given to her by David Copperfield. She turns it. Did it really cost £4.5 million?

'I don't know, I have never asked him.' Then she smiles sadly. 'But you would not have asked the seventeen-year-old that question, would you?'

I ask her about the beings who rush in from the shadows when the cameras start, and she tells me she has known them a very long time.

It is work, she says. Yes, the work will go on, one day it will be over, but she has no thoughts of retirement. Yes, one day she will marry David Copperfield.

The forty-five minutes are up and she moves towards the next set of reflecting parasols. The man rushes in to throw her hair about and his name, he tells me, is Sam McKnight, but then he stops.

'Perhaps I shouldn't talk to you,' says Mr McKnight. And the girl with the brush comes.

'This is what we call a touch-up,' Claudia Schiffer tells me and, for a moment, under those other glossy selves, the mischievousness is that of the seventeen-year-old.

I hope she caught her plane.

1995

FRIEND OF THE FAMOUS

~⌐

L ook up either Elizabeth Taylor or Richard Burton in *Who's Who*, and after the long inventories of films, spouses and children, you come to the last shared thing: 'Address, care of Major Donald Neville-Willing.' A Belgravia address and a telephone number follow.

These can lead to the film contract and the exclusive interview. And yet that rank, the hyphen ... In fiction, stars' addresses would be 'care of Solly Silverstein Enterprises', the Silverstein of which would be in conference even were the Almighty to telephone him. But when you ring the number in *Who's Who*, the Major answers. Film producers and journalist alike must have started back from those small, cold vowels on the telephone. But then at the end he thanks you, though it is you who want him to do something for you. To anyone with any experience of film stars that is the oddest thing of all.

The Major smoothed down a tailored half-cuff. He sighed. 'All my life people have come to talk to me about other people. And I do so love talking about myself.'

Friend of the Famous

But Major Donald Neville-Willing, seventy-eight, a poste restante for the shining ones, former actor, dancer, New York hotelier, former general manager of the Café de Paris in London, former private secretary to Earl Beatty, former aide to film producers and pop group czars, is at last having his revenge. After a lifetime of being useful to the great, the Major is writing his memoirs.

He has, so far, shown them to one literary agent. The man, in some confusion, wrote back to say that any publisher prepared to bring the book out would probably vanish under the libel suits. But he, however, had been unable to put the book down.

The Major, throughout his life, had a habit of popping up in the oddest places. When, during one of the most sensational divorce cases of the 1930s Edward James divorced his wife, film star Tilly Losch, who was the star witness there when a door opened, who saw the naked lover? The Major. When the former Prince of Wales was the worse for wear in St James's at midnight, who was there to lend a steadying hand? The Major.

When the present Duke of Kent was jiving for the first time at the Café de Paris, who was there to stop him kicking fellow guests to death? The Major.

He can certainly stop you in your tracks when he chooses, can the Major. The more scandalous the story, the flatter the delivery. Over tea a pair of eyes, already the size of saucers, had become the size of millstones. 'Are you sure you're twenty-one?' the Major asked kindly.

He is a small, elegant, exquisite gentleman, who in his house in a narrow street in London's exclusive Belgravia sits very still and very upright. He could pass in mandarin dress for any of the figures under the willow trees on the pieces of china about him. He is of a piece with the china. The clothes are beautiful. The white hair is glossy. A monocle hangs low on a thick black cord against the waistcoat.

The Last Human Cannonball

The only thing that jars, that hints at a world removed from afternoon tea and discretion, is the gold chain about his wrist. But you have little time to notice as the Major surfboards on his names into other stories, other decades.

The Major has, it seems, known everyone who was anyone. As manager of the Café de Paris he brought Marlene Dietrich to London in the 1950s. As the manager of the George Washington Hotel, New York, in the 1930s, he met gangsters and film actors. W. H. Auden stayed there and wrote him a poem. Noel Coward, whom he disliked, knew him as 'Major, baby'. His work as private secretary to Earl Beatty opened to him doors about which *Tatler* readers can only dream.

As he speaks there is something remorseless about the short, staccato sentences. They press down objections and arguments, and you become like one of those men in railway stations in Westerns, who sit forever taking down the messages in Morse code.

'I'm a hard person really. You get that way. Having been thrown into the world with every attitude one hundred per cent effeminate I've always tried to please people. I know if I dress properly and am clean and fit in with them I can't go far wrong.

'I was born in Manchester. We lived a real upstairs-downstairs life, though we weren't society. My father was a cotton manufacturer. There are thirty-five old people living in the house now. I send them chocolates once a year. Last year I sent them toffee: couldn't afford chocolates.

'I am the younger of two brothers. He's a cotton manufacturer, too. No sense of humour. A philatelist: that's enough for anyone. But my brother is the kindest man I know. We were such a very nice, very ordinary family. None of them knew where I got it all from. I had a prep school report: "Good at everything but excels at sewing".'

After a brief, baffled period in the cotton business, and a time in the Dutch East Indies, which it was hoped 'would make a man' of him, he came to London and the doors began to open. He got an audition for a new revue. The audition was a success, something the Major now regards with mixed feelings. 'I'd come to London full of nice thoughts. But when people ask you to sing and then they start laughing for no apparent reason ...' The words trailed away.

He became notorious in the 1920s for playing what were then known as 'effeminate' roles, so notorious that when he was offered a chance to re-enter private life he took it. He was told that Earl Beatty was looking for a private secretary to help him with his charitable work in London's dockland. In those days male secretaries who could take shorthand and could type were a novelty and so the young Neville-Willing was taken on ('He's so good, this little fellow'). They were years of high society: fifty years later he has still not got the awe out of his voice when he titles a chapter in his memoirs, 'The Duke and Duchess of York compliment me'. But in 1929 Lord Beatty decided to give up his charities – and the Major, his address-book full of introductions, left for New York. 'And my troubles really began.'

The first few years were bizarre. America had entered the Depression and there was little work. Neville-Willing spent his days working in metal cap factories and his evenings calling on the rich. Then, in his blackest moment, came the light. He was about to be thrown out of his hotel for not paying the rent when, desperately, he suggested he might work in lieu. 'And this man said, "What can you do?" So I said, "Well, vaguely, I arrange flowers." He looked as though I had hit him. A man who could arrange flowers? Then he thought about it and said that they were giving a banquet for 100 the next day and gave me 50 dollars to buy flowers. I bought bronze and yellow chrysanthemums and had 29 dollars change. When I gave him this he looked even more astonished.'

Within a year he was assistant manager of the hotel, the

George Washington, the smartest in the Hearst chain. Then he became resident manager. It could only, murmured the Major, happen in America.

He had a genius for publicity. He introduced English afternoon teas and a palm court. Visiting celebrities were invited (and scrupulously photographed), and even Hearst himself became interested in what was happening. The climax was a great press lunch. 'But over the brandy I noticed the managing director, a huge German-American, go very quiet. Finally he asked me to step outside. "Donald, you trying to make a fool outta me? You fill those glasses up, d'you hear. That's an order." It was no use arguing. So I got the waiters to fill each balloon glass to the top. Each member of the press got half a bottle of brandy. They were still there at tea time.'

He became a member of New York society, served on charity committees 'with the Duchess of Talleyrand, Princess Djordjaze, Polly Peabody, Mrs Harrison Williams ...' But he remembers other things as well; these were the years when stockbrokers threw themselves from hotel bedrooms. 'It was a terrible sound. I would ring down at once to see if it was us or the hotel opposite.'

But then came 1939. The Major tried to join up, only to be told by the Embassy that, at thirty-eight, his place was in the Home Guard. But, persuading some of his richer friends to fork up for two ambulances, he managed to join the American Field Service, a voluntary medical organisation, and was told to report on board a troop ship. And so the Major went to war.

The ship eventually got to Cairo, where he disembarked with his ambulances and where, a few days later in church, he met an old friend attached to GHQ. Strings were pulled. Telephones rang, and the Major was gently winkled out of the American Field Service. He was interviewed by the Commander in Chief, Jumbo Wilson. 'He asked why I wanted to be an officer. I said I didn't, that all I wanted was to be in the British army. So he said, "Good show." Then he looked very thoughtful and asked how I held a cup of tea. I wasn't sure. The next thing was that he'd called for a cup, and I had to hold it. Then he said, "Good show. You don't hold your pinkie out." The General said, "You won't have to do any fighting. We'll put you on the General List. You'll be a gaberdine swine." And so I became the oldest second lieutenant in the Army.'

From Egypt he was posted to India, where his duties included the setting-up of rest camps for the troops from the Front. For a while he was on the North-West Frontier and retains a sour memory of the British in India. 'All those fat women, sitting on their bottoms all day, clapping their hands whenever they dropped anything. They lost India for us, the memsahibs. I remember one coming in a great fury during my first dance there. "What do you think Stickey's gone and done?" He was her husband, a judge. "He's gone and dropped dead on me. *On dance night*."'

At the end of the war, now a major, he was transferred to the Canadian army in its invasion of Holland and was in charge of the restoration of civilian amenities like electricity and the tarring of roads. On his staff was, of course, Prince Bernhard. 'Biggest son of a bitch I ever met,' said the Major.

When the war ended he returned to the States, opened a rooming house on Park Avenue, and was involved in such theatrical enterprises as bringing the Dublin Gate Theatre to New York. But it was in 1952 that the Major's finest hour came. 'I was in a party in the Café de Paris and afterwards one of them asked me what I thought of the place. I said, "Glorious room. Terrible lighting. Ghastly food." And this man looked at me and said, "That's very interesting. You've got an appointment with the managing director on Monday." I didn't know it, but he was one of the owners.' The Major became general manager and in his seven years there brought Marlene Dietrich, Liberace and Shirley Bassey to the nightclub.

'What a showman he was,' recalled Liberace. 'Every night I was instructed to arrive in my Cadillac and to turn the lights on the moment the car hit Piccadilly so the people could see who was inside. This caused crowds to gather in the streets outside the Café de Paris ... Sometimes they had to get the mounted police.'

The opera star and nightclub singer Helen Traubel said of him: 'He ran the smartest and most exclusive nightclub in London. He was so English that when he spoke in English he had to be interpreted by the English for the English. I never understood much of what he said beyond his impeccable manners ... and the glitter of his monocle.'

Beverley Nichols, who knew the Major since the 1920s, said of him: 'He elevated the very tricky profession of publicity into genius. He had to deal with some very difficult lady stars like Marlene Dietrich, and he managed to stay friends with all of them. That is the remarkable thing. I think it's because he's such a kind man.'

Since then he has worked for the film producer John Hayman, during which time he met the Burtons. Until last year he was working for the manager of The Who. The Major seems to have liked pop stars even less than the memsahibs. 'Most of the time I was trying to stop them doing what they were doing.'

He sounded weary. Very little can shock or annoy him. A man like the Major, on whom nature has played such strange tricks of biology, cannot allow himself to be shocked or annoyed, there being so many people he himself can shock and annoy.

'The world hasn't been kind to me. I've had to sing for my supper all my life. I've heard it so often: "Ask Donny along, he'll wash up." I spend hours alone now. My neighbours look in through my windows and see me watching television. That's why I'm writing my memoirs. I could do with a little notoriety.'

In the memoirs, the great and famous appear in hilarious situations. Marlene Dietrich, Gracie Fields, Charlie Chaplin and the

Queen Mother apart, the Major is not one for hero-worship. 'The idea that the last Prince of Wales was splendid is a lot of rubbish,' he begins one chapter roundly.

He has a way with words. Edith Sitwell, he recalls, 'had a face like the back of a spoon'. Edward James 'when younger, looked like a bird, like a little pedantic bird about to take off'. But whether a publisher dare bring the memoirs out is another matter.

So in Belgravia the Major talks.

1979

PART SIX

ASGARD, WHERE ALL ROADS LEAD

MEETING MR HILL

⤳

The American film producer Jim Hill died, aged eighty-five, in 2001. I wrote his obituary for the *Daily Telegraph*, and in the course of it related a story he used to tell against himself. Hill, then a partner in Hecht Hill Lancaster, the leading independent motion picture company of its time, was making *Sweet Smell of Success*, and they had hit all kinds of problems with the script. But one morning he came into the office to tell the writer Ernie Lehman to forget the script, they had a real emergency. He wanted Lehman to write a note to accompany three dozen roses he was sending the actress already cast as the cigarette girl in the film. He then told him why.

He, Hill, had slept with her for the first time the night before, only, leaving in the small hours, he had met outside the apartment block a woman walking her dog. The two had fallen into conversation and he had gone back in with her, not knowing she was the very best friend of the actress, who, next morning, bursting in to tell her about her new-found love, found the two in bed. Lehman, who went on to script *North by North West* and *The*

Sound of Music, said the note was the most difficult thing he was ever to write.

But the *Telegraph*, which had cut 'He took a stand on pubic hair as other men took a stand on the Rhine', the best line I ever came up with, from a profile of the photographer Jean Straker, cut the story as well. Hill would have been very disappointed. His favourite quotation was 'Villainy is moonlight'.

I met him in 1974. He was then sixty, I was in my early thirties, and we met, of all places, in west Wales, at a party in a house near Llandeilo then being rented by Lynn Hughes, formerly European story editor for MGM. Hill was acting as barman. He seemed tough, distinguished and lost, all at the same time. Dressed in the casual cashmere knitwear of California, he looked like someone who had just got to his feet from under a pile of bodies after a riot he had not caused. But the air of baffled innocence was misleading, Hill would usually have caused the riot.

I noticed a twisted back, which I later learned was the result of some sports accident in his youth, though the writer Anthony Storey used to claim it was just trying to catch up with his mind. And there was something about him, something in the way he laughed and the steady way he looked at you, that suggested trouble. And, alas, fun.

'Where d'you find him?' I said.

'That, my boy ...' Hughes was then in his Welsh squire mode, 'was Rita Hayworth's husband.'

It is two years later, and we are sitting round the pool in Rita Hayworth's house in Beverly Hills, me, Jim and Rita, with whom, despite their divorce, he is still on good terms. We have been invited round to supper, though the Love Goddess has forgotten to cook anything, and from time to time, passing through the kitchen, I pass a frozen chicken which I prod moodily. The lights are on around the pool, which Rita adjusts, usually when she appears in a change of outfit; she is to change her clothes three times that night. When not doing this and making strange little confessions to me ('I don't suppose you knew I was Mexican'), she inveighs against her neighbour Glenn Ford, whose TV aerial, an enormous thing, shows above her hedge.

We have drunk about three bottles of champagne, but I know exactly where I am. I am in Asgard, among the gods, whom I have hitherto seen only against the sky or shimmering on a dance floor. Only I am not meeting them in a rented hotel suite or production office, with a PR man hovering. And the gods are head-bangers, just as they were in Asgard.

A restaurant, and Burt Lancaster has managed to stop explaining transsexuality long enough to order dinner. He has not asked Hill or me what we want: Burt, without recourse to a menu, has ordered. He has just been telling us about a part he has been offered as a transsexual, and must have noticed the blank expression on my face, for he adds kindly, in his staccato Wyatt Earp voice, 'It's what happens when you've got a cock. And balls. *And you don't want 'em.*'

In the twenty-five years I knew Jim Hill many doors opened for me, and they opened, not on contemporary cinema, but on a time of legend. For these were the stars, the directors, and the producers responsible for the films I had seen when I was young, many of whom had retired from the public gaze. The doors opened on Carol Reed, when the only other guest was the elderly gentleman who had played the zither in *The Third Man*. They opened on the world of *Sunset Boulevard*.

And it is night over Sunset Boulevard. We are in the entrance hall of a mansion so big this alone has the floor space of most modern houses; we, Hill, me and Al, an old screen-writing friend of his, are in genuine sedan chairs, each in a corner of the room, only the chairs are so far apart that to have any sort of conversation we have to bellow at each other. The house, one of many, belongs to Al's sister, with whom he lives. Her husband was a lawyer whose first client was Wyatt Earp, and his last Howard Hughes, and she has inherited. Outside in the garage are four Rolls-Royce cars and two Cadillacs. Once there was a Ferrari as well, bought by Hill's friend for his son on his eighteenth birthday.

'Bright kid,' says Hill. 'Lived a whole fortnight after he got the car, didn't he Al?'

We have been out on the town with Al. There have been other nights like this, Al, who can no longer drink, chauffeuring us from bar to bar in one of the Rolls-Royces, but this night is different. This time we have drunk coffee with him. Hill and I have drunk six cups each, and are rigid with caffeine. Al is unaffected.

We stand on the balcony outside Al's study, the Los Angeles fog drifting around us, and all that is missing is Erich von Stroheim with the sandwiches. When we come in it is into a room where the desk has been modelled on the one Mussolini sat at to overwhelm visitors, and everything is on such a scale of opulence it is on the edge of comedy.

'Gosh, Albert, this where you pick up your pencil?' says Jim, it being clear there is no need for Al to pick up a pencil in this world again.

'This is it, Jim.'

Jim Hill was the most formidable human being I ever met. He had had great wealth and had lost it. He had known some of the most beautiful women in the world, and mislaid them too. And none of this mattered in the least to him, so the man was close to being invulnerable. He just didn't give a fuck, except about writing (or 'the trade', as he called it) and mischief. In his pursuit of the latter it was of some advantage to him that he possessed no physical cowardice of any sort. I knew him twenty-five years, and in that time got into more trouble than I thought possible.

Once, having hired a car at Calais, we drove it across Europe, but couldn't operate the heater. The night came on, it was cold, and all we had was two bottles of whisky. After a while we were in no pain of any kind, so when we came on a line of cars parked, their tail lights on, I moved out and drove on. Suddenly there were men in uniform running and waving.

'Welcome to Belgium,' said Hill.

Words didn't mean that much to him, he was no great fan of poetry, except for those lines of Shelley's, 'Swiftly walk over the western wave,/ Spirit of Night!', which he said meant the pubs were about to open. What fascinated him was the practical detail of how novels and screenplays succeeded or failed. 'You have to fall in love with the lovers,' he would say, 'before the lovers can fall in love.' By this he meant that the emotional bond between two characters, which to him was the one successful engine for any narrative, only worked when you had begun to care for them. No stylist himself, he was quite simply, as Bernard Smith, Raymond Chandler's editor at Knopf, said, 'the best structure man in the business'.

We fell out badly once, when, near the end of his life, he conceived the idea that I should write the story of his company. I was lazy, he, conscious that time was running out, was impatient. All that had been written was the monologue that ends this section, before Alzheimer's Disease, like the canaries in *The Birdman of Alcatraz* (which allowed audiences to overlook the fact that the hero in real life was a murderer and a homosexual rapist), took care of everything.

2004

PLAYERS IN THE BACKGROUND

~ฺ

'It was cold the day they crucified me first ...' The head of the American film extras' agency, Central Casting, settled back in his chair to watch the effect this had. The sentence hung in the air like a Zeppelin. 'Five days I was up there, on the cross. Three hours a day, and a ten-minute break when things got too rough.

'I'd got a part as a slave in *Spartacus*. The props people had put children's bicycle seats on all the crosses. You parked a cheek on one, and when that got sore you turned the other cheek, as it were.' He beamed.

'It was bearable as long as your cross leant backwards. But that first day my cross began to lean forward and forward, until soon I was hanging from it. After a while I found it difficult to breathe. Then I realised what was happening. I was actually being crucified.' A clock ticked somewhere in the office.

'I couldn't shout. The assistant director was down the other end of the set, the ... uh ... Appian Way. If I'd shouted the whole take might have been ruined. Jobs were scarce as an extra. It was

February, just after six in the morning. All I had on was a jock-strap and a piece of cloth. Son of a bitch, did I suffer. I hung there and I thought of my wife and kids. I thought of the money. Then I thought of the guy what had been up there in the first place. I lived ...'

The sprinklers come on at dawn in Beverly Hills. Three hours later the first coach slides by the bland lawns. 'THAT, ladies 'n' gen'l'men, is the residence of Mr *Glenn* Ford. 'N THAT, behind the trees, is the domicile of the Love Goddess, Miss Rita Hayworth herself ...' The old-style Hollywood is given over to the sightseers. Universal even found that the revenue from showing tourists around its deserted lots helped to keep it in business. But there is one place the tourists do not go, though it must be one of the most legendary of all. They do not visit one of the saddest places on earth.

It featured first in the thirties version of *A Star Is Born*. The heroine was shown a great switchboard. 'Every time a light comes on there it's someone asking for a job.' The switchboard was as full of lights as a night sky in winter. The switchboard was at Central Casting. It was estimated that each afternoon something like 1000 film extras used to ring up *every hour* looking for work.

For a very few the Hollywood dream began here. Alan Ladd, David Niven, Clark Gable, began as extras; and, in recent history, Rock Hudson, Mary Tyler Moore. 'But none of them want to know me now,' said the head of Central Casting. For the Hollywood dream also ends here for thousands.

It is in the nature of things that no one remembers an extra. Who remembers the men who run forward when the gunsmoke clears? They chat vigorously at street corners; they see each other off at stations; villainous in torchlight, they press forward as a lynch mob. They are as anonymous as wallpaper. Certainly nobody remembers a plump extra going blue in the air above Appian Way. 'You can't stand out,' he said sombrely. 'If your boobs are too big, or if you're too tall, the actors say, "Get rid of it."' His use of the pronoun was brutal. 'When you're looking at the furniture you miss the show.' It is possible to get a jaundiced pleasure out of watching the faces in the margins of a film scene, all the little attempts to portray some individuality. Look at me, they say; I am a human being, too.

In the 1950s there were something like 7000 extras in Hollywood. Today there are just 2500, though of these only 1000 work on any regular basis. Yet every afternoon, between two and six, the lights still glow on the switchboard at Central Casting.

Two women sit at the switchboard behind plate glass. In an office behind them three men and a woman sit at desks. The extras ringing in are known to at least one of the four. In front of them are the production schedules of the next day.

The switchboard girls call out the names as they 'phone. 'Robert Hill ... Gwyn Jones ... Philip Howard.' If they are wanted a cry goes up from the desks, 'Hold Bob Hill...' If not, the name disappears into the ten feet of floor between switchboard and desk. After a period of waiting the light goes out on the switchboard and, with it, in some 'phone booth, in a studio or in a flat, someone's hope of a job. As many as a hundred an hour ring Central Casting.

'Fletcher Watkins ... Tony Tucker ...'

'Hold Fletcher Watkins ... Hey, Fletch, how're things. You got a tuxedo? Great. Not worked in *Marcus Welby* have you?' If an extra appears too regularly the public has been known to ring up the television sponsors and complain. It is the saddest profession: succeed, and you have to fail. 'Great. Tomorrow. Eight o'clock. Don't forget the tuxedo.'

'Brenda Neill ... Marjorie Barrie ...'

'That Marjorie still trying? Man, she's a sticker ...'

'Lloyd Watkins ... Bob Estcourt ...'

'Hold Estcourt... Hey, Bob, you wanna be a dignitary?'

Players in the Background

On the walls of the offices their photographs and curricula vitae are displayed: face after face, lovely, ageing, villainous. All the races of the earth are here. Specialities are noted. 'Grandmother'; 'can do stunts'; 'karate expert'. Past triumphs are recorded. 'Once had own daytime television show.' But for the most part this is the human being as furniture recorded on the walls of Central Casting. One was unforgettable. Under a smiling face was written, 'Specialities: smiling and laughing'.

'Michael Ryde ... Dan McGuire ...'

At the desks the dialogue would be too bizarre to use in any film. 'You remember that baby we wanted, that newborn baby? Juanita's kid is three weeks old, but it's still only eighteen inches long. That do? It's nine pounds.'

'Great. That's our boy. Mexican babies stay small longer. Known fact.'

'I hate babies. You gotta get a work permit and a stopwatch. You can only use them for fifteen minutes at a time. You need a nurse and a welfare worker. I hate babies.'

'Remember that black baby somebody wanted? Black babies are born white. Everybody knows that, 'cept this director. It takes a few days for the pigment to set in. They're kinda cream when they're born. Aw, hell, we got him his black baby.'

'And Orientals. Their babies just look American.'

'Alan Jones ... Richard Enoch ... Graham Farley ...'

'Hold Farley ... Hey Rusko, how'd the operation go?'

The head of Central Casting came to it from the casting office at Universal. Before that, for five uneasy years, he was himself an extra, 'trying to make it as an actor, like all the other extras'. A large man in horn-rimmed spectacles, he sighed. 'But I hit the business at a bad time. The pretty boys were going out and the uglies coming in. Me? Oh, I was a pretty boy.' A smile flickered across his jowls.

Nowadays as many as fifty people a day can approach Central

[217]

Casting to get taken on their books. The agency accepts between 300 and 400 a year. 'I try to discourage them,' he said. 'Most are goggle-eyed at the prospect of becoming a star. You can't disillusion them too much. They really have to love showbusiness but, more than that, they have to be able to accept defeat. Most people get crushed.

'The younger people drop out. They last five years and then they can't stand the insecurity. But the older ones have to stay in it. When you're past thirty and you're trying for an ordinary job nobody wants you if they know you've been an extra. They think you're a flake.' He shuffled through his synonyms. 'A freeloader. A lazy man. Understand?

'Eighty per cent of our people are, all the same, between eighteen and thirty. Actors like to have young healthy people about them. And you get more work out of young people. You can push them around.

'It's hard for the older people. All right, so you have to have the grey-haired banker, or the old lady running the rooming house, but not that often. Director wanted a mortuary attendant the other day. I hired a sixty-five-year-old man. Director was furious. Said you couldn't have a feller that age carting stiffs.

'It's easier the more clothes you have. You get £5 in your currency a day more if you have your own tuxedo. One of our people has £500 worth of uniforms. He's in work all the time. But the younger people ... Jesus.' He took off his spectacles and looked at the ceiling. 'Some of the young men don't know what a suit is. And the girls don't know what a bra is. Boobs bounce so you watch them. You're looking at the furniture again, not the show. We have a terrible time with young people.'

An extra gets the equivalent of £23.50 for an eight-hour day. If he works 'in close', as they say in the trade, if his face should be used in close-up, he gets £47.50. But then his features become recognisable and he can be out of work for two or three weeks:

there is no job like it on earth. And if the extra should speak just one line of dialogue then extradom dwindles beneath him, if only for the day: he is now an actor and negotiates his own salary. For extras never speak. Lips gulp noiselessly by the hitching rail. A lip reader can have a field day watching the extras in films.

In the beginnings of the industry extras were treated as cattle, Universal Studios even having what they called a bullpen. Some 300 hopefuls would gather in it just after dawn to have the assistant directors look them over; choosing extras was their great perk. A sexual pecking order was established: the producer or the star might have the leading lady, but the assistant director was a sultan among the extras.

The years between the wars, the time of Nathanael West's *The Day of the Locust*, were the years of the extras. The jetsam of the world fetched up here – Russian émigré princes with their retainers, old cowboys, aging boxing champs, Eskimos, Hawaiians, where today the students and the jobless come. But whereas ten years ago a studio would use 100 extras for a scene, accountants now decree that only half that number is necessary.

'If they handle an animal it's another £5,' said Dick Ivey, casting director at Disney. 'If they don't get to eat after five hours we have to pay meal penalties. I've known people get £40 a day in meal penalties.'

As a casting director he rings Central Casting. He orders extras as housewives order groceries. 'We're doing a New Orleans street scene. So I just say, "I want some townsfolk. Mixed ages; 25 to 55. Just average people. Put some Creole types among them. Ten men. Ten women."'

No studio request surprises Central Casting. 'Had this Clint Eastwood film about a guy who had his leg cut off. A director rang up and asked for a double for Eastwood: his height, his leg cut off above the knee. Right leg. You try to find a feller 6ft 4in with one leg. That's some strange mother. Ninety per cent of people lose

their *left* legs. It's the way they walk. You lead with the left leg.'
His work has given the director an insight into the more bizarre
reaches of human physiology. 'And usually they take the leg off
below the knee. They wanted someone with it off above the knee.
I advertised, got a feller that had been in a car accident.' He was
among his triumphs. 'I was asked for twenty-five midget women
once. Took me a week.'

It was just after dawn in the Disney studios. In the make-up
rooms women were having their hair bobbed to wear under bon-
nets. The film was *Treasure of Matecumbe* with Peter Ustinov, set
in New Orleans just after the Civil War. Men were having their
ruffs patted into shape, and their hats set at a rakish angle. They
talked of other dawns, other films. The older ones had brought
their own collapsible stools.

As this was a Disney film there were children on the set. Quiet
and grey-faced with lack of sleep, they sat beside their mothers.
The mothers talked.

'You know, this really is the era of the ugly kid.'

'You can say that again. My boy has a tooth missing. C'm
here, Tommy. Open your mouth. See that? I'm not having that put
in again.'

'No, I shouldn't. How old is he?'

'Twelve.'

'Son of a gun, he's going to be in work for a long time. He's
short.'

One little girl had been in the business since she was six
months old. In her first year she had made six commercials, and
now, aged ten, had already had a featured role in one film. One
mother paid her children two dollars a week and banked the rest
for them: it would pay their way through college. A child
yawned. 'Aw, he can sleep in the car on the way back,' said his
mother.

A small schoolroom, four partitions pushed together, had been set up in the dusty Western street, round the corner from New Orleans. A child is only allowed to work four hours a day. The law then obliges the studio to give him three hours' teaching. With a pupil-teacher ration of one to six it meant that the children had the best education possible, confided a mother. On the desks were yesterday's lessons, books open untidily as though this was the *Marie Celeste*.

'Bring on the cobweb machine,' came a roar from the set. The director had arrived and was putting the last touches to New Orleans. The mothers took out their knitting.

A set comes alive like an enchanted castle. People spring into motion. Carriages roll. A black man begins to dance outside a fruit stall. From nowhere, expressions descend on thirty faces and, then, to another signal, disappear as quickly.

A man with a dustpan and brush prowled through New Orleans, revealing why you never see horse manure in any frontier town. 'Sir, this may be hoss shit to you, but it's bread and butter to me.'

Few extras agreed to being interviewed. They looked shame-faced and wandered off. One, a twenty-one-year-old girl in silks and a long skirt, agreed on condition that her name not be used ('You see, I really do want to be an actress and you tend not to get any jobs as an extra if they know you want to be an actress'). She sat doing a crossword. She had been an extra for four months, in which time she had worked on average eight days a month. Between times she ran a store which she owned jointly with her sister: this being California, they sell stained glass.

'The waiting's the worst thing. The work isn't so bad. Yes, we do talk. It helps your facial expressions. Of course, you don't say anything.'

The extras sit and read, or do crosswords. 'You gotta do something, or your mind'd rot,' said one man. Some just sit. Terry Nichols, thirty-three, raised on a ranch, sat back on a verandah, chair tilted, feet over the rail, in the classic Western fashion. His hat was pushed forward over his eyes against the hard morning light.

'Been doing it six years now. Work on building sites between times. The uncertainty don't bother me. I say to myself, where else could I take part in a cavalry charge one day, and drive a racing car the next at 80mph? Man, they usually give me tickets for doing that sort of thing.'

Nichols, who has the sort of weather-beaten face you only find in knitwear ads now, specialises in Westerns and has a large wardrobe of boots and buckskins and black hats. He has no dress clothes ('Me, ah'm a heavy'). But even after six years he still dreams of becoming an actor. 'But you have to know the right people in this business. I hate the 'phoning in. Every afternoon you're in some 'phone booth and the 'phone rings and rings.'

The extras, for the most part, sit alone. One black woman who had ridden grandly by all morning in a landau under a parasol sat knitting. The landau came by again, empty. There was a cry from behind the cameras.

'Where's that dame, wass-'er-name?'

'Helen.'

'Helen, where are you, Helen?'

The woman continued knitting. The landau came by again. She looked at it gloomily, then put down her knitting and picked up the parasol.

'For Chrissake, Helen, didn't you hear us?'

'Mah name's Samantha.'

Dignity is a precious thing when you are part of the furniture.

A black man had danced wildly all morning outside the fruit shop. The fruit, apart from six lettuces, was all wax. After the last take of all, when the sun had begun its abrupt Californian plunge, he began quietly to load the lettuces into a large canvas bag. The set was empty. 'All adds up,' he muttered vaguely. 'Man, when ah gets among the lettuces, ah gets among the lettuces.' The job has its rewards. In the twenties he was a famous child star.

Karl Brindle was the chief executive at Central Casting at the time. He ambled among his cloudy triumphs. He talked of the dwarfs and giant Vikings he had extracted from humanity.

'Remember *The Sting*? When they made that they had this idea that the killer should have the third finger cut off at the knuckle. All you'd see would be the hand around the curtains ... that sort of thing.' He shrugged. 'But nobody loses the third finger, huh? Nobody sticks his third finger in anywhere. Anyway, I advertised. Days passed. Then one evening this feller 'phoned: "Hey, man, how much of this finger you want me to cut off?"'

He shook his head sadly. 'But that morning the studio'd rung. The director had decided it was too corny. He'd made the killer a woman.'

1977

Nobody noticed the wigs

∽

'The inaccessible he laid a hand on,
The heated he refreshed, the cold he warmed,
What Blake presaged, what Lawrence took a stand on,
What Yeats locked up in fable, he performed.'
From *A Song of Experience* by Kingsley Amis.

With women, he found very early on in his career he had an irresistible common ground. 'I made an Atlantic crossing with Burt Lancaster once, and of course all these girls appeared as they do when there's a film star around. Burt introduced me as a yacht broker, but when they found out what I *really* did everything changed. Pretty soon I'm in some cabin, while old Burt is pacing the deck.' That irresistible common ground was the fact that their obsession and his craft were the same thing in the end.

Bob Schiffer was not a star, he was not a screen-writer or a director, and when his name appeared at all it was way down the list of the credits. He was a source of amusement to his colleagues. 'I met him after the premiere of *Vera Cruz*,' said Jim Hill. 'I asked him what he'd made of the film's reception, and all he'd say was "Nobody mentioned the wigs, nobody said anything about them."' But he was also a source of mystery on account of that irresistible common ground. This is the make-up man's story.

For over forty years he walked the perimeter of the most famous faces of our time, with brush and scissors and pencil supplying what God omitted, and the years betrayed. It got to the point where Julie Andrews would not make any public appearances in Hollywood until he had ministered to her. Marlene Dietrich would not appear in *Judgement at Nuremberg* until he had made her up, and as he was already working on another film he had to fit her in at 4.30 a.m. The make-up man saw many dawns.

'You're like a psychiatrist with the women. They start confessing things to you, it's like a laying on of hands. For you meet them that early, the way few of their husbands have even seen them. They come in with bandanas on, and don't show themselves until I've finished.

'The result is a man gets cynical, seeing the humorous side to film stars, that insecurity the public don't get to see. Who would believe that anyone would get up that early to have grease smeared all over them, how do they explain that to the kids? I think acting's a silly profession.'

But then, as he acknowledged, so was his own. Once he worked on *Blonde Venus* with Marlene Dietrich. 'At five o'clock in the morning I had to apply body make-up to thirty naked women in a tent.' He shook his head ruefully. 'If that doesn't make you into a queer nothing will.' And nothing did. Now in his sixties, large, amiable and elegant, a hairline cunningly lowered to hide receding temples, this man in his beginnings could have been the greatest womaniser of all. The studio then would not allow him to put make-up on Norma Shearer without an entourage present.

And his beginnings were bizarre. He was sixteen, and a seaman on a passenger liner when there was a fancy dress ball. Schiffer noticed the ship's barber charging passengers £2 to be made up, so, something of an amateur painter, he undercut the man by offering to make them up at £1 a head. That was his first encounter with a world which was eager to pay him for sticking false beards on its faces and lining its eyes.

He got into films by taking rooms in a house in Los Angeles, the owner of which was in the make-up business. Through his influence Schiffer got a job in studios where every day was a fancy-dress ball, and people were prepared to pay him far more than £1. By the age of twenty he had his own plane, and was among the women.

His favourite was Rita Hayworth. 'I kept her looking good for many years.' He grinned. 'But then she *did* look good for many years, I think she had the most perfect face of all. I made her up for *Gilda*, *Cover Girl* and *The Lady from Shanghai*. She had this one eye that appeared smaller than the other, so I compensated for that by applying a few false lashes upward in the corner at a forty-five degree angle, which opened the eye and made it larger. I used an invention of my own on her face, a powder which gave her face a luminescent look.'

He is actually one of the few men to have created a standard of beauty for a generation. In the past it was painters like Charles Dana Gibson with the Gibson girl who did this, now it is the make-up man. The 1940s look is generally acknowledged to be of Schiffer's begetting, as, red-lipped and thin of brow, his creations settled like snow in the dreams of millions ... Rita, Dietrich, Lana Turner.

But it is the peculiar sadness of his craft that its recipients never acknowledge it. 'They'd hate to admit they needed me, but without make-up most of them would go down the tube. They like to think they look like that all the time. If I were to write my memoirs some would be very worried. As for the rest, there would be the curiosity. Whose face had I lifted? Whose was the ugliest? I couldn't.'

With the men he took refuge in professionalism. 'In *The Birdman of Alcatraz* I had to age Burt Lancaster from eighteen to seventy-five, and the problem was that there was so much strength in his face. I had to weaken it, take the jaws away. It took two and a half hours a day. I put these rubber appliances round his eyes, stippled his face, then pulled it down with tapes so it stretched, then wrinkled. I ordered his costumes two sizes too big so they hung on him.' Lancaster sent him a photograph of himself inscribed 'To the Old Master'. So at least he noticed once.

The rest of the time Schiffer indulged in fascinated mockery of a star who was also his friend. 'Burt never looked in a mirror. I remember when he was filming *The Hallelujah Trail*, I put two moustaches on for his eyebrows, and he went on set looking like that, with everybody falling about. He looked like Groucho Marx.'

Then there was Humphrey Bogart. 'The first thing he said to me was, "You can't do anything with this face, I've lived in it too long." They all say they don't want make-up, yet they're the first in the chair in the morning. Bogart asked me for a mirror one day. I took it from him. "If you don't trust me, you don't need me."

'I played a lot of backgammon with Bogart.'

That way he got some of his dignity back, and could forget the hours spent waiting for a nose to get shiny. The other was special effects. For *Camelot*, wanting to give Merlin the illusion of blazing eyes, under vacuum pressure he fused tiny mirrors into contact lenses so the eye itself became a mirror and glittered. There was a small hole in the lenses so the actor could see. 'I wonder if anyone noticed,' said Schiffer wistfully.

But in one film everyone did. Required to turn the actor Dean Jones into a dog on screen, he broke the process down into six stages. In the first the face had become slightly hairy, a small moulding on the nose making it hairier.

In the second the man was beginning to lose a lip and his ears were floppier. By the third the ears had flopped over and the nostrils were dilating. By the fourth the lower lip had gone and the nose was a dog's nose. In the fifth it had become a muzzle. In the sixth and last stage Schiffer animated the lower jaw by means of an extension spring. Large teeth had grown, a long tongue attached to the actor's own tongue, and blue contact lenses fitted to blot out the whites of the eyes. There was hair everywhere.

It makes for one of the most bizarre pieces of film ever seen. 'The man's on the phone, you see his nose grow, his mouth extend. He puts down the phone. He barks.' Schiffer has kept all six severed heads in his studio. 'Whatever you think of all this,' he said grimly, 'it was one piece of make-up nobody missed.'

He was cynical about the qualities he looked for in would-be make-up men. 'I ask them about their art backgrounds, I look at their drawings, I ask the odd technical question.' Then he grinned. 'Remember the make-up man's is the first face a star sees in the morning. In the end I pick the guys who are the most attractive physically.'

We were in his studio at Disney, with a South African couple he had met on holiday. The wife, a woman in her late forties, was in the chair, and Schiffer was working on her. Now her husband was there, I was there, but Schiffer and the woman were oblivious to our presence, there were just the two of them and the mirror. They did not speak, and if we said anything neither seemed to hear, they were in a dream of their own, the woman's breathing quickening until I could see her bust rise and fall. I thought then, and still think it the most erotic tableau I have ever seen. It went no further, but I was watching a seduction.

'I like women,' he told me later. 'I find myself in restaurants looking at them in this odd and detached way, thinking about where they've gone wrong and how easy it would be for me to change them. It's like going to a house and seeing how you could alter the garden.

'You can take ten to fifteen years off by mechanical means, taping the face up, but it's not that, it's just that most of them, I'd say eighty per cent, just don't know their faces. So on a plane, after a couple of drinks, you sometimes do tell them. You lean across, and forty-five minutes later you're still telling them. Some write years after, saying how you've changed everything.'

He paused, and then said the strangest thing. 'Then you feel how sad it all is.'

> 'And so he knew, where we can only fumble,
> Wildly in daydreams, vulgarly in art;
> Miles past the point where all delusions crumble
> He found the female and the human heart.'

2004

Nameless Faces in the Celluloid Graveyard

╰╮

The name will mean nothing to you but the moustache will, the fine hard features and those eyes. You would recognise their authority if you met them in the street, but you would also be puzzled because they would seem so familiar. Only you never will meet them. The actor John Dehner has died in California and another icon has been taken down.

In over 100 films he was the man in charge. Dehner was the gang boss, the crooked chairman, the cold-eyed sheriff. He died many times but without showing fear, for Robert Middleton, in similar roles, jowls wobbling, held the franchise on fear. Dehner never got to kiss the girls, either, his assignations being only with Nemesis, which he met in curtained nightclubs or in the dust of a cattle town, and now will forever meet at midnight all over the world in that eternity of old late-night films.

When actors like Dehner go it's like a death in the family. The stars were different; they had names and private lives relayed through the publicity departments of film studios. But the character actors were men without families or names. They played a version of themselves, that either they, or others, had fashioned, always cynical or weak or evil or honourable – and at some stage in their typecast careers even stopped being actors altogether. They became incarnations.

James Hill told me of the chaos he had known on a location for a Western in Mexico, when the actor Jack Elam vanished off the face of the earth. Remember Jack? The rolling left eye, and the crooked eyebrow going up and down like a blind as new dark vistas opened up for him?

They had to stop filming, and the accountants were beginning to fight each other when Jack was found in a local jail. The Mexican police, film fans all, had locked him up for being evil.

You will not see the likes of such men again, for their careers needed the regular output of studios. And, with the studios gone, the actors themselves are beginning to die, so that those of us who are over forty find we are staring at obituaries and faces to which at last we can put names.

For them this was the one irritant in those long and industrious careers, and it is ironic that this should be removed only in death. The actor Peter Bull, who specialised in explosive foreigners and in eighteenth-century vicars with high blood pressure, ruefully entitled his memoirs, *I Know The Face But ...*

The obituaries come regularly now. Three years ago there was George Coulouris who said so wistfully, if only he had been allowed to play, just once, an English barrister, 'with some sensible lines to deliver'... It was not to be. George was doomed to twitch, stare and rant – also, to play foreigners.

He was the scruffy Greek sea captain, the east European spy, the South American dictator. Remember George? Or rather, remember those eyes, mad with drink on the bridge of a tramp steamer, swivelling in street shadows, bulging above the gold braid? George also died many times, and, being highly qualified to do so on account of his eyes, was allowed to show fear.

But here comes the grand master of fear, facial muscles twitching, eyes wide: Elisha Cook Jr, who perspired and perished in every film he ever made, to the enormous satisfaction of cinema audiences, for Elisha always had it coming to him. He specialised in being the rat caught in the trap, though once, on one fleeting occasion, he was allowed a moment of heroism. Terrified (his masters would never allow him to waste his expertise) but game, Elisha faced Jack Palance (the gunfighter all in black with gloves) in *Shane*. Elisha then died again.

You can imagine his telephone conversations with his agent. Got a great part for you, pal. Do I get to die? Does the sun rise, Elisha? OK, where do I get to die this time? Outdoors, in the mud – it's a Western. At the end? C'mon, Elisha, you know you never make the final reel. Nor did he.

But then we didn't want him to, for whatever happened in our own lives there were some things which never changed. In the Western town more familiar than our own home towns, there was always the store, kept by James Griffith, the tall one with the Adam's apple, who at some point could be relied on to show his yellow streak or to head the lynch mob.

Percy Helton, small, bald and squeaky, would sit on the board-walk watching the world go by, ready to misdirect the posse. Remember him as Sweetface in *Butch Cassidy*? In his films Percy was always misdirecting someone.

You can play this game yourself, filling the town with your own familiar ghosts. In the rooming house Jane Darwell, that prop-forward of a matriarch (usually photographed against the sky by John Ford), is cooking steaks, often helped by S. Z. Sakall, eyes twinkling behind his spectacles, who specialised in lovable immigrants and pastry cooks. In a corner, crusty Edgar Buchanan is grumbling about the food.

Bad men never get to eat in Westerns. Have you noticed that? If they order a meal, like Lee Marvin in *Liberty Valance*, trouble intervenes before they start chewing; in these films the steak is the sacrament, and once you eat it you are filled with the Frontier virtues. So down at the saloon Jack Elam and Robert Middleton and John Dehner are noisily starving, helped by the special bottles of whiskey kept under the counter just for them.

They are drinking, too, in the office behind the nightclub: gangster Lionel Stander, crooked policeman Ray Collins, town boss Eugene Pallette, and Mike Mazurki, the ultimate heavy and former professional wrestler who died just over a year ago, having mumbled monosyllables in all his films.

A change of scenery, jackboots on the cobblestones, and there, between the peaked cap and the SS runes, are the hooded eyes of Anton Diffring. In life no SS man had Anton's eerie glamour, just as no managing director born was incisive like Geoffrey Keen, no sergeant major so powerful as Harry Andrews.

The result was that if these men played anything else you felt bewildered, as when Geoffrey Keen was a cockney gangster and Anton Diffring on stage at the Mermaid was Henry V, and that could destroy the whole production for you. James Hill blamed the commercial failure of his company's classic film *Sweet Smell of Success* on the fact that everyone was waiting to see Burt Lancaster jump out of a tree.

So watch as they pass – Burt Kwouk, hand on samurai sword, Oscar Homolka crinkling his KGB eyes, Roland Young and Roland Culver on their way to the races, C. Aubrey Smith on his way to the Khyber Pass.

And now it's that summer morning again in an English country village somewhere in the Home Counties. Dennis Price is facing bankruptcy at the Hall, Raymond Huntley, bank manager or solicitor, is looking at himself in the mirror with great satisfaction, and Joan Hickson is arranging flowers. Michael Hordern is humming.

The Last Human Cannonball

Down at the racing stables David Lodge, honest but dim, looks on as Sam Kydd, rat-faced in a polo neck, is up to no good with a doping syringe, while Victor Maddern talks out of the corner of that gloriously crooked mouth. But soon the sounds they fear most will come, the slamming of the car door and the crunch of gravel, and Bernard Lee will be there, police sergeant or superintendent, stern, kindly and smoking a pipe.

These men were never stars, but then neither were they 'the furniture', as one casting director called the extras.

They were always in work and they knew their place, which was in that long roll call after the titles. When you mourn John Dehner it is yourself you mourn, and your own lost certainties.

1992

This old acrobat

~

I t looks like a transport café where the lorries no longer stop. There is a wooden hut in need of paint, a broken electric sign, and a locked door. There is no menu outside. If you knock, and are admitted, you come into a small room with a bar and a few tables. Yet being allowed to reserve one of these counts as a major social triumph. It might prove marginally easier talking your way into the Kingdom of Heaven than into Dominick's Restaurant in Los Angeles.

It would certainly be less puzzling: in Dominick's you keep getting the feeling that you are among people you know, for at almost every table there is a face which seems familiar. Then you remember. The sharp-faced man against the wall is Robert Redford. The ageing redhead in the shadow is Rhonda Fleming. The door here is locked against the world, the cameras, and the gossip columnists. For over twenty years Dominick has kept it so.

'I keep the door locked because I don't want people to feel wanted,' said Dominick, rattling a cocktail shaker. 'I only want people *I* want to see.' He underscored the pronoun. A man laughed at the corner of the bar. He had entered unnoticed. But the laugh echoed back across the years of your own life. It was not a pleasant laugh: it held no amusement. Two rows of even white teeth flashed as you knew they would.

It is a brutal face. The great stars always had some endearing feature; even old Wayne, slaying his tens of thousands, has a friendly smile. But there is nothing endearing about Burt Lancaster's face. It belongs to the streets.

The only features which come close are those of Charles Bronson, but they look like a piece of stone even the winds have forgotten. With Lancaster you feel the energy pounding out of the face, and with age the menace in it has become more pronounced, the pale eyes sunken. In the shadows of the bar the great jaw muscles seemed to belong to some earlier stage in human evolution.

He stood there at his ease, grinning his terrible rictus grin, a very large man dressed like an eccentric lorry driver. Lancaster has always been the despair of film publicists. 'I think he has one suit,' said a friend. 'I know he has one shirt, a dark one. And a red tie. He used to have a white tie as well, but he lost that. What kind of film star is that, for Chrissake?'

He was wearing his dark suit. There was no sign of the red tie. Over the shirt he wore a long woollen Mexican waistcoat like an old rug. He had some kind of yachting cap on his head. He wore spectacles with thick rims which glittered. As he showed in *Sweet Smell of Success* he can make spectacles look the cruellest prop ever devised. Photographed at Heathrow two years ago, passing through after filming the television series of *Moses*, he was wearing a dark shirt and a Mexican waistcoat. He had some kind of yachting cap on his head.

It is a peculiar experience, meeting a film star. In a way you are meeting yourself, or what you once were. When you were ten, Lancaster embodied all your feelings of adventure; at twenty he was romance and vengeance; at thirty he was your fantasy of power.

This Old Acrobat

He did not look older, or smaller, or gentler. At sixty-two the old acrobat is in a fearsome state of fitness, and could pass for a man of forty. It had always been difficult to think of him as an actor. The old stars were the gods.

They played themselves in film after film, smiling the familiar smile, walking the familiar way, getting the girl, triumphing, grander and simpler in a world that was grander and simpler.

It is hardest on the women. To be a Love Goddess at sixty-one is the cruellest joke the business has played on its creations. They sit in darkened rooms, or dine at each other's houses, or in Dominick's. They talk of scripts they still receive, but the films do not get made.

But after more than fifty films Lancaster is still there. Even now his presence in a cast brings the money-men hurrying: *Executive Action* got off the ground only when he got into it. Others have disappeared into television or thin air, he remains the star. Oh my Victor Matures and my Rock Hudsons, long ago.

'Burt has never faltered in his career,' said the director Alexander MacKendrick, who came to Hollywood in 1959 to direct Lancaster in *Sweet Smell of Success*. Before that, in *The Ladykillers* and *Mandy*, he had worked with most of the great English actors. 'One of the things he has, that the stars had, is that he can walk into a room, and there is a change in the heartbeat. If you had some instrument you could measure it, it's like having a wild animal there suddenly. It has to do with aggression and potential violence. I think some politicians have it, but no English actor.

'I was very conscious that here was an ego different to others. The stars had this, a neurosis which goes right to the edge. You have somehow to use this to get performances from these deep-sea monsters. There was this enormous difference between him and Tony Curtis. Tony has a fantastic vanity, but no ego. He could act Burt off the screen, but he will never be a star. He hasn't this granite quality of the ego.'

The Last Human Cannonball

The film director Visconti once called Lancaster 'the most perfectly mysterious man' he had ever met. Certainly his press-cuttings must be the thinnest of any of the stars. There is the odd reference to his appearance at a Civil Rights rally, or to one of his brushes with the Californian police over a speeding offence. The last follows a pattern: Lancaster refuses to sign the summons demanded by state law, spends a night in jail, and is acquitted. He has no love of the police. But there are no personal details.

He once made one of his rare television appearances on a chat show and the interviewer departed from an agreed list of questions. There was a monumental scene. After a commercial break the cameras came back on a rumpled interviewer in an empty studio. Lancaster's dislike of personal publicity has become worse since the break-up of his marriage in 1971, after almost thirty years and five children. He now lives in a flat in Los Angeles with Jackie Bone, a forty-seven-year-old hairdresser, but sees a great deal of his children. Only one, Billy, has followed his father into the business, as a scriptwriter.

He does not give interviews, except when prevailed upon to publicise a new film, and what then emerges is a brisk lecture on his craft. Part of his attitude is that such things are just not necessary. 'Life's too short for that sort of shit. The questions have all been asked. You've answered them time and again. It's not *worth it.*' A thick forefinger stabbed the darkness above the burnt pork chops. He had come because James Hill, his former partner in the production company of Hecht, Hill, Lancaster, had asked him to come. It was, insisted Mr Lancaster, to be a social evening. That is to say, he talked.

He talked as he did when he played the evangelist Elmer Gantry ('What is *lerrv*? Lerrv is the *Mornin'* an' the *Evenin'* Star'), in sharp staccato sentences, the syllables bursting out of his mouth. He underlined words. He did not listen. 'Great *beers* here. You wanna beer? Three beers.' Like jesting Pilate, he did not wait for an answer. The Panzer tracks of his ego were over and gone. The beers came.

Nothing could be further from the taut monosyllables of his Westerns, for Mr Lancaster likes to explain things. He explained films and stars and studios and history. He even wandered along the wilder shores of sexual psychology.

Every film he has made had brought its little bit of knowledge. *The Leopard* had the Risorgimento in Italy; Mr Lancaster explained the Risorgimento. Even *The Flame and the Arrow* trailed some history. 'Barnaross, I guess it was,' said Lancaster, then added kindly, 'famous emperor of the twelfth century.' Lancaster, the old circus performer, must be unique in having conducted his own education in full view of the entire world. In the shadows a god began to die, and a mad adult education lecturer took his place.

People who know him talk of a vein of cruelty in his nature. There was a scene during the filming of *Gunfight at the OK Corral*. Lancaster and his co-star Kirk Douglas had just walked off set. A crowd of autograph hunters surrounded Lancaster. He turned to them, 'Why don't you ask Mr Douglas for his? Great performer. Of course, you don't recognise him without his built-up shoes.' The big egos are hypersensitive. When they finally got to the cars Douglas was weeping.

Lancaster grinned. Only he doesn't grin: he just unleashes his teeth. They flashed. He must be one of the few men in the world to be able to grin with both sets, like an Alsatian dog. The teeth have a curious history. A Californian dentist in the 1950s pioneered the theory of the perfect bite, that a man's mouth could be so remodelled that the two sets did not grind against each other, so no fillings would be subsequently needed. Lancaster bought the treatment. It cost something like $10,000 then. His two partners, to save him any embarrassment, also bought the treatment. It must have been very strange, entering into business negotiations with Hecht, Hill and Lancaster and having the three perfect bites flashing at you across the table.

He began life as an acrobat, was spotted by Hollywood, and became a contract star to a studio. 'All the junk got thrown at me. The Sunken Treasure. The girl on the island. "Here come the natives."' But he extricated himself almost immediately to become an independent producer. With Harold Hecht and, later, James Hill, he headed the most successful production company of the 1950s, making *Marty*, *Vera Cruz*, *Elmer Gantry*, *Sweet Smell of Success*, *Trapeze*. His success hastened the decline of the once all-powerful studios, a chapter in the history of Hollywood closed with Hecht, Hill, Lancaster. The company was dissolved mysteriously in the early 1960s.

In Dominick's Burt Lancaster was explaining the difference between stars and actors. 'There is something about the man, his appearance or his personality. You just want to see him again. An actor may have the skill, but not the *presence*. It's so much more important in a film when your face is nine feet across in close-up. So people like myself might be *schlepps* as actors, but ...' He spread his hands like Elmer Gantry.

'I never saw Barrymore as Hamlet. I saw John Gielgud and he was *extraordinary*. But I don't think you'd have cast him as Wyatt Earp.' The teeth glittered.

Yet Lancaster was always aware of the dangers of being a star. Very early on he had played parts that were out of character. In *Sweet Smell* he was the megalomaniac newspaper columnist. The film had a critical success, but a commercial failure. Later he played the ageing Prince in *The Leopard*. 'I actually went to see that,' said Lancaster. 'There was this man behind me who kept asking his wife, "When's Lancaster going to screw Cardinale?"'

He shrugged. 'And that's all he wanted to know. But I made a *hell* of a lot of money out of that film.'

But by 1976 he could play a lonely, ageing professor in Visconti's *The Conversation Piece*, without the public expecting him to leap up and annihilate the rest of the dramatis personae. 'At thirty-three, he was a thing of beauty,' said Hill. 'But now he's had to make this transformation into an actor. How many of them have? He's a rarity.'

'These old dames, they go on,' said Lancaster of women stars. 'They're fifty, they're fading. They can't cope. They sit in make-up chairs for five hours with straps holding their faces up.'

Bob Schiffer, now head of make-up at Disney, was Lancaster's make-up man for years. It seems to have been a bizarre experience. 'We were going on a train to Kansas City, Burt, Hill and I. Burt and Hill were sitting opposite me in the restaurant car. Behind me sat a man and his wife. The woman had on a low-cut dress.

'Hill was eating olives, and he began to flick the stones over my shoulder. One finally went down the woman's dress. Burt didn't see any of this. He was spooning up his soup. The first he knows of it is that this man is standing over him, wanting to punch him. But that's the lovely thing about old Burt. He never stops to ask himself, "Why should this be happening to me?" The man is standing there and wants to punch him, so Burt just stands up and is … magnificent.

'The next minute all Hell is let loose. Burt's fighting the man. The conductor starts fighting me. Then they want to throw us off the train. We're in the middle of the bloody desert. All the time Hill is sitting there, sweet as pie, eating his olives. Anyway we finally talk our way out of it.

'So I'm fed up with these two idiots. Burt was on about his next film, *The Rose Tattoo*. I hadn't read the part or anything, but I said to him, "You can't play it with all that hair." He'd just done a Western and had all this long golden hair. I ended up cutting it all off to about a quarter of an inch. With nail scissors.' Lancaster's peculiar tonsure in the film puzzled many critics. 'I think if you smeared dung all over his face and told him he looked great I think he'd believe you. I've never seen him look in a mirror.'

Lancaster talked about the new film he was thinking of making with Anthony Burgess. 'Film about a *transsexual*. You know what a transsexual is? It's quite different to being a transvestite,' explained Burt. 'Well, this man really thought he'd been born into the wrong sex. He was a judge in Germany in the nineteenth century. He reacted against it by growing *breasts* when he was in a state of tension.' He paused, then said thoughtfully, 'We don't know what'll come of it yet.' He did not notice the eyes big as saucers across the table.

'Anthony Burgess. Wonderful man. Great novelist. But doesn't understand motion pictures. Thinks he can walk away after he's done a script. But a picture's a concerted thing. Like the Russian Ballet, with Nijinsky and Diaghilev and Prokofiev all working away there in Paris.' The old Adult Extension lecturer is untiring.

'I think Burt's the most moral man I've ever met,' said Hill. 'He really cares about segregation. I think he's the only actor I've known never to have made a commercial.'

He is also one of the few big stars prepared to waive his customary commercial fee to appear on American public service television in the classics. He had agreed to do Ibsen's *The Master Builder*. In some euphoria the station had commissioned someone to adapt it and the ending had been changed.

'No,' said Lancaster shortly. 'We're going back to the original ending. No argument about that. *None*. This *man*, he wrote a scene in which a dwarf walks into a lake. Nothing happens. *Bubbles*. No dwarf. So the producer asked him to explain it. He said there was no need, that it was all a piece of symbolism. *Symbolism*. What right had he to say that? *What bloody right?*' There was a loud cracking noise in the darkness. Mr Lancaster was beating on the wall.

His next film was to be a thriller in Rome, produced by Lew Grade. 'Know him? *Wonderful man*. Great businessman. But he does have this occasional wish to interfere.' Lancaster looked pained. 'The film's about a plague. It ends with me ordering a train blown up. So he rings up and says, can't I say something like, "My wife and two children were on that train." He always wants these happy endings.' He was quite serious: Mr Lancaster does not make jokes.

A week later he made one of his rare public appearances. A priest, the son of one of Lancaster's oldest friends, an old boxing pro, had asked him to address a small film seminar at the Jesuit Loyola College in Los Angeles. Lancaster is loyal to old friends.

He was late. The students had just watched him as Wyatt Earp ride off into the sunset. The priest, playing for time, told the students it was a 'good Grade B movie' then broke off. The grin in the Mexican waistcoat had arrived.

Three hours later Burt was still talking. He told the bemused students about grosses and percentages and profit situations, overheads and overdrafts. A question was like a match applied to blue touch paper. He did a lot of explaining. He explained more history. He explained the differences between Italian Communism and Chinese Communism. 'I don't know what you think about Communism,' he gave the old cocksure grin, 'and I *don't* care.'

He talked about parts he had turned down. 'I didn't do Ben Hur because I disliked the approach to Christianity. I thought it cheapened it.' Then Burt, the old ham, turned to the priest, 'But as you know, Father, the *flesh* is weak.'

'A movie,' he told his audience earnestly, 'is like a love affair. If you don't mind me talking about such things.' He beamed at them. 'You mustn't doubt your sense of *manhood*.' He was enormous, coarse, wordy, a healthy egomaniac with an audience. He looked very happy. The next day he was due to fly off to Rome, but meanwhile there was an audience, and Burt talked. He was still talking when I left. 'What was he this time?' asked one of his friends. 'The World Sophisticate?'

A fortnight later, on a yacht belonging to another old friend, there was a visitors' book in which guests were expected to write their comments.

'Burt came out with us a few months back.'

'What did he put?'

'"Burt Lancaster."'

1997

THE LINGERING SMELL OF SUCCESS

~

The Israelites beat it by three, being forty years in the Wilderness. But when *Sweet Smell of Success* was chosen this year to be one of twenty-five films from the history of cinema for inclusion in the Library of Congress, it had completed thirty-seven years of bizarre wandering – from the personal and financial disaster it was, to the cult *film noir* it became, to the classic it is now.

The producer was James Hill. For him it ended a run of box-office hits, being the first major setback for Hecht-Hill-Lancaster, which had broken the hold of the studios on the picture business and, until then, could do no wrong. In London Hill remembered one partner's reaction as they came out of the preview. 'Well, there goes the company,' said Harold Hecht.

The director did not even wait for that. Alexander (Sandy) MacKendrick, whose first American production this was, had seen the audience's reaction to their most popular stars Burt Lancaster and Tony Curtis being portrayed as the biggest shysters of all time. 'It was a direct insult to what they'd come to the cinema to enjoy.'

The Last Human Cannonball

'We never saw Sandy after the preview,' said Hill, now seventy-nine. 'He made a bolt for home like a convict let out of a penitentiary.'

MacKendrick was off.

They were the final additions to a casualty list that had already claimed Ernest Lehman, the author of the novella on which the film was based, who had a breakdown while working on the script with Hill. ('If you must have a coronary, Ernie, have it on the couch so I don't trip over you on the way to the can,' said a solicitous Hill.)

The film was made under conditions of hysteria, loathing and despair, which meant it was off to a flying start. *Sweet Smell of Success* is about hysteria, loathing and despair.

To Lehman the main character had been Sidney Wallace, the New York press agent he himself had been, dealing with columnists like Walter Winchell whose cold little voice on the telephone each morning he had come to dread. 'Ernie, what's *new*?' In his novella Winchell is Harvey Hunsecker, all-powerful and venomous, and self-disgust permeates a narrative in which every character – with the exception of Sidney's wholesome Jewish family – is out to screw the others.

'I wanted to dump the wholesome Jewish family from the moment I first read it,' said James Hill. 'They got in the way of the unremitting darkness which I loved. This summed up all my experience of the motion picture business.'

Yet this is that same film of which Tony Curtis wrote so fondly in his autobiography this year, 'there was never anything like *Sweet Smell*.'

It is the film which, thirty years after it was made, Tom Cruise and his girlfriend watched on television in *Rain Man*. Characters in other films have quoted from its dialogue, something unique in the history of cinema, and you too must have met someone given to phrases like 'match me, Sidney' or 'go make yourself a holiday', both extracted from Clifford Odets' script.

But all this is in the future in late November 1956 as the Super Chief train pulls out of Los Angeles bound for New York. There the locations have been found, a crew of forty has been hired and the high command is riding to the war.

On board are Hill and MacKendrick both at the peak of their careers, Hill having produced *Trapeze*, the top money-spinner of the year, and MacKendrick's *The Ladykillers* having just opened. With them is the scriptwriter Clifford Odets, and all that is missing is a script.

'I think that worried MacKendrick most,' said Hill. 'After what he had been used to at Ealing Studios it must have seemed to him as though he had fallen among lunatics. 'We'd meet in the corridor of the train and he'd say, "Anything on paper yet?" Of that there was nothing, but Clifford was so interested in everything, in the landscape, in the history, we didn't have the heart to bring up the fact that the only paper we'd seen in his hands was the menu. I said to Sandy, "I have this horrible feeling he thinks he's on holiday." And Sandy began to move his arms like a puppet – as he did every time he got into a state of tension. He went sort of fluttery.'

Beyond the windows the plains unroll like stair carpet, meal times come and go with Odets ordering everything ('Know what lunch costs today?' asks a production executive), and at every halt in the flat nowheresville of middle America there is a wire waiting from Harold Hecht, the business head of the company back in Los Angeles. 'Any script yet? Burt now very concerned.'

After three days the Super Chief arrives in Chicago, where they are to change trains and where suddenly, not only is there no script, there is no scriptwriter either. As Hill boards the New York train a wire is delivered from Clifford Odets to say that he has gone to see a sick aunt in Philadelphia.

In their own panic they have not noticed that the tourist Odets is also a worried man. To make *Sweet Smell* he is returning to the scene of his early triumphs in the theatre, but this is a city he abandoned twenty years before to go to Hollywood. Since then he has become even more an object of vituperation to its leftwing intellectuals as the man who has named names before McCarthyite tribunals. Odets is in no hurry to get to New York.

'For us it was like coming to Death Row,' said Hill. 'We're stuck in this hotel, and Sandy's got the crew out filming every hydrant and every dustbin they can see. That's why it killed me when Carol Reed said the exteriors of *Sweet Smell* were the finest he had ever seen. You don't need a script to film streets.

'On the third day Odets turned up. What did I say to him? I'll tell you what I said to him. I walked up, looked him straight in the eye, and I said, "Hello Clifford, how's your aunt?"'

For of course, by now, there is nothing they won't do now for their errant writer. MacKendrick moves out of his own room so that Odets can enjoy its great view of the city, only to find that Odets has drawn the curtains in the daytime and taped paper over the windows; the last thing he wants to see is New York. He emerges from the hotel to eat in restaurants after midnight.

'I was standing talking to Sandy when we heard it, the sound we had been waiting to hear. Tip-tap, tippety-tap. Clifford was at the typewriter and it was that moment in Westerns when fellers turn their faces up to the sky as the rains finally come.

'We opened his door and old Clifford was going great guns. The first piece of paper fell from the machine and I picked it up to hand it to Sandy. I could hear him start to read. "The quick brown fox leaps over the ..." Jesus! Sandy went down as though somebody had hit him over the head. But it was odd, in spite of everything I knew once Clifford got going we would be all right.'

Odets, while hardly changing a moment in Lehman's original plot – except to jettison the wholesome Jewish family ('Holy smoke, who are the bums going to *like* now in your crummy movie?' howled Harold Hecht) – changed everything through language and the poetry of his structure.

Wonderful lines flowed from the typewriter. 'Hold the good thought.' Or the hat-check girl describing her attempted seduction: 'But Sidney darling, the man must be out of his mind – it was only eleven o'clock in the morning.' In the moral vacuum of *Sweet Smell* the timing is the one thing which disturbs her. 'Everybody knows Manny Davis except *Mrs* Manny Davis.' Entire scenes were being shot the day Odets wrote them; only later were they gathered up to be included in the script.

But the major change was in the structure, thrown up by the new emphasis on the columnist Hunsecker. As MacKendrick recalled, Odets had been uneasy about this character. 'He said to us both in a challenging way, "Why in hell does the Tony Curtis character just sit there and take this from the man?" And Jim said, "Come on, Clifford, you know who he is. This is a man who can tell presidents what to do." There was a slight beat while Clifford wrote that down, and it's in the movie.'

In Odets's script a good quarter of an hour goes by before we meet Hunsecker (Lehman's Harvey Hunsecker is now the bleak J. J. Hunsecker, a man without even the intimacy of a Christian name), but his photograph is everywhere on the billboards, and we approach him through the orbits of his readers, his press agents and his fellow columnists, all the swirling debris of his world, until finally we reach the heart of darkness. Even then, in the nightclub, we feel we are on the slopes of a monolith as Sidney frantically pleads into the telephone, 'JJ, I need your ear for two minutes.'

The fact that Hunsecker now towered over everybody got Burt Lancaster interested in what became the most extraordinary casting against type in cinema.

In the film, while Tony Curtis forever fidgets, Lancaster, the old acrobat, hardly moves – he who in earlier films spent most of his time on ropes and the trapeze is still. You feel the menace seeping out of this immobility as the light puddles the cruel spectacles Lancaster chose to wear.

'So we'd blown it there as well,' said Hill. 'Not only did the audience want to like Tony Curtis, they also wanted to see Burt jumping around with bananas.'

And all this time they had no ending. Hill, pursuing the darkness, wanted a complete massacre at the end, but even Odets drew back from that. ('They won't let us get away with it.') The compromise, with Hunsecker looking down from his eyrie as the Tony Curtis character gets beaten up by corrupt cops, is at best satisfactory.

After the preview came the notices. In America, with the exception of Pauline Kael of *The New Yorker*, they panned it; Miss Kael said that Lancaster had become an actor. In Britain the critics were kinder, and some months later, Hill, coming out of the Dorchester, found young autograph-hunters waiting for him. 'I said to Burt, "Holy cow, we're getting ourselves an audience."'

But it was too late, for by then two partners in what had been the most successful film company of the day were communicating only by memo, and a director who had only known success was glumly recording, far away, 'It didn't dawn on me until the first preview that the fans were not only going to *resent* it ...' Thirty-seven years ago there was just recrimination and bitterness.

Now, finally, the world has caught up. 'And I have just one question to ask,' said Hill. 'What took you so long, you bastards?'

1995

ALL THINGS PASS

❧

'**M**y name is Jim Hill, by trade I was a screen-writer. That is to say, I tried to make some sense of things that happen to all of us: if you like, I rewrote life. The blurred, the commonplace, the monochrome, these were not my stock in trade. Thus in a film bad news comes to a man when he is at the summit of worldly success, it comes when he rises to speak at his daughter's society wedding. It comes at Christmas. It is in life that bad news doesn't realise its dramatic potential.

I was stuck in traffic on a six-lane carriageway when the news bulletin came, anonymous as the music which had preceded it. I was half listening to wars taking place in lands I would never visit, to people starving I would never meet, to politicians fucking up this and that, when, like something falling from a great height, there was this.

'The film star Burt Lancaster has been admitted to hospital. Lancaster, the only actor to come out of the War and become a living legend, is believed to have suffered a stroke, though as yet there is no word on this ...'

The Last Human Cannonball

Of course then I couldn't get off the fucking freeway. No place to pull in, no exits, just the rush-hour traffic, bumper to bumper, crawling along at 15 mph in second gear. And me thinking about a man in whose company I had spent more time than in that of any other human being. We had our own film company, Hecht Hill and Lancaster. Harold Hecht, Jim Hill, Burt Lancaster, that was us. *Trapeze. Marty. Vera Cruz. Sweet Smell of Success, Separate Tables.* Jesus, we almost took over MGM.

'Guess this'll have to be called the James Hill Building,' said Burt. We were being shown over the Irving Thalberg Building on the Metro lot where I'd started as a junior writer on seventy-five dollars a week. I said, 'No, the first thing, if you plan on stepping into L. B. Meyer's shoes, will be for you to invest in a decent pair of your own.' God, he was a scruffy son of a bitch. But we were young, there didn't seem to be anything we couldn't do.

I don't know if you have any idea what it was like to have your own motion picture company back in the 1950s, but believe me, it was as close as a man will ever get to being God. The laws which applied to ordinary mortals, they didn't apply to you: men waved you through Customs, they awaited your arrivals, attended your departures. Anything you wanted, you got given, clothes, cars. Put the good guys in Fords, and Ford gave you the cars. Next year, if you'd got tired of Fords, you put the good guys in Chryslers. As for women, give them a few more pages of dialogue, and the greatest beauties in the world stretched out in the back of those cars, women who today can't even smile on account of their face lifts.

I remember when our company was making *Vera Cruz* with Gary Cooper down in Mexico, and there was this scene where Burt playing the gunman Joe Erin shoots someone without even turning round. This troubled Coop. 'Gee, a man sizing up the targets with the back of his head,' he said with sarcasm. So we went over the details again with him, and for a long time he was silent.

Then he said, and I can remember the tone, it was so wistful, 'Must be nice, having your own production company.' And it was.

Burt and I, we went to play golf the other day. Burt was driving and he was explaining something, Burt was always explaining something, so he didn't notice the car in front had braked. Next thing is, this feller's coming round to the open window. 'Now just you sit there, d'you hear? I'm going to get some paper and take down your details.' And Burt sat.

Muhammad Ali in his prime acknowledged he wouldn't have liked to have got into a ring with him, whatever age Burt would have been then. In his *Adventures in the Skin Trade* the screen-writer William Goldman said he was a man who 'just exuded physical menace'. And now there was old Burt sitting there like a garden gnome. 'Oh to be twenty years younger,' he said when the man had gone, but that might have had something to do with the fact that the asshole had written 'Burt Lancaster' on his bit of paper, and it had meant nothing at all to him.

The first time we met, we were on Fiji, making *His Majesty O'Keefe*, and Borden Chase, my collaborator and I, we were frantically trying to get a script together. Borden saw himself as some kind of Southern gentleman, and had this secretary, an English girl, taking the bullshit down. Anyway the door opened and the star of the picture burst in. Lancaster was only wearing shorts and had been on a fifteen-mile run; he was dripping with sweat.

He was already famous then, and the secretary stared as people do when confronted with film stars or royalty, but there was no greeting or exchange of names. Burt crossed the room to the wash-basin in the corner, dropped his shorts and began to piss in the sink. The girl gasped.

But Borden knew his role; he moved to her side, put his arm round her and gently led her from the room. Me, I just sat there, staring at my employer's white ass. 'You know, Gandhi used to relieve himself in the Ganges every time he had some important ritual to perform,' he explained to me over his shoulder. And that was my introduction to Burton Stephen Lancaster, and to his explanations. It was my introduction to wash-basins too.

Later, when we had our company, I found myself twitching whenever we had a conference in a room with a wash-basin, for at some point Burt would get up and make for this like some heat-seeking missile. Mind you, it had its advantages. Accountants, studio executives, all those bums that had sat there querying everything in our books, they'd agree to anything as soon as they saw old Burt at the wash-basin.

There was another bulletin on the radio. 'He suffered the stroke this morning while visiting an old friend confined to a home with Alzheimer's Disease.' That figured. He remembered old friends, he visited the sick, it was part of his rag-bag personality.

Remember him in *From Here to Eternity*, rolling in the surf with that English dame, Deborah Kerr? He came into the office one day to tell me he was in love. I told him not to be silly. I mean, she had kids, and Burt, he had a house full of them. Amazing people, actors. Ten days later he couldn't remember her name. A month later all he talked about was the way the water went up his ass when they made that scene.

And could he talk...When I first met him he was practically a mute, he'd come into an office, pick something up, then walk out again. That is, if there wasn't a wash-basin. Later on there was no stopping him talking. I read an interview he gave when he turned seventy. 'Getting older means you have to keep your mind open, try new things. Some of us finally realise that maturity means consideration for other people, I think it is the ability to love yourself and consequently others.' But, give credit where it's due, he didn't claim to have learned to love himself and the human race at the same time, he seems to have given himself a head start.

It's only once in a blue moon that a film star like him comes along, and when he does there are all these people hanging to his shirt tails. And I should know, I was there, hanging on with the rest of them, me and Harold, Harold Hecht. Burt was our trump card, things happened around him, but it was only years later I realised that it was Harold who made them happen, this absurd little man with his vanity and paranoia and his energy.

Burt was a struggling actor when they met, appearing in his first play on Broadway. That lasted just twenty-three nights, but on the twenty-third night there was this little man waiting for him, who bought him supper and told him that within five years not only would Burt be a star but the two of them would be producing their own films, *producing* their own films. I mean, it was then the heyday of the studios. It should have been a scene in comedy, these two maniacs sitting there, the golden giant and the manikin of 5 feet 4, in this cheap restaurant, for they were both broke. And it all came true.

It came true because no one ever found it possible to disentangle the reality and the fantasy in Harold Hecht: he told them something, they believed what he told them, and in a while the fantasy became reality. I should know, I was his business partner, and if he was a mystery to most people, think what he was like to Burt and me. He was said to have started life as a dancer, but the two of us were sports nuts and we never saw any evidence of this in his movements. Yet ...

When we were in Fiji that time, we were way over budget, there was a production crew hanging around with the meter running, yet I went out one day and there was Harold the producer rehearsing the fucking cannibals for a dance number. Given his head, he'd have had the Earp brothers dancing in the OK Corral. If someone asked me what it was like working with Harold, that was it, immaculately choreographed cannibals and no script.

We did *The Birdman of Alcatraz*, and we were in all kinds of trouble. Frank Stroud the Birdman, he'd done two murders and was a raving aggressive fruit, and he was the hero. Somehow the first got worked into the script, but what were we going to do about the other? We were casting Burt against type anyway, but all Harold said was, 'Just let the canaries take care of it.' That's what happened, the canaries took care of it.

I remember staying in Palm Springs, and I couldn't sleep. Around 4.30 I went out, just as the dawn was coming up, when only the bolder desert rats were about, who of course got the best grub. And amongst them was one small, tricky bastard who didn't move as I approached, just ate. I said to myself, Jesus, that's Harold.

He had this ocean-going yacht, 90 foot long, which for years Burt and I used to admire, until we realised we owned it as well. It was there in our company accounts. But even that was nothing to what was under 'Sundries'. We'd always been unnerved by Harold's show of authority in script conferences. We weren't sure he could read, but he'd intervene suddenly over a script, saying 'My people say' or 'My people tell me this or that.' This made him difficult to contradict, until we discovered who his people were.

We knew his wife had been to college, and presumably he talked to her, but the others were a mystery until we noticed how often items like 'shirts' turned up in the company accounts. Now Burt and I, we probably had five shirts between us, and we knew we were not in the mail order business. But here were all these silk and cotton shirts by Yvel, which is Levy spelt backwards. We had it out with Harold, and it was then he confessed. Every time he wanted an opinion on a script he took it to Levy to read, which meant he had to buy a shirt. Really tricky shirts meant a visit to his tailor, which was why Harold was usually in cashmere. Then we remembered when we hit real problems Harold never had more than a half inch of hair and went round in a cloud of eau de cologne. Real problems meant his barber.

He was keen on psychoanalysis, though the fees those birds

charged ruled them out as script readers. Harold had himself psychoanalysed, he put his wife and his kids through it, and when his wife's poodle jumped out of the car window on Wilshire he had the animal psychoanalysed as well. God, he spent money. When our company moved into the old William Morris building he had this special bathroom built for himself with ultraviolet bulbs around the mirror, so he could pop in, put dark glasses on and top up his tan. I knew none of this when, working late on a script, I used the mirror to shave in and woke up in the middle of the night unable to see. I got up, fell flat on my face, and, like any lapsed Catholic, assumed God had caught up with me. By morning I was beginning to see outlines again.

He hired a head of company publicity, whose duties, he told the bewildered man, included testing hotel beds for the three partners. Lancaster, he told him, was to be treated like the President, me like the Secretary of the Interior, while he, Hecht, was the Secretary of State. When I went to London to start work on *Trapeze* this man was sent on ahead, but when my plane touched down he wasn't there. He had followed his orders to the last detail, tried out my bed at the Savoy, and fallen asleep on it like Goldilocks.

We had a complete aviary in the front hall of our offices, canaries everywhere. I think it was Ernie Lehman who said that if you could get through that without being shat on there were still the three partners waiting their turn. But we were a company without collateral, we lived, literally, from day to day, so any film which was a financial disaster could destroy us, as in the end one, *Sweet Smell of Success*, did. We lived off our wits. I oversaw the scripts, Lancaster starred in the films, Harold faced the accountants. But his main worry was that Burt, around whom the company turned, would in the end walk out and like that other nut, Samson, bring everything down around him. Which he did.

So any film that had Burt interested was considered, and options taken on the craziest books, like Max Catto's *The Killing*

Frost, not a word of which went into *Trapeze*. But it was about a circus, Burt the old acrobat was fascinated by circus, so the book was bought. Had Harold seen Burt with his nose in the Sears-Roebuck catalogue, he'd have taken out an option on that, and some kind of script would have been knocked into shape.

We'd call budgetary meetings from time to time to stem the escalating costs. We'd start with personnel, because, apart from the yacht, we had a story editor, a public relations and a production manager, casting director, controller, a top legal firm on stand-by, contract writers on top salaries, and a whole army of secretaries ... Someone would read out the first name, Max Arnow, head of casting: none of us put up a defence for Arnow, so he'd duly get entered on the firing list. But then, as we worked his way through the alphabet, one or other of us had something to say for each name that came up, so when we'd finished only Arnow had lost his job. But the accountants would say that firing him wouldn't make much difference, so Arnow was reinstated. The number of times Jack Arnow was sacked and reinstated ... And he never knew.

All this was when we had our film company, and were young.

I think the sight of Burt aging affected me more than what time was doing to me. He was like a god once, a golden-haired god, albeit a scruffy one. That business with the motorist was the first shock, the big operation was the second, the triple or quadruple bypass or whatever it was he had. His old doctor, whom we'd shared for years, had told him it wasn't necessary, but he'd gone on holiday and his stand-in assured Burt it was the answer to everything. So the surgery was booked, the nurses hired, the lights set up, and the old ham, with a potential audience, went through with it.

It was months before I plucked up enough courage to go and see him after his stroke, for yes, I did get off that freeway in the end. He'd come home from hospital, and was back in the flat that occupied the whole eighteenth floor of a thirty-storey building just over the road from a golf course. That was the only reason he'd bought it in the first place, and from the greens I'd look up from time to time at his windows. That was where the silence started, Burt didn't talk any more.

Odd tales circulated. A golf pro who was an old friend of Burt's said he was a vegetable, but his investment manager came away, saying they'd had a productive meeting: for the first time in his life Mr Lancaster hadn't objected to anything he proposed.

When the day came when I did finally call I didn't go alone. There was the golf pro, and Mike Starkman, another golfer, and me. The door opened, a huge thing he'd got out of some castle, which once he'd have been swinging on or shooting arrows at, and there was Burt in a chair. And Burt was *immaculate*. This is what made me stare, for this was the man who only ever had two shirts. Now there were clearly many shirts. And a tie, for Godsake. In all our time together, outside film sets, I only saw him wear a tie once, and that was the time he went to collect his Oscar, when he called on my mother to tie it for him.

We went up to him one by one, like ambassadors presenting our credentials, and each of us in turn pressed the back of Burt's hand where it rested on the arm of his chair. We told him how wonderful it was to see him again, and how well he looked, for he did indeed look well. Then we told him stories out of the past, which was when the others gave way to me, for he and I went back that much further, and I reminded him of the villainies we'd shared.

I told him about the time we were staying in the Georges Cinq during the making of *Trapeze*, when he got into his head to climb the drainpipes of the hotel to the penthouse where we were staying, watched by this crowd which didn't realise that had anything happened to him there would have gone the film. And the night he stormed off the *Mike Wallace Show* when Wallace departed from the agreed list of questions. When we got back to the hotel where we were staying there were all these messages of approval. One was from this Princess Radziwill to say how much she and her sister Jacqueline Kennedy would like it if we came over. So there I was telling Burt what we could do to the President's wife and her sister, only Burt was an honourable man. All he wanted to do was tell me what he was going to do to Mike Wallace.

Me and him and old Mr Lancaster at a football game.

'Have a burger, Dad.'

'Don't have my teeth, Boitie.'

'Gum it, Dad.'

Soon everyone was laughing, except one. Not a smile crossed Burt's face. But we were so jolly, the three of us, that after we left we talked all the way to the lift, and it was only when the doors closed that the silence came. 'I thought he recognised Hill,' said Mike Starkman, 'His eyes never left you after you pressed his hand.' And for some reason that irritated me.

'Don't you think that might have been a good time to have got your own back?' I said.

Some years before Mike had had a row with Burt on the golf course, which ended with Burt taking a club out of his bag and threatening to break it over his head. I can't remember why, but Burt almost went out of his mind, that ugliness was always lurking in his nature somewhere.

'Come on, Jim,' he said.

So we parted. It was odd, but suddenly we were eager to be rid of each other, as though we couldn't wait to think our own thoughts.

It was then it really hit me, what if the old Burt was still there, locked behind that silence? The old Burt who had been locked up so many times in films, led out onto scaffolds, who, with a bound and a flash of the crockery, which was what Borden Chase called his teeth, had always got free.

I owed him so much. When we met I was a writer with a fair to middling situation, nothing more. He was already a star. And, without a word to me, he had followed what contributions I'd made to the films his company made, until he turned over to me the final word on each script. And I'd written him out of so many desperate situations.

'You all right, sir?' It was the parking attendant.

'You're damn right, I am all right,' I said so loudly the man stepped back.

For suddenly I knew what I was going to do. I was going to write the story of our lives and our company, and I was going to read the lot aloud to him, chapter by chapter, until I got his attention. And if I didn't then I would rewrite it, as I'd done so many times in the past for him, for whatever else I am, or was, I had one thing going for me. It was this.

"Chapter One.

"My name is Jim Hill, by trade I was a screen-writer. That is to say, I tried to make some sense of things that happen to all of us: if you like, I rewrote life ..." '

So we had the structure, but that was all we wrote. It might have made a good book.

2004

THE LAST HUMAN CANNONBALL

⤺

I saw it, I was there. I feel obliged to tell you this because however often you have the act described, nothing prepares you for what happens. First they dragged in a thing the size of a naval cannon, and a man climbed into the muzzle, which was then cranked up to an angle of sixty degrees.

It was the bleakest night of the year, rain drilling into the mud of Wanstead Flats, and in Gerry Cottle's Big Top a poor first house of about ninety people, most of them light-headed at being out at all, sat huddled together. At just after six o'clock there was a huge bang and they saw a man shot from a cannon.

Forty feet above our heads a frail assembly of blood and bone hurtled through the air. He did not land, he fell ninety feet away like Icarus, and the whole thing was over in about a second. Remember, in a second. After the introduction and the build-up this should have been an enormous anti-climax. And it wasn't.

It would have been a spectacle anywhere, on television or under the lights of a big arena, but here, on a night like this, with such a small audience, it was extraordinary. There was no trickery of any kind, it was just honest and terrifying. An amiable lunatic fell out of the safely net, checked he could still walk, and grinned at us.

'Vell, I always bin acrobat,' said the lunatic, a gaunt man with shoulders like a coathanger. 'Doing somethings unusual you know. I find no human cannonball left in Europe. I think to myself, Christ is time I start.'

The Last Human Cannonball

Name, Osci Tabak. Age, 'Oh, about forty-two.' Nationality: this, as it has to be, is Hungarian. Long wild hair to his shoulders, a moustache like Vlad the Impaler's, the sort of Magyar horseman who brought terror over the rim of Europe. Occupation, bullet. 'Bin doing this nine years now. Must be getting somethings right.'

The human cannonball act is as old as the twentieth century and is littered with young men in wheelchairs, the last of them, Elvin Bale, crippled after a performance in Hong Kong when he reportedly failed to take account of the humidity and over-shot a sagging net.

'Yes, is very dangerous,' agreed Mr Tabak, who pronounced it 'dangerouse'. 'Is somethings I wouldn't recommend to enemy. But perhaps I would ...' He leered, it was a wonderful leer full of black teeth and mischief, and I could have listened to Mr Tabak all day. 'First time I do this I am shaking, I don't know where I am.'

'You were in the cannon,' I said.

'Yes, yes, I am in the cannon but next thing, bang, I am going faster than aircraft. One blink, and is sixty miles per hour. I am torpedo. We get pressure of 150lb per square inch, the cannon is biggest air gun in whole world, and I am human torpedo. All I not got is motor in bottom.'

The acceleration is so extreme, from nought to sixty in a fraction of a second, that when he leaves the cannon a man's vertebrae are compressed to the point that he becomes an inch or two shorter. So not only do you see him fly, you see him grow in the air.

'Lissen, flying not bad, even coming out of cannon not too bad. What is bad is impact and that can be very bad. I am twenty-five to thirty stones when I hit the net. If I hit cable then I snap it just like that, I am going so fast. And if I don't reach that net you call safety I die.'

He has wonderful phrases, and it is like hearing the language being invented in front of you. 'That net you call safety...' But of course it must be that to him.

The history of the act is mainly the history of a single Italian family, the Zacchinis, starting with an engineering forebear so fascinated by cannons he started cramming his relatives into them. Before the compressed air cannons there were some which were just huge catapults. These are about the only things which terrify the Magyar Tabak.

'I have old friend, he do this. They point the gun wrong and he miss the net. Now he is in wheelchair and cannot cope. Bang.' He put a forefinger to his temple. 'Was great artist, but his cannon was elastic not airgun. Air cannon you can change distance when you use low velocity, high velocity. But elastic, whoooosh and you go.'

The Zacchinis appeared for Bertram Mills and later for the Ringling Brothers. In the huge big tops of the 1920s and 1930s, they set records which still stand, being shot distances of 140 feet and so high they cleared the Big Wheel in a fairground. But every generation had its cripples, and the family finally got out in 1970 when a husband and wife act slammed together, being shot from a double cannon, and there was a broken neck and broken spine.

Tabak, if I managed to unscramble his English correctly, got into this business when his old tutor in the State Circus School lost an eye doing it. There was a danger of the man, a Pole, being deported so his pupil stood in for him.

'Is there skill?' The circus owner Gerry Cottle had told me the only skill was 'the ability to withstand being shot up the arse each night by 150lb of compressed air'.

'Lissen,' said Mr Tabak. 'I throw knives, I damn good clown like my father. You name it, I do it. But you want to do something people can't see any other place. So you do this. Daily people could not do this thing. Daily people have not got the muscle.'

Daily people? Of course, people who know what they will be doing tomorrow. Like walking.

'Being acrobat I am used to jumping off things, so I lie there in cannon, arms folded, head crouched to my shoulders in case it comes off. In air is not much to prepare landing. How you end up you don't know but it is just little time for you to support this leg or that leg.

The Last Human Cannonball

'Worst time for me is when piston stuck. I am pushed just halfway out and then, *bang*, it goes off and I am not ready. I break my pelvis and for months I have a blue dicky. But lucky there is doctor in audience, he put me together. My wife, she also puts me together good.'

Mr Tabak married into the Fossetts, an English circus dynasty. His brother-in-law fires the cannon. 'He is very important, he point it and he get the right pressure.' His wife administers first aid. 'Knees go, elbows go, ankles … I take painkillers, I take whatever I get my hands on. Funny thing, you know. People say "Circus is cruel to animals" but nobody give a damn when circus people cruel to themselves.'

He hopes his son Osci junior, a friendly monster of sixteen, will join him in the act, for which he plans the old terror of a double-barrelled cannon. 'Is great chance for British engineering, no?' Curiously enough, Osci junior is enthusiastic.

'I've done it four times and it can be a bit frightening when you are up there and the net is the size of a bath towel. But you speed up and you can open your arms and steer a little bit. No, I'm really looking forward to it, perhaps because I've got guts or, more probably, because I'm barmy.'

'I've been after an act like this for years,' said Gerry Cottle. 'It's something unique to circus. You can get clowns and animals anywhere, but you can't put something like this on at the London Palladium. We found him in Europe.'

In the Big Top the ringmaster was booming into the microphone. 'And now he's disappearing into what is surely the loneliest place on earth, the barrel …'

'I think perhaps I do this for another ten years and then I retire,' said Mr Tabak.

'You ever hear of a human cannonball retiring?'

'No,' said Mr Tabak sheepishly.

1998